Getting the Word Out
Academic Libraries as Scholarly Publishers

Edited by Maria Bonn
and Mike Furlough

Association of College and Research Libraries
A division of the American Library Association
Chicago, Illinois 2015

The paper used in this publication meets the minimum requirements of American National Standard for Information Sciences–Permanence of Paper for Printed Library Materials, ANSI Z39.48-1992. ∞

Library of Congress Cataloging-in-Publication Data

Getting the word out : academic libraries as scholarly publishers / edited by Maria Bonn and Mike Furlough.
    pages cm
  Includes bibliographical references.
  ISBN 978-0-8389-8697-4 (paperback) -- ISBN 978-0-8389-8698-1 (pdf) -- ISBN 978-0-8389-8699-8 (ePub) -- ISBN 978-0-8389-8700-1 (Kindle)
  1. Academic libraries--Publishing--United States. 2. Libraries and publishing--United States. 3. Libraries and electronic publishing--United States. 4. Library publications--United States. I. Bonn, Maria, editor. II. Furlough, Mike, editor.
  Z716.6.G48 2014
  050.5'94--dc23
                            2014045104

Chapter 6, "Library-as-Publisher: Capacity Building for the Library Publishing Subfield," by Katherine Skinner, Sarah Lippincott, Julie Speer, and Tyler Walters originally appeared in *The Journal of Electronic Publishing*, Volume 17, Issue 2: Education and Training for 21st Century Publishers, Spring 2014 (DOI: http://dx.doi.org/10.3998/3336451.0017.207). Used here with permission.

Copyright ©2015 by The Association of College & Research Libraries, a division of the American Library Association.

All rights reserved except those which may be granted by Sections 107 and 108 of the Copyright Revision Act of 1976.

Printed in the United States of America.

19 18 17 16 15   5 4 3 2 1

In Memory of Julia C. Blixrud, 1954–2014
Passionate and tireless advocate
for scholars and for libraries

Table of Contents

vii   Foreword
Dan Cohen and Kathleen Fitzpatrick

xi   Acknowledgments

1   Introduction. The Roots and Branches of Library Publishing Programs
Maria Bonn and Mike Furlough

Section 1: Why Libraries Publish

17   Chapter 1. Scholarly Publishing as an Economic Public Good
Paul N. Courant and Elisabeth A. Jones

43   Chapter 2. We Scholars: How Libraries Could Help Us with Scholarly Publishing, if Only We'd Let Them
J. Britt Holbrook

Section 2: How Libraries Publish

57   Chapter 3. Toward New-Model Scholarly Publishing: Uniting the Skills of Publishers and Libraries
Monica McCormick

83   Chapter 4. From Collaboration to Integration: University Presses and Libraries
Charles Watkinson

113   Chapter 5. The Evolution of Publishing Agreements at the University of Michigan Library
Kevin S. Hawkins

119   Chapter 6. Library-as-Publisher: Capacity Building for the Library Publishing Subfield
Katherine Skinner, Sarah Lippincott, Julie Speer, and Tyler Walters

111	Chapter 7. **Nimble and Oriented towards Teaching and Learning: Publishing Services at Small Academic Libraries** *Lisa Spiro*

Section 3: What Libraries Publish

177	Chapter 8. **Textbooks and Educational Resources in Library-Based Publishing** *Cyril Oberlander*
193	Chapter 9. **More than Consumers: Students as Content Creators** *Amy Buckland*
203	Chapter 10. **Archival APIs: Humanities Data Publishing and Academic Librarianship** *Matt Burton and Korey Jackson*
221	Chapter 11. **Peering Outward: Data Curation Services in Academic Libraries and Scientific Data Publishing** *Patricia Hswe*
239	About the Authors
247	Index

Foreword

Dan Cohen and Kathleen Fitzpatrick

Thinking about academic libraries as scholarly publishers requires both historical perspective and a sense of the future. It also requires a reconsideration of current scholarly publishers and their evolution.

University presses, for instance, were invented as a means of getting the work of an institution's faculty out to the world. They were created not as a means of establishing professionalized publishers on campus, but as a way to work around a publishing industry that found the academic market too small to bother with. University presses were literally the institution's printing office, and they often sent the work they produced to other universities' libraries for free in exchange for the work being produced at those universities.

Over the course of the twentieth century, university presses, for a host of good reasons, became professional—and scholarly publishing benefited from that professionalism—but as a result, the press operation grew increasingly distant from the campus, its mission, and its needs. While university presses continue to produce a wide range of important and extremely high-quality work, their economic model (and in particular the declining levels of support most such presses receive from their institutions) has somewhat restricted their ability to conduct the research and development necessary to experiment both with new publishing models and with the kinds of content for which there simply isn't much of a market.

This work is licensed under the Creative Commons Attribution License 4.0 (CC-BY 4.0).

This situation has opened up a potential space on campus for different kinds of publishers, working once again to support the work being done locally, focusing on using the best technological means of getting that work out to the world. That the technology of the Web provides entirely new and open ways to do such dissemination has only expanded and strengthened the possibilities.

Despite facing budgetary difficulties of their own, academic libraries may be the ideal place for this new kind of publishing model to flourish. These libraries are still relatively stable, long-term institutions that are a core part of the university infrastructure and that are filled with people who have the requisite skills to move into the creation, as well as the storage and discovery, of published works. They have long supported the collection and preservation of the products of scholarly research, both through the development of their research collections and, more recently, through the establishment of institutional repositories.

Libraries have the potential to become the crucial nexus for knowledge flows on campus, working both—as they have long done—to collect the knowledge produced around the world for study on their campus and—as they are increasingly doing—to disseminate the knowledge produced on campus around the world.

And indeed, a host of new models for library-based publishing have emerged in the last few years, including intensifying relationships between the library and existing university presses, as well as the establishment of entirely new publishing enterprises within library structures. Libraries are also thinking more creatively about the wide range of services that they can provide, ranging from data and technical services to distribution and marketing. They are developing and leveraging networks of institutions and scholars. In short, libraries are coming to understand their latent strengths and to see how these strengths might be applied to publishing as well as preservation and access.

These new library publishing enterprises are not just changing the nature of publishing, however; they are also, of necessity, changing the libraries they inhabit. Libraries are of course already undergoing many of the same kinds of changes that are taking place across the institution. The global reach of today's networked scholars means that they are decreasingly using their home library as their first point of research and instead looking to online tools. For scholars, the importance of discovery and the problems related to abundance are very real, and libraries have an increasingly uncertain role in this workflow. By becoming publishing agents as well as storehouses for published works—that is, by working on both sides of the equation—libraries can insert themselves into the cycle of scholarly research more effectively.

How might academic libraries get to this goal? Some practical knowledge, as well as some dreaming, is necessary. This volume brings together practitioners who have deeply considered, experimented with, and implemented a variety of models, ranging from new startups within the library, to the repurposing and expansion of existing modest enterprises, to the importation of university presses into the library (for some, a reunion). They also draw from views and innovations from across the landscape—from digital startups outside of academia, to new technologies that hold promise for publishing workflows and cost containment, to the products of new fields like digital humanities and others that are undergoing transformations and thus are looking for more expansive publishing platforms and opportunities.

From those sources and experiences, the authors try to address some critical questions. For instance, organizationally, should publishing be a distinct unit within the library or connected to other units and services? How can a library handle complicated and sometimes contentious functions such as peer review, sales, and dissemination? There undoubtedly needs to be a psychological shift as well since publishing requires more outward-facing and discipline-specific skills. And from the modern researcher's side, it requires a similar psychological change since it creates an utterly new relationship with an institution that, while beloved and critical to independent work, has not generally been seen as a gatekeeper or manager of the scholarly process beyond the first stage of research.

We believe that a publishing landscape with a strong set of libraries involved is a healthier one. At the very least, the presence of robust library-based publishing can put important economic and social pressure on commercial and even society-based publishers to act more in the interests of the university and the scholar than themselves. But competition is a poor solitary reason for library publishing to increase. It should have its own inherent value, and indeed the pieces in this volume articulate well why libraries make excellent places for publishing and how they can become even better places for this activity in the future. Although libraries are likely to remain a relatively small sector of the publishing apparatus, in certain domains they will play a critical role in the sustainability of fields. As the contraction of monograph sales continues, libraries can keep alive the specialized but commercially unviable works that publishers have increasingly let slip from their lists. Ideally, they can also bring to life new subjects and new formats, including formats of varying length and composition, that have been shunned by traditional publishers. In this way and so many others, the academic library as scholarly publisher can expand and diversify the realm of publishing at the same time that it remodels that realm for the next century.

Acknowledgments

The Editors wish to thank many people:

First, the authors of the essays in this collection, from whom we have learned much, and who have all been unflaggingly cheerful throughout the publication process.

Kathryn Deiss, who was always enthusiastic and never impatient.

Judi Lauber, the copy-editor of this volume, who saved us from Chicago Style and helped everyone look good.

The ACRL New Publications Advisory Board members, who saw merit in the idea for this book.

In addition, Maria Bonn would like to thank: The staff of Michigan Publishing, unflagging and enthusiastic partners in developing an academic library publishing program: they were ever ready to learn and were my best teachers. And John Wilkin, always there to support and willing to spend dinner time talking about publishing, libraries, and the intersection of the two.

Mike Furlough would like to thank: Martha Ney, who provided him with critical support when this book got going. His former colleagues at Penn State University Libraries and Penn State Press, from whom he learned why publishing is so hard and so critical, and last, but best of all, Ellie Goodman—for reasons too many to list.

INTRODUCTION

The Roots and Branches of Library Publishing Programs

Maria Bonn and Mike Furlough

In recent years, library publishing activities have drawn increasing attention within the professional world of academic libraries, from the scholars those libraries serve and from established scholarly publishers that seek to assess both opportunities and threats presented by this activity. This work goes by a number of names, with varying connotative values: *library publishing*, *publishing libraries*, *library publishing services*, *library publishing support services*, and even just *publishing*, Whatever this work is called, a sufficient number of libraries engaged in it so that when the Library Publishing Coalition (LPC), a collaborative effort to "support the emerging field of library publishing" (Skinner, Speer, and Watkinson 2012, 2) was formed in 2012, more than

This work is licensed under the Creative Commons Attribution License 4.0 (CC-BY 4.0).

fifty college and university libraries paid their membership fees and added their names to the directory (LPC 2014a). Its first Library Publishing Forum, in March 2014 (LPC 2014b), was filled with people engaged with publishing and libraries, eager to share their experiences and their challenges. The 2015 edition of the directory, just released as of this writing, contains 124 entries and represents fifty-six member libraries (Lippincott 2014). LPC is not the only indicator of increased academic library attention to and engagement with scholarly publishing. In the Association of Research Libraries' (ARL) current "Strategic Thinking and Design" process and the subsequent planning (ARL 2014), developing a strategy for at-scale library-based publishing has been prominent. Characterized variously in the emergent outcome documents (e.g., research libraries as "scholarly dissemination engines, promoting wide reaching and sustainable publication of research and scholarship" (Neal 2014, 614), the focus has been on aligning publishing with the broader institutional mission and ensuring that the economics of that effort are sustainable.

Over the past decade, a number of reports on library-based publishing have been sponsored by organizations such as ARL (Hahn 2008), Ithaka (Brown, Griffiths, and Rascoff 2007), and IMLS (Mullins et al. 2012), each of which has provided a high-level overview of the state of the field at that time. In addition, a number of practitioners, including the editors of this book, have published articles and chapters on related matters. However, there have been few collections or at-length studies that highlight the diversity of library publishing programs, services, and philosophies. We have sought to rectify that through this volume, having invited some of the most talented thinkers in this area of librarianship to explore the issues in depth, giving decision makers and service providers a single resource to understand the current state of the field and the prospects for its future. Our goal has been to examine library-based publishing with both a clear-eyed realism about the challenges faced by libraries as publishers and a confirmed optimism that libraries are well suited to address and overcome these challenges. From this perspective, we hope this collection will inform the current conversation about academic libraries as publishers and encourage academic libraries to expand into this important area of academic activity.

Although library publishing efforts are flourishing and multiplying, the history of library engagement with publishing is longer than is generally discussed. At root, libraries have always been keenly interested in the methods, models, and economics of publishing as libraries exist in a symbiotic relationship with publishers that it is at times a mutually profitable partnership and at others an antagonistic battle of wits, budgets, and negotiating skills. But beyond their role in the consumer-producer relationship, academic libraries have long been a site of publishing. "Many of the earliest US academic presses got their start in university libraries in the decades surrounding 1900," note Paul Courant and Elisabeth Jones in their extended and articulate discussion of a "number of powerful economic arguments in favor of the proposition that research libraries are natural and efficient loci for scholarly publication," found in Chapter 1 of this volume.

The current focus on library publishing began around twenty years ago. At the tail end of the twentieth century, the possibilities inspired by digital technology and networked communication, paired with increasing (library) consumer dissatisfaction with the costs and use constraints imposed by commercial publishers, led some libraries to actively explore alternative means and models for scholarly publishing. Throughout the 1990s, this exploration often took place through partnerships with commercial publishers, through advising and helping to shape innovative scholarly publishing ventures, and through providing infrastructure and guidance for scholar-driven publishing or providing sources of collections for digitization (and relicensing back to libraries). This period saw libraries keenly interested in and often supporting such efforts as JSTOR, Project MUSE, HighWire Press, the Text Creation Partnership, the *Bryn Mawr Classical* and *Medieval Review*s, and the development and distribution of primary source databases by Chadwyck-Healey, later subsumed by ProQuest. Early experiments in distributing Elsevier content to libraries (TULIP and PEAK) appeared in this period, as did the first online instantiation of the *Oxford English Dictionary*, the *Bibliography of Asian Studies*, the Thesaurus Linguae Graecae, and Perseus. Libraries also partnered in the delivery of large image databases, such as the Advanced Papyrology Information System.

In these early efforts, the focus was often on online search and retrieval of legacy collections and backfiles, not the full set of functions often associated with publishing new, original material. But these activities demonstrated capacity and built infrastructure that created the potential to expand into a wider and more theoretically and pragmatically defined publishing practice. Concerns over the increasing costs of subscriptions to scholarly publications led the library community to turn attention to the publication of original work. In 1998, ARL developed and launched the Scholarly Publishing and Academic Resources Coalition (SPARC), designed to engage both in publishing activism and advocacy and in publishing content that would be competitive with high-priced commercial products. Around the turn of the millennium, some academic libraries began to fund, develop, and deploy publishing efforts. Best known among these at the time, at least in the United States, were the University of California's eScholarship, established in 2000;[1] Cornell's Project Euclid, launched in 2003 (Koltay and Hickerson 2002); Columbia's CIAO (Columbia International Affairs Online), dating to 1997 (Wittenberg 1998); and the University of Michigan's Scholarly Publishing Office (SPO), begun in 2001 (Bonn 2002). SPO's statement of its goals at its founding reflects those of both its contemporaries and of many of the publishing libraries that have become active in recent years:

> Supported by the infrastructure of the digital library, [SPO] provides an alternative to commercial publication for faculty, scholarly societies and non-profit organizations. Its goal is to create online academic publications that meet the needs of authors, libraries and individual users. Its projects range from campus-based publications… to new electronic journals… to large-scale publishing partnerships…. SPO represents a new direction for the Library. Through the lessons learned and the skills acquired in building the digital library, the Library is now poised to become a producer as well as a consumer of publications. (Bonn et al. 2003, 39)

These early efforts originated at about the same time as the emergence of open-source and commercially produced software to support publishing and distribution of scholarly work. Such tools allowed libraries without the capacity to develop original software to begin to experiment with publishing-related services. DSpace, first released in 2002 by MIT and

---

1. For the history of eScholarship see Candee 2001.

Hewlett-Packard Labs, launched the institutional repository movement and provided libraries with a means to systematically collect and openly share the research and scholarship produced by the faculty and students they served (Smith et al. 2003). Berkeley Electronic Press, founded in 1999 and later renamed bepress, published its own journals and later bundled its publishing tools with its Digital Commons repository software adopted by many libraries (bepress 2014). Cornell University partnered with Penn State University to create DPubS (released in 2006), a generalized open-source version of software used by Cornell's Project Euclid (Thomas and Eaton 2005). Many libraries, which were just beginning to experiment with publishing before committing significant resources to the efforts, found DPubS more complicated and less attractive than Open Journal Systems.[2] OJS was first released in 2001 by the Public Knowledge Project at Simon Fraser University and over the next decade was adopted by thousands of journals published by academic units and libraries worldwide (PKP 2014).

With a variety of tools available to them, more North American libraries adopted publishing services. In 2008, when Karla Hahn surveyed the ARL membership, thirty-five libraries reported having publishing services in operation (Hahn 2008); today, the Library Publishing Coalition's most recent directory lists 124 in libraries of all sizes (Lippincott 2014). There is a great deal of variety in the nature of this publishing, so much so that one would be hard put to assert a uniform definition of library publishing. Although publishing may be, and often is, understood to encompass a bundle of activities ranging from and beyond acquisition and development to production to marketing, sales, and distribution, academic libraries vary in the extent to which they prioritize and assert capability in each of these functions. Nevertheless, scanning the broad field of library publishing, we can see clusters of activity, programs, and projects. These clusters suggest a kind of taxonomy that can help us to understand how libraries are engaging in and with publishing in order to serve and advance the missions of the academic institutions in which they reside.

The digitization of library holdings, both independently and in partnership with commercial ventures, has provided many libraries with relatively simple publication opportunities through the sale of reprints.

---

2. See, for example, an internal report prepared by Ohio State University Libraries (Samuels, Griffy, and Kaliebe 2008).

These programs build off of the roots of library publishing programs in 1990s-era digitization projects, such as the Making of America, which was based at Michigan and Cornell. Books digitized at sufficient resolution and attention to quality will result in master files can be used as the source for creating high-quality facsimile reprints. This, coupled with the easy availability of print-on-demand services, such as Lightning Source and Amazon's CreateSpace, and with venues for online sales, has made it possible for libraries to make portions of their collection available for private ownership in print, usually complementing free public availability online. For example, the University of California Library and the University of Michigan Library both have hundreds of thousands of titles available for sale. Other libraries make portions of public domain historical and special collections available for purchase. At Penn State, the university libraries and university press partnered to create Metalmark Books, a series focused on Pennsylvania history and culture, drawn from public-domain titles in the libraries' regular and special collections (Penn State University Press 2014). Such publishing tends to garner good will from the user community, as users are able to purchase older, difficult-to-find books that have special use or personal significance, and the sales can provide a supplemental revenue stream for the source library.

However, we also see academic libraries functioning as original publishers, developing full-fledged imprints that bring publications to fruition under library management and auspices. In 2013, Amherst College garnered considerable media and academic attention for this kind of publishing initiative in launching Amherst College Press through its library with the goal of "facilitating the free, electronic distribution of high-quality literature and scholarship" (Amherst College Library 2014). An increasing number of university presses are now situated as organizational units of their university libraries. (At these authors' last count, twenty AAUP member presses reported within their home institution's libraries.) The degree of the library's involvement in its press's operations varies widely. In many cases, the relationship is primarily one of courtesy administrative reporting on the part of the press director to the head of the library, but the press is largely independent in matters of both budget and strategic direction. In other cases, there is much more active alignment of organization, goals, and management. In the latter case, we begin to see press and library staff collocated in library facilities, sharing the benefits of library organizational support and infrastructure, and cooperating on projects that arise out of both conventional press activities (such as development of a marketing website) and activities closer to the generally understood mission of the library (populating the institutional repository and promoting its use). As both publishing and library professional organizations increasingly foster shared discussion about the optimal organizational alignment for presses and libraries, we may well see rapid development of models for interaction and effective publication. In this volume, we include two perspectives on both the aspirations and practical aspects of library-press integration. Monica McCormick and Charles Watkinson, both veterans of university presses, libraries, and the merger of the two, share their perspectives as librarians in the publishing house and publishers in the library in Chapters 3 and 4 of this volume. In, respectively, "Toward New-Model Scholarly Publishing: Uniting the Skills of Publishers and Libraries" and "From Collaboration to Integration: University Presses and Libraries," they each highlight the ways in which both the missions and skill sets of these organizations complement and support each other.

Another form of library publishing activity is enacted through academic libraries forging publishing partnerships with other mission-aligned bodies, such as scholarly societies and nonprofit academic organizations. In such partnerships, there is often a division of labor in which the "partner" (say, a scholarly society) provides editorial oversight and content development, while the library contributes production and distribution support. For an exemplar of this kind of publishing engagement, one might turn to *Elementa: Science of the Anthropocene*, one of the earliest publications devoted to this newly emergent research subject. *Elementa* is the result of a partnership between BioOne and five academic libraries: Dartmouth, the Georgia Institute of Technology, the University of Colorado Boulder, the University of Michigan, and the University of Washington. In this partnership, Dartmouth Library provides operational support, hosting the infrastructure and managing the staff producing the journal (*Elementa* 2014). An earlier instantiation of this kind of partnering to publish can be seen in the American Council of Learned Societies' History E Books Project, produced in collaboration with Michigan Publishing at the University of Michigan Library (ACLS 2014).

Partnerships such as *Elementa* and the History E Book Project are the result of libraries reaching beyond the walls of their home institutions and finding partners with complementary needs and skills. Far more common are internal partnerships, in which libraries provide publishing support for locally based publications, often created by their institution's faculty or academic departments. Such partnerships can be seen as a natural outgrowth of the service orientation of academic libraries striving to develop capacity to meet the needs and achieve the goals of their user populations. Again, the exact nature of these publishing library services varies across institutions. Many libraries run Open Journal Systems (and now Open Monograph Press) to provide a turnkey publishing platform to their communities but leave all editorial and production functions to the publications' developers. Others "catch" the publication at some point after development and perform functions like copy-editing and markup. Others may broker relationships between faculty and campus publications and freelance specialists who can help bring the publication to print or to the screen.

Many such campus-based partnerships are driven by the imperative to support academic faculty, but, increasingly and especially at colleges and smaller universities, the library is developing capacity to support student publications. Graduate and undergraduate student publications, often journals, serve multiple ends: they showcase and disseminate the work of students, who in the apprenticeship stage of their careers might have difficulty finding other publication venues; they engage students in thinking about paths to publication, a habit of mind that may become important in later academic careers; and they provide opportunities for students to garner experience in publishing as a possible professional path. For many libraries, support of such publishing is an opportunity to both capture the research output of their campuses and to demonstrate support of student development. In Chapter 9 "More than Consumers: Students As Content Creators," Amy Buckland prompts us to think "of our students as future researchers" and to consider how this "offers libraries many reasons to support those students as creators in the scholarly publishing world," strengthening the role of libraries as partners, not merely resources, in undergraduate education. Chapter 7 presents a related discussion, but one that addresses a broader spectrum of topics. Lisa Spiro in "Nimble and Oriented towards Teaching and Learning: Publishing Services at Small Academic Libraries," inventories and analyzes how by offering publishing services, small college libraries can bring attention to the institution's research (including student research), promote open access initiatives, partner with faculty, and demonstrate their expertise in supporting emerging scholarly communication models. Spiro's essay offers a valuable overview of the publishing work conducted at these schools, which is often overlooked in this field.

In a perhaps natural extension of academic libraries' support for their institution's educational mission and interest in keeping education affordable, some libraries have also begun to explore educational publishing. As is discussed in Cyril Oberlander's Chapter 8 essay "Textbooks and Educational Resources in Library-Based Publishing," "the State University of New York (SUNY) library system supports open textbook publishing and had fifteen titles in production in the first year of the initiative, garnering contributions and drawing upon the skills and resources of SUNY administration, libraries, and instructional faculty. Other libraries have assisted faculty in self-publishing texts and have reissued commercially published texts when rights reverted to the authors. While the ongoing funding and organizational model for such projects is not yet clear, it is apparent that, with its ability to have a positive impact on many students at a low cost to those students, textbook publishing is an opportunity for publishing libraries to raise their visibility and gain considerable good will.

The first years of library publishing programs have focused heavily on more traditional models of journal and monograph publishing. However, spurred by shifts in government policy and funder requirements, the expressed needs of scholars and long-rooted library concerns about access and preservation, libraries have recently invested heavily in developing capacity to support digital humanities, e-science, and the management of research data. The integration of these services pose special challenges for libraries, especially because needs can vary greatly by discipline. In this volume, we approach this question from the perspective of both humanities and scientific research. Korey Jackson and Matt Burton focus on publishing humanities data, in Chapter 10 "Archival APIs: Humanities Data Publishing and Academic Librarianship," while Patricia Hswe explores scientific data publishing in Chapter 11 "Peering Outward: Data Curation Services in Academic Libraries and Scientific Data Publishing." All of these authors delineate the convergence of scholarly need, academic library mission, and resources that argues for an increased role for academic libraries in data curation and dissemination.

One last area of work bears mentioning, although it may be more closely described as libraries *and* publishing than libraries *as* publishers. Academic libraries are seeing a growing need for publishing support services, and as they develop these services, they are increasingly playing a role as publishing educators and advisors. As noted above, these services might take the nuts-and-bolts (or perhaps bits-and-bytes) approach of offering hosting and distribution architecture, perhaps through an institutional repository or an instance of publishing software. The services might also take the form of education about and consultation on authors' publishing contracts, negotiating permissions for use of third-party materials in publication, or talking with graduate students and junior faculty about the best way to prepare their materials for publication. Such efforts have a range of institutional homes. In some cases, they are squarely aligned with library publishing efforts; in others, they might be attached to a scholarly communications office or the responsibility of a designated scholarly communications specialist librarian. In some places, education, advocacy, and consultation in regard to copyright and publishing are seen as such overwhelming needs that academic libraries have established dedicated copyright services offices to serve their campus communities. In this volume, our authors share their experience and expertise in building the service components of library publishing with particular attention to the skills and knowledge required to get the work done. Katherine Skinner, Sarah Lippincott, Julie Speers, and Tyler Walters, in Chapter 6, "Library-as-Publisher: Capacity Building for the Library Publishing Subfield," delineate both the ways in which publishing skills are compatible with traditional library skills and the areas in which new capacity has to be built to have in place a staff ready to publish and provide related services. Kevin Hawkins, in Chapter 5 "The Evolution of Publishing Agreements at the University of Michigan Library," provides a case study of the development of publishing agreements that serve the needs of both authors and publishers and are designed to support the best possible scholarly communication outcomes. Both essays should prove an invaluable resource for any academic library in the emergent stages of its publishing program.

Of course, no library service of any kind can be successfully offered without a deep and thorough understanding of the community it serves. The necessity of library publishing services seems to be a foregone conclusion in many library circles, but not in the rest of our universities and colleges.

Publishing, perhaps the most determinative factor in the career success of most academics, often may be a fraught subject of discussion. Promotion, tenure, and publishing are all premised on the fiercely protected concepts of academic freedom; library-based publishing, J. Britt Holbrook warns, may be seen by some academics "as a threat to academic freedom." In his Chapter 2 essay "We Scholars: How Libraries Could Help Us with Scholarly Publishing, If Only We'd Let Them," Holbrook, a visiting assistant professor in the School of Public Policy at the Georgia Institute of Technology walks us through various conceptions of "academic freedom" to better understand how our rhetoric around open access and publishing can be counterproductive, urging librarians to "approach the issue of scholarly publication… in terms of empowering scholars to pursue their scholarship with maximal freedom and creativity."

This collection of essays, which surveys our current academic publishing landscape, reveals that rather than a uniformly designed and implemented set of activities constituting a commonly understood function called publishing, there is a rich array of services, imprints, and attempts at intervention taking place across the library world. What does seem increasingly widespread is an acknowledgment on the part of academic libraries that their traditional support of the research, learning, and teaching happening upon their campuses encompasses support for publishing. That support takes many forms. It is that very multiplicity which may make this burgeoning work most effective, as academic libraries address the problems and fault lines of existing publishing practices on a number of fronts. That multiplicity also makes it imperative that academic libraries share their experiences, and, over time, come together to combine their strengths in order to sustain and share scholarship and extend its impact.

Works Cited

ACLS (American Council of Learned Societies). 2014. "ALCS [sic] History E Books Project." Accessed October 25. www.historyebook.org.

Amherst College Library. 2014. "Amherst College Press." Accessed October 25. https://www.amherst.edu/library/press/node/440154.

ARL (Association of Research Libraries). 2014. "ARL Strategic Thinking and Design." ARL website. Accessed December 10. www.arl.org/about/arl-strategic-thinking-and-design.

bepress. 2014. "The Story of bepress." Accessed October 25. www.bepress.com/aboutbepress.html.

Bonn, Maria. 2002. "A Case Study in Library-Based Scholarly Publishing: The University of Michigan Library's Scholarly Publishing Office." *New Review of Information Networking* 8, no. 1: 69–80. doi:10.1080/13614570209516991.

Bonn, Maria, Patricia Hodges, Mark Sandler, and John Price Wilkin. 2003. "Building the Digital Library at the University of Michigan." In *Digital Libraries: A Vision for the 21st Century: A Festschrift in Honor of Wendy Lougee on the Occasion of Her Departure from the University of Michigan*, edited by Patricia Hodges, Maria Bonn, Mark Sandler, and John Price Wilkin, 22–41. Ann Arbor: Michigan Publishing, University of Michigan Library. doi:10.3998/spobooks.bbv9812.0001.001.

Brown, Laura, Rebecca Griffiths, and Matthew Rascoff. 2007. *University Publishing in a Digital Age*. New York: Ithaka, July 26. www.sr.ithaka.org/sites/default/files/reports/4.13.1.pdf.

Candee, Catherine H. 2001. "The California Digital Library and the eScholarship Program." In *Libraries and Electronic Resources: New Partnerships, New Practices, New Perspectives*, edited by Pamela L. Higgins, 37–60. Binghamton, NY: Haworth Information Press.

Elementa. 2014. "About Us: Open Science for the Public Good." Accessed October 25. http://home.elementascience.org/about/about-us.

Hahn, Karla. 2008. *Research Library Publishing Services: New Options for University Publishing*. Washington, DC: Association of Research Libraries.

Koltay, Zsuzsa, and H. Thomas Hickerson. 2002. "Project Euclid and the Role of Research Libraries in Scholarly Publishing." *Journal of Library Administration* 35, no. 1: 83–88. doi:10.1300/J111v35n01_06.

Lippincott, Sarah K., ed. 2014. *Library Publishing Directory 2015*. Atlanta: Library Publishing Coalition. www.librarypublishing.org/resources/directory/lpd2015.

LPC (Library Publishing Coalition). 2014a. "Background." LPC website. Accessed December 10. www.librarypublishing.org/about-us/background.

———. 2014b. "Library Publishing Forum 2014." LPC website. Accessed December 10. www.librarypublishing.org/events/lpforum14.

Mullins, James L., Catherine Murray Rust, Joyce L. Ogburn, Raym Crow, October Ivins, Allyson Mower, Daureen Nesdill, Mark P. Newton, Julie Speer, and Charles Watkinson. 2012. *Library Publishing Services: Strategies for Success*. Final Research Report. Washington, DC: SPARC, March. http://wp.sparc.arl.org/lps.

Neal, James G. 2014. "A New Age of Reason for Academic Libraries." *College and Research Libraries* 75, no 5 (September): 612–15. doi:10.5860/crl.75.5.612.

Penn State University Press. 2014. "Metalmark." Accessed October 25. www.psupress.org/books/series/book_SeriesMetalmark.html.

PKP (Public Knowledge Project). 2014. "History." Accessed October 25. https://pkp.sfu.ca/about/history.

Samuels, Ruth Gallegos, Henry Griffy, and Kyle Kaliebe. 2008. "Digital Publishing Systems Comparison Report: A Review of DPubS and OJS." Internal report, Ohio State University Libraries. http://library.osu.edu/staff/techservices/sri_epublishing_ComparisonReport_final.rtf.

Skinner, Katherine, *Julie* Speer, and Charles Watkinson. 2012. "Library Publishing Coalition (LPC): A Proposal." Edited by Spencer Keralis. August 14. www.librarypublishing.org/sites/librarypublishing.org/files/documents/lpc_proposal_20120814.pdf.

Smith, MacKenzie, Mary Barton, Mick Bass, Margret Branschofsky, Greg McClellen, Dave Stuve, Robert Tansley, Julie Harford Walker. 2003. "DSpace: An Open Source Dynamic Digital Repository." *D-Lib Magazine* 9, no. 1 (January). www.dlib.org/dlib/january03/smith/01smith.html.

Thomas, Sarah, and Nancy Eaton. 2005. "The Right Tool for the Job: The DPubS Publication Management Software." Project briefing, CNI Fall Membership Meeting, Phoenix, AZ, December 5–6. www.cni.org/topics/e-journals/the-right-tool-for-the-job-dpubs-publication-management-software.

Wittenberg, Kate. 1998. "CIAO: A New Model for Scholarly Publishing." In "Moving from Print to Electronic Publishing," special issue, *Journal of Electronic Publishing* 3, no. 4 (June). doi:10.3998/3336451.0003.405.

SECTION 1
Why Libraries Publish

students · learning · print · educate · asssociation · peer · book · research · author · open · editor · digital · teaching · librarians · information · faculty · journals · collaboration · publishing

CHAPTER 1

Scholarly Publishing as an Economic Public Good

Paul N. Courant and Elisabeth A. Jones

In this chapter we take an economic perspective on library-based publishing, and that perspective leads us to conclude that there are a number of powerful economic arguments in favor of the proposition that research libraries are natural and efficient loci for scholarly publication. We also note that this idea is anything but original: many of the earliest US academic presses got their start in university libraries in the decades surrounding 1900 (Kerr 1949, 17–26; Hawes 1967, 31). And although the technological constraints and economic realities of printing and physical distribution soon pushed many of these early presses to become freestanding units within their universities, the fundamental alignment of mission between the library and the press remained. More recently, with the radical changes in printing and distribution afforded by digital technologies, the reasons to

This work is licensed under the Creative Commons Attribution License 4.0 (CC-BY 4.0).

keep these symbiotic entities divided have largely gone away, and we argue that it is time for scholarly publishing to return to its roots in the library. Our argument relies on economic reasoning, but it is not principally an argument about either cost or profit—rather it is about efficient and effective production and use of scholarly work. We take the position that scholarly work ought to be treated as a pure public good.

Alignment of Missions and Functions

Although it is quite common for both press and library directors to focus narrowly on the prosperity and survival of their respective institutions, it is impossible to make sense of the missions of either university presses or university libraries without explicitly recognizing that both are derived from the missions of the universities in which those entities are situated. Individual universities—like the libraries and presses they contain—operate in cooperation and competition with other institutions, individually and collectively contributing to advancing scholarship and its purposes. Thus, as we consider how best to situate the apparatus of scholarly publishing, our evaluation must derive from what is best for advancing the purposes of universities and research institutes, viewed individually and as a system. At the same time, we must acknowledge that the best interests of individual universities will not always align perfectly with the best interests of the system as a whole—a problem that arises frequently in economic systems other than the perfectly competitive markets so beloved of economics textbooks.

Before delving into current business models and our proposals for adjusting them, it will be useful to more specifically outline the features of and dependencies among the underlying missions and functions at issue here: those of the university, its library, and its press.

The University

Broadly, the mission of both individual universities and of the university system as a whole is to advance knowledge, both within and beyond university walls. While a great deal of this work takes place via teaching, our focus here will be on research and on the creation and use of new knowledge. Scholars and researchers fundamentally strive to *learn*, and that learning leads to more learning through processes that are invariably cumulative and accretive: current scholars build upon the work of past scholars, and future scholars will build upon scholarship created now. Effective accretion of this kind requires both publication and preservation of academic work. Publication is essential because if scholarship is not made public, it becomes the proverbial candle under the bushel; nobody can see it, much less build upon it. Preservation is essential because once scholarship is made public, it cannot reliably persist for reuse without assistance—in order for future scholars to build on past scholarship, that past scholarship needs to be someplace where it can be found, and the easier it is to find, the better. In order for all of this to happen, the system needs both reliable channels for publication and dependable repositories to preserve and organize those (and other) publications for reuse.

The University Library

Broadly speaking, the mission of the university library is to provide its patrons with access to as much of the scholarly record as it can, both now and in the future. To take a nearby example, the University of Michigan Library declares that its mission is to "support, enhance, and collaborate in the instructional, research, and service activities of the faculty, students, and staff, and contribute to the common good by collecting, organizing, preserving, communicating, and sharing the record of human knowledge."[1]

As this statement suggests (and there are many libraries with similar statements), the library's *mission*—the provision of access to information in support of scholarship—is closely related to the *functions* it serves—the collection, organization, preservation, communication, and sharing of scholarly and cultural materials. Notably, at U–M, as at most similar institutions, the faculty, students, and staff of the university are the primary audience for the library's services; service to the broader scholarly community and the general public are desirable, yet secondary goals. Whatever the audience, however, it remains the case that the fundamental

---

1. U–M 2013a. Notably, similar language also appears in the mission statement for the University of Michigan as a whole, which pledges to serve "Michigan and the world" in part "through preeminence in creating, communicating, preserving and applying knowledge, art, and academic values" (U–M 2013b).

mission of the university library for the past few centuries has been to facilitate long-term, reliable access to the cultural and scholarly record by collecting, organizing, and preserving the materials that it contains.

These functions of the library support all of the academic disciplines because by performing them, the library assures the integrity (in the sense of authorship and good metadata, not necessarily the quality of the work) of the scholarly record. Still, different disciplines stand at different levels of remove from the record the library maintains. For chemists (to pick a group of laboratory scientists arbitrarily), the library's value is almost completely as a keeper of the scholarly record—chemistry itself is usually done at some distance from the library. For humanists, on the other hand, the library's value is not simply as a repository: its resources often stand at the very core of their actual day-to-day work. In such disciplines, the library *is* the laboratory, by virtue of both its ordering and authentication of scholarly work and its provision of the cultural materials that form the source material for humanistic inquiry.

Until quite recently, the research library delivered these vital services of scholarship largely from its own collections, although individual libraries would also assist faculty and students in finding relevant work that was not held locally. One of the consequences of widespread use of digital technologies is that an increasing fraction of the source material used in university-level research and teaching is held elsewhere, and often its physical location is diffuse and unimportant and its connection to the local library contractual or even incidental. Yet, even in many of these cases, library intervention is needed to make these services function usefully for scholarly work. For example, a great deal of preliminary literature review is now executed using tools like Google Scholar, which seem to displace the library and its many (costly) subscription databases by offering free article-level searching of the academic literature. However, actually reaching the full text of articles found on Scholar often requires the user to be logged onto the very library systems that system superficially appears to replace. The functions of the research library—being able to find and deliver works relevant for scholarship and to do so reliably for a long and indefinite period of time—have remained unchanged, but as those works become more diffusely held in the digital world, those functions are becoming less and less visible to those making use of them.

It's worth noting that not everything that the research library does is in the direct service of scholarship. The library provides study space, coffee shops, teaching support, printing facilities, and a host of other more or less useful amenities of the academic world. Many of these activities contribute to the ability of the library to do its primary work because they serve the local university efficiently and effectively—sometimes (consider coffee shops) even by turning a profit that can be used to support the library's academic missions.[2]

The University Press

If the university library's mission is to provide its local user base with reliable access to information over long periods of time, the university press has the more outward-facing mission of making scholarly work available beyond the walls of any one university. Publication is an essential part of scholarship, as we have argued above (and elsewhere; e.g., Courant 2006), and is therefore essential to the purposes of the research university. One cannot build on the work of others without that work being available, and the library cannot do its business (which is the university's business) without having such a scholarly record produced in the first place.

The university press provides a mechanism for populating the research library with scholarly works. The press is not the only such mechanism. In principle, after all, the work of university presses could be done by commercial publishers, and indeed commercial publishers do publish a small subset of scholarly work that has market appeal beyond the academy.[3] However, in a fully commercial system of scholarly publication,

---

2. Burton Weisbrod, working with a number of collaborators, has developed the argument that mission-driven organizations, such as universities, may well be able to attract resources to serve their missions through activities that are profitable in the commercial marketplace. As long as the profit-motivated work is recognized as being subsidiary, rather than a goal in itself (and there are real risks here), such activities can contribute to the nonprofit missions of academic institutions (see, e.g., Weisbrod, Ballou, and Asch 2008).
3. Most of the published cultural record that serves as source material for work in the humanities and some social sciences is published by commercial publishers, rather than scholarly publishers—thus the research library contains many works that are not the products of academic research. The distinctive feature of the university press, however, is that it specializes in works whose purpose is the advancement of knowledge.

the misalignment between commercial and academic objectives would soon result in a paucity of outlets for useful—but unprofitable—scholarly output (one of the conditions that, in the eighteenth and nineteenth centuries, led to the establishment of university presses in the first place). Commercial presses are bound to select works to publish based on their potential for sales, while university presses are (or ought to be) more concerned with selecting works based on their potential contribution to the advancement of knowledge. This mission-driven orientation (often in conjunction with university subsidies) creates vital space for the publication of important, yet low-selling scholarly works. As a director of the Harvard University Press put it decades ago, "The university press publisher has as his objective the publication of the maximum number of good books this side of bankruptcy" (Kerr 1949, 13). Research universities and their faculty and other research staff depend on the availability of outlets for the publication of scholarly work that use merit rather than marketability as their core criterion for selection. Effective scholarship requires the publication and dissemination of useful ideas that libraries can gather up for future scholars to find and build upon in their own work—and the nonprofit, mission-oriented university press has provided a vital mechanism for fulfilling that requirement.[4]

And, like the library, the press often performs functions that are not in direct support of scholarship, either locally or more generally. University presses often seek to publish trade books at a profit, and they also often publish regional history and regional natural history, also motivated at least in part by profit. Of course, the profits can be used to support the core mission of making scholarship public—but especially as universities increasingly expect presses to provide more and more of this kind of self-support, it is not surprising that the publishing and pricing strategies of university presses sometimes become misaligned with the mission of making as much useful scholarship as possible available to the "great conversation" (Guédon 2011) in which scholars are engaged.

---

4. Effective scholarship in "journal article fields" requires exactly the same sort of publication and dissemination of useful ideas, and libraries play the same role with respect of published journal literature that they do with respect to monographs. There are several important differences between journals and monographs (and differential publication norms by fields) that are beyond the scope of this discussion.

Mission-Driven Business Models

Mission-driven institutions, like profit-driven ones, require resources in order to survive, although they have different motives (maximize the good, subject to avoiding bankruptcy, rather than maximize the difference between revenue and expenditure) and operate in different economic environments. The fact that mission-based institutions like university presses and libraries are not "in business" in the conventional sense does not mean that they can survive without effective mechanisms that reliably deliver the resources that are essential to their functions. Generally, whether market-based are not, such mechanisms go by the name of "business models" (as outlined, for example, in the NSF Blue Ribbon Task Force report on digital sustainability; Lavoie et al. 2008, 32–33). Part of our argument is that changes in publishing and library technologies have led —or ought to lead—to changes in business models and business arrangements while the basic missions of scholarly publishing and research libraries have remained unchanged. Still, as these shifts in business model occur, it is important to keep the mission squarely in focus. In order to clarify the relationships between mission and business model within university libraries and university presses, this section will describe the genesis of each entity's business model in the print world (focusing mainly on the United States, but also a bit on Europe), and then, following an interlude on the basic economics of public goods, will delve into how those business models might shift to optimize scholarly production in the digital world.

University Library Business Models in the Print World

Although the history of libraries in general can be traced even further back than the history of the book itself (e.g., Harris 1995, 10–15; Lerner 2009, 1–4), university libraries are a much more recent phenomenon whose history is bound up with that of the universities in which they are situated. And in the United States, universities began to take up their current orientation toward research—an orientation requiring the sort of sizable, well-rounded collection now expected of university libraries—only as recently as the mid-nineteenth century or even later (Lerner 2009, 112; Bivens-Tatum 2011, 47–48).

The research-oriented model of the university, built on Enlightenment ideals of learning as a grand dialogue rather than a unidirectional flow of received wisdom, was pioneered by German universities in the eighteenth century. Emphasizing the production of scholarly writings as an essential role for university faculty, it effectively set a precedent for the "publish or perish" system that remains in place today. In the mid- to late nineteenth century, this model gained traction in the United States, with institutions like Johns Hopkins, Cornell, Harvard, and the University of Michigan all beginning to place a strong institutional emphasis on research—in some cases as a founding tenet, and in other cases as a gradual part of institutional growth.[5] And as Lerner (2009, 112) points out, this shift in the form and purpose of the university—toward a more active, productive engagement with research and knowledge creation—required a parallel shift in the form and purpose of the library collections the university had to maintain:

> A university that sought to transmit existing knowledge saw its library mainly as a mechanism for the safe keeping of books. But as universities sought to increase the sum of knowledge, a more dynamic sort of library was called for. And as knowledge—and the publications by which it was transmitted—increased rapidly, as it did in the latter half of the eighteenth century, university professors and other scholars could not hope to collect private libraries sufficient to their needs. The universities had to provide the intellectual resources with which their senior members could sustain themselves.

Before 1850, university libraries tended to be, as Harris (1995, 249) puts it, "small and unimpressive collections of books—poorly housed, little used, and strictly guarded"—but when the universities began to focus more on research, the libraries were required to expand their collections and services to support that shift. Gradually, over the course of the late

---

5. Jagodzinski 2008, 2–3; Bivens-Tatum 2011, 68–82. Harold Shapiro (2005), in his discussion of the evolution of American universities, argues that the German model as such was not as important as is often asserted. However, he also documents the co-evolution of the American research university and the research library during the latter decades of the nineteenth century.

nineteenth and twentieth centuries, university libraries would amass extensive reference collections, expand their open hours, liberalize their circulation policies, and begin to collaborate with other institutions on cataloging, collection development, and interlibrary lending—all to the benefit of undergraduates, graduate students, and faculty alike (Lerner 2009, 116–23). Eventually this evolution would lead to the institutions we recognize and utilize today.

This model of the university library as a toolkit of the raw materials for scholarship has largely been organized around balancing the joint and related objectives of preservation and access in a world where the contents of that toolkit are generally made of paper and bound in codex form. As described earlier in the chapter, the mission of the university library is fundamentally to provide access to recorded knowledge. However, because that mission is not restricted to the present but extends far into the future, and because paper is not impervious to wear, choices must be made between access now and access in years to come. In a world of paper information, libraries must constantly weigh the benefits of increased access for current users against their ability to sustain that access into the future: the more fingers that touch a page, the more quickly the paper degrades; the more times a spine is cracked open, the sooner the binding will require repair. Increasing access to paper materials at best increases preservation costs—and at worst leads to the loss or destruction of crucial information.

Indeed, even the relatively straightforward process of storing and moving paper books turns out to be quite an expensive endeavor over time: depending how long the book is kept and in what sort of shelving, the cost of simply holding on to it can easily exceed the original cost of purchasing the book, possibly many times over (Lawrence, Connaway, and Brigham 2001; Courant and Nielsen 2010). Given these realities, many of the limitations libraries currently impose on their physical collections—access or borrowing only for those with a university ID card, purchasing (and often retention) limited to those volumes deemed most useful to the local academic community—make a great deal of sense. However, where the pragmatics of storing and preserving paper no longer dominate, it becomes worthwhile to call these restrictions into question lest the legacy of the print world and associated behaviors interfere with the central goal of scholarly progress.

University Press Business Models in the Print World

The genesis of the university press, much like that of the university library, is bound up with the history of the research-oriented university and its vast capacity for both use and production of scholarly work. While the library's role was to acquire and provide local access to scholarship produced throughout the academy, the press's role was more outward-facing: to take the work of scholars (often, but not always, local scholars) and transmit it to other scholars and other universities' libraries as well as, to a limited extent, to the public at large. But where American university libraries followed a fairly consistent pattern in their early years—a centrally located building or buildings containing a set of resources arranged systematically, accessible to faculty and then later to students, with librarians inside to act as both guides and gatekeepers[6]—American university presses were more variegated from the very start. Some began as printers of other university materials (e.g., newspapers, course catalogs) and only later moved into book publishing. Others started as publication agencies tasked with gathering and editing manuscripts but outsourced the printing. Still others established a printing division in order to serve the needs of the press or established a university imprint in order to unify a diversity of press-like entities on campus (Kerr 1949, 15–32).

A key reason for this variegation lay in the fact that university presses, unlike university libraries, were not unique in providing their particular function to the scholarly community. Rather, as is still the case today (despite the general withering of the industry), commercial publishing houses were often happy to entertain submissions from university faculty—just perhaps not as many submissions as those faculty tended to produce (as noted above). The university press thus emerged as a way of bridging the gap between faculty publication objectives within the new research-oriented universities of the late nineteenth century and the limited capacity for and interest in publishing these manuscripts in the commercial sector.

In fact, the strictly noncommercial nature of the university press was held up as a key virtue of such entities in the early years of their existence:

---

6. Some university libraries, such as Harvard's, which were established before the nineteenth century, started out as loose confederations of departmental and field libraries without any centralized structure; however, given their early (pre-research university) genesis, they seem rather like exceptions that prove the rule.

lacking a central focus on profits, the university press remained free to publish scholarly work because it was significant, and not simply because it would sell. As one commercial publisher expounded in a 1931 issue of *Publishers Weekly*, "It seems also increasingly clear that the day is at hand when the commercial publisher must frankly admit his limitations... and turn the whole protection of knowledge and the publication of works of learning and scholarship over to endowed houses"—that is, to university presses. And these presses, he continued, should be substantially supported by their institutions, in order to insulate them from the potentially anti-meritocratic pressures of the market: "Any profits they make should be a source of grateful surprise; the question of whether the book will sell or not should never be for them a criterion for the acceptance of the manuscript or project.... The only criteria for the acceptance of a manuscript for such houses should be the intrinsic merit and value of the book itself and the question of whether there is a bibliographical need for it" (Kerr 1949, 35).

This sort of praise for the almost *anti*-commercial business model of the university press is echoed throughout Kerr's early history of those institutions, by publishers, by faculty, and by Kerr himself (1949, 43, 52, 72, 105–6, 262–63).

Given this orientation toward diffusion of meritorious works and away from profit, it is perhaps unsurprising that several of the earliest North American university presses—including those at Johns Hopkins, the University of California, the University of Toronto, the University of Washington, and the University of North Carolina—were initially created under the administrative aegis of the university library.[7] After all, the university library's job was already to take university money and hand out books for free, at least within the university. The press simply took that same role and turned it inside out—taking university-subsidized faculty work and disseminating it as widely as possible, including through market channels, with that dissemination also university-subsidized. And while most presses did recoup some of their costs through book sales, such

---

7. Kerr 1949, 17–26; Hawes 1967, 30–31. Indeed, several even disseminated their publications at least in part via direct library-to-library exchange. This strategy was most fully developed at the University of California, which in the early twentieth century shunned "all commercial or semi-commercial practices" in favor of strictly non-monetary transactions between libraries (Muto 1993, 48).

calculations were not at the core of their business model; rather, that model remained tightly coupled with the presses' mission, which, like the mission of universities themselves, remained the dissemination of knowledge.

Interlude: Some Basic Economics of Scholarly Communication

Before delving into the new business models available for pursuing library and press missions in the digital world, it will be useful to step back for a moment and lay out a few of the basic economic principles at play in this domain—and particularly the concept of public goods.

Information is what economists call a pure public good: it has the distinctive feature that additional use of the good is feasible without additional cost.[8] For example, if I tell you that Pluto is no longer considered a planet, your acquisition of that knowledge does not in any way diminish my possession of it. Similarly, if you read something in a book (or on a screen), or use an algorithm to perform a computation, neither the information in the book nor the source code of the algorithm is harmed; the only costs associated with your acquiring the information are your own cost of time and information processing (and the tiny electrical costs of running your local processor and screen). The classic statement of this property of information comes from Thomas Jefferson, long before the term *public good* was ever technically codified:

> If nature has made any one thing less susceptible than all others of exclusive property, it is the action of the thinking power called an idea, which an individual may exclusively possess as long as he keeps it to himself; but the moment it is divulged, it forces itself into the possession of every one, and the receiver cannot dispossess himself of it. Its peculiar character, too, is that no one possesses the less, because every other possesses the whole of it. He who receives an idea from me,

---

8. Indeed, this is a foundational principle of information economics (e.g., Shapiro and Varian 1999).

receives instruction himself without lessening mine; as he who lights his taper at mine, receives light without darkening me. (Jefferson 1813)

In economic terms, we would say that information, like fire passed from one candle to the next, is "non-rivalrous": use of it does not change the quantity available to be used. Such non-rivalrousness is a definitional characteristic of a pure public good.[9]

Further, in Paul Samuelson's (1954, 1955) original formalization of the theory of pure public goods, he specifies a second attribute—non-exclusion—such that everyone accesses the same quantity of the good. Views of the sky, for example, are both nonexcludable (assuming the absence of a coercive mechanism to prevent people from looking up) and non-rivalrous. Information is plainly non-rivalrous, but there are a variety of market and nonmarket mechanisms that can be used to exclude some users (often those who do not pay) from access to it. For the purposes of our analysis, however, the important attribute of public goods and of information is non-rivalry in consumption.[10]

What does non-rivalry imply about the optimal price of a public good? As a general matter (conditional on a textbook's worth of side conditions), economic efficiency requires that the price of a good be equal to the marginal cost of producing that good, where the marginal cost is defined as the cost of producing the last unit of the good. In competitive markets for rivalrous goods, this condition will hold. When consumers pay more than marginal cost, increased supply will be induced, bidding

---

9. In fact, it should be noted that in economics, public goods are defined purely technically, rather than normatively: some pure public goods may in fact be bad. Global climate change, for example, affects everyone, and the effect (although not the cause) is approximately independent of population size; it is thus a pure public good. The key feature is that using the good does not change the quantity available to be used (for good or ill, with joy or pain) by others.
10. Indeed, there are many reasons an individual might wish to exclude others from access to a particular piece of knowledge; for example, a desire for financial gain (as from a trade secret), a need to protect private personal information (like medical records), or a desire to be "first" in exploiting a particular data set or newfound corpus of documents.

the price down (and increasing quantity consumed) until what people are willing to pay for another unit just equals the costs of production of that unit. At this point, further production would cost more than the consumer price. For non-rivalrous goods like information, however, competitive mechanisms fail. The marginal cost of adding one more consumer, by definition, is zero. If the good is non-excludable (e.g., views of the sky), there is no problem because the price is also zero. But if a non-rivalrous good is excludable (e.g., electronic access to a recent *Nature* article) and the holder of the good chooses to exclude users who are unwilling to pay a price for access, that price will be greater than marginal cost and the outcome will be economically inefficient. That is, by pricing the non-rivalrous good at zero, it would be possible to increase the welfare of those who want to use that good without reducing the output of any other good being produced by the economy. To be sure, the owners of the excludable non-rivalrous good would be worse off—they would lose revenue and profit—but the consumers who were paying the price would be better off by the same amount, and new consumers would now be able to derive benefit from consumption of the good so that the overall effect on welfare would be positive.

Thus, given the existence of a non-rivalrous good, pricing it at zero is economically efficient. The problem is that at a price of zero, the good will often not be produced at all.[11] This is the basic argument for having

---

11. A strong argument can be made that in most cases, authors of scholarly works would produce their articles, books, and other forms of communication without being specifically paid for such works. Above all, scholars want to be read and to have an effect on the development of their fields. They get paid to do their research (and generally would not be able to function as productive scholars without being paid), but direct payments for their books and articles are a tiny part of their compensation except in a fairly rare set of cases where a scholarly work—usually a book—has a market that extends beyond the scholarly community. And of course, for scholars, the reputation that derives from high-quality academic work often translates into both prestige and increased income, though not necessarily through sales of the work itself. Steven Shavell (2010) argues vigorously that copyright protection is not required to induce academics to produce academic publication and that such protection should be removed. We find his arguments to be persuasive. Pamela Samuelson has argued in legal

public goods of various kinds provided collectively—for example, national defense, the judicial system, roads and bridges, and many others. It is also the argument for the basic business model of libraries, whether academic or public. Libraries are expensive to operate: they must acquire books and other materials, catalog and store them, maintain and preserve them, help patrons use them, and more. They do all of this in the interest of making the information contained in their collections available to their patrons. Their costs are covered on a collective level—via tuition, taxation, or other mechanisms—so that at the individual level they can remain free of charge.

As noted above, university libraries generally target their services at an authorized set of users—the members of the university community and, often, unaffiliated individuals willing to pay for privileges. The existence of such a group allows for an elegant solution to the problem of getting the library paid for while still charging zero at the point of use. Tuition, grant overhead, gifts, and various other university revenue streams are used to cover the costs of running the library and its programs. Effectively, each member of the library's user group has thus actually paid for the right to use the library "freely" (though some have done so more directly than others).

In the economic literature, non-rivalrous goods whose use is restricted to a group of people who pay for access via membership fees are called "club goods." Community swimming pools are a ubiquitous example, as are various amenities provided by local governments that are restricted to local residents. Because the university wishes to provide library services to its faculty and students so that they can engage in scholarly production and learning, and understanding that the nature of such information is locally non-rivalrous (except in the unusual case where there are many readers wanting a specific resource at the same time), universities choose a level of library services to provide their authorized users and compete on that level in their efforts to attract faculty and students. The "club good" model describes this behavior quite well.

As is the case with most public goods, works held in academic libraries may be approximately non-rivalrous in use (and therefore efficiently priced

---

filings (e.g., 2010) that the Authors Guild does not represent the interest of academic authors because academic authors are principally interested in having their works broadly available, not in receiving royalties on those works. Again, we agree.

at zero marginal cost); however, they are costly to produce, at least in the first instance, and those costs must be paid. It is costly to produce books and journal articles, even once the research has been done and written up. There are costs of selecting, editing, and reviewing (as well as, in the case of print, printing, binding, and distributing). Thus while the marginal cost of using the information in a book may be approximately zero, the cost of producing the book in the first place is well above zero, and those costs must be covered in order for that production to occur.[12] We have already established that covering costs by selling access to academic literature is inefficient—the information is non-rivalrous. Given the mission of the university to advance scholarship, a strong case can be made for subsidizing the costs associated with publication through author subventions or university general funds. Authors want their work to have maximum impact, and the additional costs of publishing once the first copy has been produced are relatively small.

Although a system of subsidies would serve the academy as a whole, individual institutions would have an incentive to let others pay for such a system—that is, to "free ride" on their peers' contributions. This free-rider problem arises frequently in the provision of public goods.[13] In the case of scholarly publishing, universities that produce scholarly output but that do not subsidize university presses are free riding on the system. Provosts at institutions that provide such subsidies often grumble at this state of affairs.

---

12. Of course, many journals, especially in the STM fields, are made available to libraries on terms where price greatly exceeds cost. Our point here is that it makes sense for libraries to pay to acquire scholarly resources. At the same time, we believe that pricing in parts of the industry is both inefficient and inequitable.
13. Another example of free riders in the university library/university press sphere would be library patrons who are unaffiliated with the university and do not pay access fees but are allowed to use the collections within the library buildings. In this case, however, the increased social welfare produced by their free riding (i.e., the increase in public access to information) more than outweighs whatever minor cost impact their relatively circumscribed free-riding behavior might have on the provision of the library's resources. This is also one reason members of the public are generally charged for services like borrowing: such services are costly to provide, and it makes sense to recover some of these costs from users who have not already paid through their membership in the community.

There is no general solution to free-rider problems. In the case of scholarly publishing, one could imagine a system in which publication was subsidized by the institution where the scholarship is performed, regardless of where it was published. Such a configuration would align the costs and benefits of scholarly publishing more closely than the current system—publication in the service of scholarship would be paid for along with all of the other costs of scholarly production, and institutions would continue to compete on their ability to provide good environments for faculty production of scholarly work.

The non-rivalrous nature of information is relevant to publishing and library behavior no matter what the technology of publication may be. Crucially, the purposes of scholarship and the non-rivalry of information call for mechanisms that support robust production of relevant literature while charging essentially zero prices for access to the user. As we have seen, and will see more, the digital world changes the business models available to universities and their libraries and presses. And with that in mind, we now return you to your regularly scheduled program.

Digital Business Models: A Convergence of Purpose

In the digital environment, many—though not all—of the costs associated with the production, storage, and distribution of paper-based scholarly work disappear, and this creates significant opportunities for university presses and libraries to work together to increase the accessibility, utility, and stability of scholarly information. As organs of the university, the press and the library share a mission-based interest in the dissemination and preservation of scholarly work. Where the costs of dissemination fall, so should the price of access; where the costs of preservation are not increased by extending access to larger populations, such extensions should be granted. And both of these conditions obtain for digital information.

For digital works, many of the library's costs for retention and lending fall sharply or even disappear. Once the requisite digital infrastructures—big hard drives, fast networks, powerful servers—are in place, there is essentially no marginal cost to providing digital access to scholarship throughout the connected world. While market arrangements with publishers can and do hold libraries back from opening access to licensed electronic resources—and this is unlikely to change—it seems clear to us that where legal and contractual arrangements permit, the mission of the academic library demands the provision of the broadest possible access to its digital resources, at least at a basic level. This conclusion also follows from the public goods logic discussed above. Where goods are non-rivalrous, charging for their use is economically inefficient because doing so excludes people who benefit without imposing costs on others.

For publishers, the digital shift has been a source of greater tension, though its effect with respect to *scholarly* publishing is, at least in principle, quite straightforward. The mission of the academic press, aligned with the mission of the research university, is to disseminate research and scholarship. As for libraries, once a digital work is on a server, the marginal technical cost of making it available to another user, or another thousand users, is essentially zero. Thus selling the products of scholarly work ceases to make sense as a means of financing any part of publication; attaching a cost to scholarly information simply diminishes its reach. Publication is an essential part of university work—a public good both within and beyond the academy—and like most public goods, the most efficient way to produce it is to pay for it in advance (along with paying for the faculty, the research library, the graduate students, the trips to archives, the laboratories, and all of the other apparatus of research) and then give it away for "free." Additional services can then be sold (e.g., print copies, digital bells and whistles), and the revenue from them can provide an additional line of support for the underlying mission.[14] But whatever add-on services might be offered, the basic welfare economics of public goods in the digital world leads us to conclude that there should be a readable and usable version of scholarly work openly available without charge to the user.

Interestingly, in this scenario, the press and the library begin looking much more alike: in extending access to its collections beyond the walls of the university, the library takes on the outward-facing aspect of the press; in paying for materials up front and then giving them away, the press assumes

---

14. The models of National Academies Press and of Open Humanities Press are apposite here (e.g., Pope and Kannan 2003, Kimball 2009). Interestingly, there is still a market for printed versions of works, and some of the costs of producing a work that can be distributed over the Internet or via print on demand can be recouped—such sales can be part of the business model that supports mission-driven scholarly publication.

the basic dissemination model of the library. This, of course, brings us to where we've been heading all along: in the digital world, the press and the library need no longer be separate. Given the symbiosis in their missions, functions, and optimal business models in the digital world, they should unite. Within such a partnership, the library can teach the press how to give information away for free and how to hold on to it over the long term, while the press can teach the library how to reach beyond the university for both authors and audiences and how to extract mission-enhancing revenues from the value-added services it provides. Ultimately, a new form of university agency should emerge—for now we'll call it the "library-press."

And by the way: this kind of merger should occur not at just one university or a few, but at all of them. The optimal scale of provision of digitized resources (whether born-digital or digitized from tactile media) is virtually unlimited and implies that the individual university in many cases is not the ideal locus of production for digital access but that much larger consortia can do the job more efficiently by sharing the costs of initial provision and preservation. Once the relevant works are placed (with appropriate redundancy) on the network, the cost of subsequent provision is very close to zero. Thus, for works in the public domain, the ideal is to share high-quality digital access widely. For works not in the public domain, this would also be the ideal except for (and it's a big exception) copyright law.

Thus, via digital technologies and collaborative arrangements, it can become possible, at essentially zero added cost, to extend the mission of the library-press to making scholarship ubiquitously accessible. Provided that such an expansion can be accomplished without substantially harming the interests of the local university community, we can think of no principled basis for not doing so, although the current state of copyright law substantially reduces the benefits that can be made available to both scholars and the general public. Providing such widespread access both increases the reach of scholarship and improves its quality and depth by permitting scholars to find and draw upon (and critique and question) works from other times and places that would otherwise have been difficult to access and reuse. Making access to scholarly resources as ubiquitous as is consistent with the law would amplify both the library's mission of providing long-term access to the scholarly record and the press's mission of broad-ranging dissemination; the problem is simply (or perhaps not so simply) organizing the collective will, across the university system, to implement such an expansion in access and mission.

Putting the Pieces Together: Optimizing Scholarly Production in the Digital Age

The first definition of *publish* in the OED is "to make public." Taken literally, this definition implies that libraries in general, and research libraries in particular, have always been publishers. The library is itself a means of scholarly publishing or scholarly communication. After a certain period of time, if you can't find an academic work in the library, it is as if it had never been published because as a general matter it is lost. And conversely, if you can find the work in the library, it continues to be published—made public—even if it is out of print. The publisher, by producing and distributing the work in the first place, provides an essential, but time-limited service to the life cycle of scholarly work. The library provides an equally essential and, in principle, time-unlimited service by making the work available—publishing it— to the relevant publics indefinitely.

Publishers have never been directly concerned with assuring that there is an archival record of their works. Libraries have made preservation part of their mission, partly because of an accident of print technology: the only way to provide access to print was to own a copy of the item and keep it in good enough shape to be used. In the current environment, where electronic works often sit on publishers' servers, their long-term durability is at risk both technically and economically. Works can be lost because hardware breaks or because commercial entities fail. If the server is in the library, however, and the library takes long-term usability (access via preservation) as an essential element of mission, the chances that works published today in electronic form will be reliably found and used in one hundred years are much better than if those works are not held in libraries. The library is already the de facto publisher for the future of works published (and collected by the library) in the past. With digital technology, and recognizing the mission of the university to make scholarly work public, the library is ready to take on the role of making public most of the scholarly record as it is produced.

A Proposal: Move Forward by Looking Back

In a brilliant essay published in 1980, August Frugé, director of the University of California Press from 1944 to 1976, suggests that scholarly publication should be organized to deliver two complementary functions: "full publishing," which looks very much like traditional scholarly publishing, and "recording," which Frugé identifies as a form of "fractional publishing." The first form is to be reserved for books (he was writing only about books in 1980) that are "of great distinction and usefulness" (271). The latter would "preserve and make available a host of competent but secondary writings" (271). Most scholarship is of precisely this latter nature, as are most scholarly publications, be they in monograph or journal form (1954).

Frugé's differentiation of these two types of publishing harks back to the University of California Press under his leadership, which undertook two programs divided much along these lines. It also coheres with the experience of the older author of this chapter (Courant). One of the striking things about scholarly publishing, viewed from the perspective of an economist, is the discussion around scarcity in the world of monograph publishing. Some of the time, especially in conversation with editors and press directors, what is scarce is good books—"books of great distinction and usefulness" (Frugé 1980, 271). University presses and editors compete vigorously with each other—and, where there is substantial commercial potential, with commercial presses—to attract authors and projects that will contribute to the reputation and commercial fortune of the press. Moreover, commercial presses are better equipped to deal in the trade market, to provide advances and excellent dinners and all of the other goodies that publishers lavish on authors whose works are deemed especially desirable, which leaves university presses at a disadvantage in these cases.

At the same time, from the perspective of the young scholar attempting to make a career or a scholar at any level wanting to contribute to the literature in her field, what is scarce is a place on the front list of a respectable academic press. Many "competent" writings are never published, and many scholars are frustrated by the fact that scholarly publishers, seeking works of "great distinction"—or perhaps grasping for greater commercial success—do not have places for good scholarly work on their lists.

The obvious solution to this problem is to bifurcate the list, much as was done at the University of California Press for decades, when that press published both a "monograph series" and a more conventional book series.

The monograph series published UC work only (we would probably not keep this sort of local-only feature) and the costs were paid directly from what we would now call general funds (Frugé 1980, 271). In the digital world, we can build upon this model in a much more flexible and nimble way. That is, in our model, Frugé's "recording" or "monograph series" level of publication becomes the *baseline digital edition*: a lightly edited, open-access edition of the text made available online, something like the digital OA versions of books available through the National Academies Press or the way public domain works are presented on HathiTrust—that is, accessible, but not exactly the Platonic ideal of usability. Upon this baseline, myriad additional levels of publication could potentially be built—paperback or hardcover editions, enhanced digital editions, various bundles or indices, and so on—but all of the library-press's editions would receive at least this level of publication. The purpose, much like that of *PLOS ONE* in the biological sciences, would be to assure that competent scholarship could become part of the scholarly record and remain so. Libraries—and library consortia like HathiTrust—would be natural homes for this kind of publication, given their expertise in assuring both accessibility and permanence of the scholarly record. Still, it's worth noting that in this setup, many of the activities of the scholarly press continue—ideally paid for via publishing subventions that would be allocated to scholars in fields where book-length publication is the norm, for just this purpose.

And what of the works of great distinction and usefulness? Some of these, surely, would still be produced through the editorial work done by academic publishers seeking excellent projects and developing specialized lists. But some could also emerge in a more data-driven fashion from the list of baseline digital editions that we sketched in the preceding paragraph: should one of these lightly published works prove especially popular or useful in its field, it could be converted or revised into a more full-featured edition—electronic, print, or both—at any time. We would expect that the library-press in that scheme would continue to have the right to distribute a readable and usable open-access (baseline) version of the work. The author (or conceivably the author's employer) would have the right to further commercial exploitation, including the right to negotiate the terms of such exploitation with a publisher. That publisher could be the original library-based press, a more full-featured imprint of same, or some other publisher. Thus books with commercial promise, or even books that seem open to extended editorial improvement and enhancement or distribution through channels beyond the relatively utilitarian baseline edition,[15] could receive such, with the profits being shared by the publisher and the author, much as is the case now.

Is it plausible that works that are available open-access can also be sold? Yes, it happens every day. For example, the National Academies Press (NAP) has a sweeping and longstanding open-access policy, yet many people still prefer—and are willing to pay for—hard copies of NAP works. A 2003 University of Maryland study (Pope and Kannan) showed that a striking 58 percent of individuals at the point of purchasing a NAP book would still go forward with their purchase even after being offered a free PDF version of the same book. Although that percentage has undoubtedly diminished over the decade since the study was conducted, as e-reading technologies have improved, many readers still prefer paper books—or would be willing to pay a small premium to add various bells and whistles to the electronic versions available to them. Many open-access journal articles and monographs have substantial print sales even though they can be read online.[16] (The same is true of more popular literature, which still enjoys robust sales in both print and electronic formats, despite low-priced or free availability through providers that infringe copyright.)

Finally, we believe that a plan along these lines is economically feasible. Currently scholarly monographs are supported in part by research libraries that buy them. The more commercially viable ones also sell to a broader public. The cost of producing a well-reviewed and lightly edited scholarly monograph to be distributed digitally through libraries is not well established in the literature, but, accounting for reduced marketing and sales expenditure relative to current norms, it is unlikely to be more than $12,000 for the average humanities monograph, some of which is already being spent for the research library to acquire the work. Additionally, whatever the cost of producing the baseline digital edition might be, it is

---

15. To be clear, we do not use *utilitarian* as a pejorative here. It simply reflects a lower-cost and fewer-frills approach.
16. Indeed, the University of Michigan Libraries sell hundreds, or perhaps even thousands, of reprints of digitized works that are out of copyright via their print-on-demand program every year (e.g., via the Espresso Book Machine services section of the library website, www.lib.umich.edu/espresso-book-machine).

surely less than producing a full-fledged print-published book, and since under this new regime at least some books that presses might previously have print-published would get only the baseline digital treatment (until and unless they found an audience to pay for more), some cost savings could undoubtedly be realized in this area.

If the average length of time it takes to produce a useful monograph is six years, the $12,000 (or less) would be a tiny fraction of over $500,000 in salary and benefits, plus the indirect cost of space, HVAC, libraries, stipends for graduate students, and more that it costs the university to employ a humanities faculty member for six years.[17] And, of course, all of these amounts are tiny when compared to startup packages in the sciences.

Crucially, a plan like this is feasible because the library already holds the means of acquisition, cataloging, preservation, and distribution, and in the digital world, the "first copy" can be distributed widely over time and space without incurring any appreciable additional cost.

Conclusion

At the heart of our argument for placing the press (or at least many of its activities) in the library is our observation that the missions and methods of the press and the library tend to converge in the digital world. Both have always been part of a system of scholarly production whose purpose is to document and preserve forever the record of scholarly work. That record is costly to produce and costly to preserve, yet it is non-rivalrous in use—

---

17. This is a back-of-the envelope calculation. Salary and benefits for a beginning English professor at the University of Michigan are about $80,000. Michigan's indirect cost rate is just over 50 percent. It's likely that in the humanities, indirect costs are somewhat lower than in the sciences, but building and grounds, heat, light, security, administration, and the library benefit humanists as much (or as little) as scientists. Conservatively, if we use a 30 percent rate, we get total annual costs of about $104,000. Multiply by 6, and the total is well over $600,000. Of course, the professor is paid in no small part to teach, but producers of scholarly monographs get release time and other assistance precisely so that they can do research. The $500,000 estimate is not unreasonable. And, of course, pay and other costs rise with time and experience.

once it exists, the cost of allowing another user to have access to it is essentially zero once the user has the works in sight. In the print world, the press produced the book (sometimes with subsidy), the library purchased and cataloged the book and arranged for its preservation, and the user walked to the library to use the book. In the digital world, the first parts of the story are unchanged, but in the end the library can come to the user, pretty much anywhere in the world, via the Internet. Thus the library is equipped to make the work public—to publish the work.

Moreover, the library is equipped to publish the work without charging for its use, consistent with the requirements of economic efficiency in pricing non-rivalrous goods and consistent with the long-standing practice of research libraries of providing access to their collections (to an authorized population) at no charge. In the digital world, the authorized population can be everyone with access to the Internet. The remaining problem is covering the initial costs of producing a work of sufficient quality to merit publication in this form. There are many ways that this could be done. We have suggested a *PLOS ONE*–like model in which the institution that employs the scholar pays for the cost of library-based publication of an open-access baseline digital edition of scholarly works.

Whatever the details of the business models of publication and preservation, in the digital world the vital goals of distribution and preservation can piggyback on the existing capabilities of the research library, with the result that the academic literature in "book fields" will be robust and secure.

Works Cited

Bivens-Tatum, Wayne. 2011. *Libraries and the Enlightenment*. Los Angeles: Library Juice Press.

Courant, Paul N. 2006. "Scholarship and Academic Libraries (and Their Kin) in the World of Google." *First Monday* 11, no. 8.

Courant, Paul N., and Matthew Nielsen. 2010. "On the Cost of Keeping a Book." In *The Idea of Order: Transforming Research Collections for 21st Century Scholarship*, 81–105. Washington, DC: Council on Library and Information Resources.

Frugé, August. 1980. "A Two-Level System for Scholarly Writings, or, Is Publishing Necessary?" *JGE: Journal of General Education* 31, no. 4 (Winter): 265–77.

Guédon, Jean-Claude. 2011. "Between Quality and Excellence; from Nation to Region: Strategies for Latin American Scholarly and Scientific Journals." In *Calidad e Impacto de la Revista Iberoamericana* [Quality and Impact of Ibero-American Journals], compiled by Ana Maria Cetto and José Octavio Alonso Gamboa. México: Facultad de Ciencias, UNAM. www.latindex.org/ciri2010/parte_01/01_01/01_01_00.html.

Harris, Michael H. 1995. *History of Libraries in the Western World*. Metuchen, NJ: Scarecrow Press.

Hawes, Gene R. 1967. *To Advance Knowledge: A Handbook on American University Press Publishing*. New York: American University Press Services.

Jagodzinski, Cecile M. 2008. "The University Press in North America: A Brief History." *Journal of Scholarly Publishing* 40, no. 1: 1–20.

Jefferson, Thomas. 1813. Letter to Isaac McPherson, August 13. The Founders' Constitution, Document 12 on Article 1, Section 8, Clause 8. http://press-pubs.uchicago.edu/founders/documents/a1_8_8s12.html.

Kerr, Chester. 1949. *A Report on American University Presses*. Washington, DC: Association of American University Presses.

Kimball, Shana. 2009. "Scalable Library-Based Publishing Services at the University of Michigan: Partnering with Open Humanities Press." Paper presented at LIANZA Conference, Christchurch, NZ, October 12–14, 2009.

Lavoie, Brian, Lorraine Eakin, Amy Friedlander, Francine Berman, Paul Courant, Clifford Lynch, and Daniel Rubinfeld. 2008. *Sustaining the Digital Investment: Issues and Challenges of Economically Sustainable Digital Preservation*, interim report Blue Ribbon Task Force on Sustainable Digital Preservation and Access. December. http://brtf.sdsc.edu/biblio/BRTF_Interim_Report.pdf.

Lawrence, Stephen R., Lynn Silipigni Connaway, and Keith H. Brigham. 2001. "Life Cycle Costs of Library Collections: Creation of Effective Performance and Cost Metrics for Library Resources." *College and Research Libraries* 62, no. 6 (November 1): 541–53.

Lerner, Fred. 2009. *The Story of Libraries: From the Invention of Writing to the Computer Age*, 2nd ed. New York: Continuum.

Muto, Albert. 1993. *The University of California Press: The Early Years, 1893–1953*. Berkeley: University of California Press.

Pope, Barbara Kline, and P. K. Kannan. 2003. "An Evaluation Study of the National Academies Press's E-Publishing Initiatives." Washington DC: Association of American University Presses, January 31.

Samuelson, Pamela. 2010. "Academic Author Objections to the Google Book Search Settlement." *Journal on Telecommunications and High Technology Law* 8, no. 2 (Spring): 491–522.

Samuelson, Paul A. 1954. "The Pure Theory of Public Expenditure." *Review of Economics and Statistics* 36, no. 4: 387–89.

———. 1955. "Diagrammatic Exposition of a Theory of Public Expenditure." *Review of Economics and Statistics* 37, no. 4: 350–56.

Shapiro, Carl, and Hal R. Varian. 1999. *Information Rules: A Strategic Guide to the Network Economy*. Boston: Harvard Business School Press.

Shapiro, Harold T. 2005. *A Larger Sense of Purpose: Higher Education and Society*. Princeton, NJ: Princeton University Press.

Shavell, Steven. 2010. "Should Copyright of Academic Works Be Abolished?" *Journal of Legal Analysis* 2, no. 1 (Spring): 301–58.

U-M (University of Michigan). 2013a. "About MLibrary." Accessed October 25, 2014. www.lib.umich.edu/about-library.

———. 2013b. "Mission Statement." Office of the President, accessed October 25, 2014. http://president.umich.edu/about/mission.

Weisbrod, Burton A., Jeffrey P. Ballou, and Evelyn D. Asch. 2008. *Mission and Money: Understanding the University*. New York: Cambridge University Press.

CHAPTER 2

We Scholars
How Libraries Could Help Us with Scholarly Publishing, if Only We'd Let Them

J. Britt Holbrook

> Universities easily fall into ruts. Almost every epoch requires a fresh start.
> —*Daniel Coit Gilman*
> *Inaugural Address as First President of Johns Hopkins University*

> Research has become the dominant source of instinct, meaning, status and revenue in higher education, especially at the top of the university totem pole.
> —*Simon Marginson*
> *"Ideas of a University" for the Global Era*

> Postmodern knowledge is not simply a tool of the authorities; it refines our sensitivity to differences and reinforces our ability to tolerate the incommensurable.
> —*Jean-François Lyotard*
> *The Postmodern Condition:*
> *A Report on Knowledge*

We scholars[1] value scholarly publication above all else. Since the library can help us with research—mostly by providing access to the scholarly literature we need—we also value the library. However, we scholars are not, as a group, convinced that librarians really understand the value of research. Yes, librarians understand things like cataloging and preservation, but even when librarians are technically considered members of the faculty, we scholars presume that libraries and librarians are there to serve our research needs.

Put differently, for us scholars, where scholarly publication has intrinsic value, the library and librarians have instrumental value. It goes without saying for us scholars that whatever has intrinsic value (such as research) and is valued for its own sake is inherently more valuable than anything that has merely instrumental value (such as the library) and can be seen as a means to another end. This attitude, which Nietzsche would have termed the order of rank of our scholarly values, is literally ancient— it was clearly expressed by Aristotle in his *Nichomachean Ethics* (written ~350 BCE). We scholars have institutionalized this attitude in the form of the university.

As we shall see, this attitude has several implications for libraries as publishers. One such implication is that we scholars tend not to work in a collaborative manner with libraries and librarians; instead, we expect not to encounter any resistance from them (a book should always be on the shelf, we should have easy access to all the journal articles we need, and so forth). We may in fact resent it when libraries try to move beyond this minimal role. For instance, if libraries really understood scholarly publishing, they would not do things like impose open-access mandates.

---

1. Throughout this chapter, I include myself in the set "we scholars" in contrast to librarians, a group of which I am certainly not a member. Whether I really ought to be included among "we scholars" will, I hope, remain unclear. For the sake of argument, however, I definitely mean to exclude librarians from that group and to treat librarians and scholars as separate entities with different values.

So the idea that libraries might themselves enter into the publishing arena strikes many academics as silly at best.[2] At worst, depending on how it is implemented, many academics will see library publishing as a threat to academic freedom. This chapter attempts to reconstruct how we scholars think about these matters in an effort to help libraries that are venturing out into the world of scholarly publishing. It also attempts to construct an argument that we scholars ought to adjust our own thinking about the library, as well as about scholarly publishing.

On (Academic) Liberty

The university is founded on freedom. At the same time, the university instantiates many ideas of freedom. Although I agree that it is important for librarians to understand the difference between the sorts of academic freedom we scholars enjoy and the intellectual freedom accorded to librarians (see Danner and Bintliff 2007 for an excellent account of this distinction), these are not the different sorts of freedom I plan to address here. Instead, I shall begin with an examination of the philosophical issues that underlie several different understandings of freedom operative in the university where "the university" is understood to embody many different contexts. These different understandings—which are usually implicit—provide ample opportunity for miscommunication among us scholars, between us scholars and university administrators, and between us scholars and librarians. Until we begin to understand—and perhaps to reconceive—academic freedom, libraries have little chance to succeed as scholarly publishers.

Academic freedom itself varies from context to context. Different countries, and even different universities within the same country, have different views of academic freedom. This fact is fairly well known and is very well discussed in the literature on academic freedom. Less well discussed, however, at least outside of the circle of academic philosophy, is the question of whether we have different ideas of freedom itself. This

---

2. I am aware that some libraries have been engaged with publishing for some time; but I believe I am in the minority and that most scholars remain ignorant of this fact. I spend more time than most scholars engaging with librarians, and I was surprised to learn while writing this chapter that there had once existed an International Group of Publishing Libraries.

chapter is not the place to go into detail about this philosophical debate. However, a brief tour of some of the issues—something no scholar of philosophy would respect as true scholarship—will prove enlightening.

Isaiah Berlin (1958) distinguished between two concepts of liberty: *negative liberty*, which can be summarized as freedom from constraint, and *positive liberty*, which can be summarized as freedom to pursue a self-determined course of action. Although Berlin's account was specifically about liberty in a political context, these two concepts of liberty are also relevant to the sort of freedom we scholars understand when we think of academic freedom. Indeed, the history of the notion of academic freedom suggests that we scholars have moved away from thinking of academic freedom as positive liberty and toward a notion of academic freedom as negative liberty. The most obvious evidence of this shift is the evolution of our attitudes toward tenure.

Tenure—From Means to End

Tenure is meant to be a means to secure the end of academic freedom. In fact, however, tenure has become the end we seek, and academics have become so beholden to the idea of tenure that we sacrifice the pursuit of positive freedom. Instead of what Fuller (1999) describes as the "right to be wrong," we scholars assert the "right to be right—or at least to avoid being wrong—in our own little world."

The idea that tenure is meant to be a means to secure academic freedom is explicitly and clearly expressed in the American Association of University Professors' (AAUP) *1940 Statement of Principles on Academic Freedom and Tenure*:

> Tenure is a means to certain ends; specifically: (1) freedom of teaching and research and of extramural activities, and (2) a sufficient degree of economic security to make the profession attractive to men and women of ability. Freedom and economic security, hence, tenure, are indispensable to the success of an institution in fulfilling its obligations to its students and to society. (AAUP 1990, 3)

As competition for tenured academic jobs has increased over the years, tenure has increasingly been identified with the end of economic security. Those lucky enough to secure a tenure-track position these days are typically advised to "do what it takes" to be granted tenure. "What it takes" is typically expressed in terms of a set of criteria for tenure, including especially publishing a certain amount of scholarship (a number of articles or a book) in certain venues (top journals or academic presses). The first seven years or so of a scholar's career are thus spent with one aim in mind: securing tenure. Moreover, scholars are trained to adhere to strict disciplinary standards of what counts in order to achieve the end of tenure. The idea that tenure is meant as a means to freedom of teaching and research has dropped out, replaced by the idea that tenure equals economic security, provided one follows the rules.

Once tenure has been granted, scholars *do* view themselves as free—*free from* the overwhelming pressure to publish or perish. Once tenure has been granted, the scholar is safe. Provided that minimal standards are met, the tenured scholar is generally permitted to go about her or his business of teaching and research without too many external constraints. Academic freedom has been effectively reduced to the idea of negative liberty.

Insofar as we scholars tend to view tenure as the end and scholarship as the chief means to that end, we also tend to undervalue the positive aspects of academic freedom. We scholars care not what we are *free to* do, but only what we are *free from* being required to do. (This insight, by the way, should be an important lesson for those in charge of assessing scholarly research.) That scholars tend to undervalue the positive aspects of academic freedom has important ramifications for the course of scholarship. Nowhere is this fact more evident than in the process of peer review.

Our Twisted View of Peer Review

According to Biagioli (2002), peer review was originally used as a complement to state censorship—foreign products were censored, while those produced within the state under the auspices of national academies were subject to "internal," that is, intrastate, peer review. The notion of an internal peer gradually moved away from the state, shifting the locus of power to academic disciplines. Today, particularly in terms of the scientific community, peer review is treated as a guarantee of epistemic warrant, as well as viewed as another means of securing academic freedom. However, the sort of academic freedom peer review secures is negative—peer review erects a barrier against outside, nonacademic interference. What is lacking is any sense that peer review could also be used to expand our positive freedom (Holbrook 2010). We seek assurance from our peers that what we say is right, or at least not wrong, rather than insurance from peer review to take intellectual and academic risks.

Disciplines define peers, and peer review is generally designed to uphold disciplinary standards—of rigor, of method, of subject matter, and generally of what counts as good research within a discipline. When a piece of research is subject to peer review, then, it typically means that disciplinary standards will determine whether it passes muster to be published (in the case of a manuscript submitted for publication) or to be funded (in the case of a grant proposal). Decisions regarding promotion and tenure typically involve a larger body of work, but this work is also typically subject first and foremost to disciplinary peer review (by peers within the department and external referees, who are typically scholars of high standing within the discipline). Tenure decisions usually also involve review by members of the faculty from disciplines other than that of the person up for tenure review. These tenure review committees tend to rely heavily on the reports of the disciplinary peers within the department and the external disciplinary reviews. The largest factor in their decisions, however, remains the candidate's record of *peer-reviewed publications* (National Research Council 2012; Harley 2013). Such publications ideally appear in the top journals within the researcher's field of expertise. In other words, nondisciplinary "peers" place their trust in the judgment of disciplinary peers.

This sort of respect shown by members of review panels for the disciplinary expertise of other reviewers is also sometimes evident in the peer review of grant proposals. Lamont, Mallard, and Guetzkow (2012) identify several "rules" adopted by panelists, including "deferring to expertise" and "respecting disciplinary sovereignty" (431). Peer review, then, whether of manuscripts or grant proposals, is typically dependent on disciplinary norms. As such, peer review is typically conservative, encouraging adherence to normal rather than "potentially transformative" research (Frodeman and Holbrook 2012).

Although tenure depends on peer review, the conservatism of peer review is reinforced by the need to secure tenure. Scholars seeking tenure are warned against—since they are typically not rewarded for—publishing in lower quality (according to peers) venues, much less in venues outside their native disciplines. The combined forces of peer review and tenure requirements pose the greatest threat to the emergence of libraries as publishers.

On (Academic) Libraries

I see an ongoing effort aimed at re-envisioning the academic library. The source of this effort is, as far as I can tell, internal to libraries themselves. Libraries face a slew of problems. Most pressing, perhaps, are issues regarding space and increasing strains on library budgets. Technology promises some help for issues of space. Digitized collections, after all, take up less physical space than books. But technology may also help ease the strain on library budgets—or so the thinking goes.

As far as I can tell, forward-thinking librarians, many of whom have training in information science as well as in library science, see an opportunity in the advance of information technology. This opportunity is linked to the increase in subscription prices for scholarly journals, including the practice of many scholarly publishers of bundling journals together. Why, these forward-thinking librarians wonder, should subscription prices for journals go up while the price for publishing them, because of advances in information technology, continues to go down? Armed with knowledge of both the economics and technology of publishing, librarians have begun to think in terms of *business models*.

The open-access (OA) movement also seems to be linked with this new way of thinking. Opening access to scholarship is good, philosophically speaking, especially from a librarian's (or a research funder's) point of view. Technologically, OA is viable. As a business model for scholarly publishing— or rather, for scholarly publishers—however, OA presents many difficulties. Scholarly publishers have generally balked at OA, though the combination of funder mandates, new OA journals, and increasing pressure from librarians has led to some publishers at least appearing to move in the direction of OA (though one suspects a movement akin to "greenwashing" businesses).

Sensing an opportunity, libraries have begun to promote OA policies at an increasing number of universities. Faculty senates across the land have been convinced that such policies are good for scholarship—we scholars certainly want our research to be more readily available, perhaps even more read and more cited! We also love it if we can simply and easily access others' research without having to navigate pay walls or sign in to our library website, only to find that our library has dropped a subscription (it was too costly, after all, given that it was bundled with little used journals) to a journal that contains an article we need to write the next sentence! OA seems a win-win-win for libraries, for research funders, and for us scholars. If OA undermines the current business model of today's scholarly publishers, well, so much the better! Libraries can act as publishers to fill the void left when today's giants of scholarly publishing collapse.

This sort of enthusiasm is infectious, of course. In fact, one can make a case that something like infectious enthusiasm is a necessary requirement for any revolution to succeed. But for all its promise, OA should also be seen as an opportunity for libraries to learn some lessons. The simplest and biggest lesson of OA is that librarians do not yet understand us scholars and our scholarly culture. This misunderstanding is demonstrated by the fact that many OA policies *mandate* that scholarly work (starting with peer-reviewed journal articles) be submitted to an institutional repository.

Lessons to be Learned from Open-Access Mandates

The first lesson to be learned from OA mandates is the extent to which we scholars value our academic freedom—specifically in the sense of negative liberty or *freedom from* constraints. To mandate that we upload some version of our scholarly work to an institutional repository—no matter how easy libraries make that task—automatically places an additional constraint on us scholars. Insofar as mandates place additional constraints on us, they by definition limit our negative liberty.

The second lesson to be learned from OA mandates is that we scholars tend to see our academic freedom in disciplinary terms. Even if we scholars (in the form of a faculty senate, say) voted in favor of an OA mandate, which seems to respect our academic freedom, OA mandates can be seen as a threat to our academic freedom insofar as they fail to respect disciplinary sovereignty. Historians, to take one example, tend to resist OA mandates that apply to dissertations. A historian's dissertation typically becomes that historian's first book. Making the dissertation openly available automatically makes the historian's research openly available. This openness poses two threats to the historian's disciplinary sovereignty. First, many historians are concerned that an openly available dissertation will be viewed by book publishers as prior publication, thus making the prospects of securing a book contract more difficult. Second, once the research is made openly available, other historians who are working on similar areas may come in and "scoop" the research, including it in their own book already under contract. A footnote in someone else's book does not equate to one's own book, and if the research is already published in someone else's book, that, too, would undermine one's efforts to secure a book contract.

The third lesson to be learned from OA mandates is that it is sometimes possible—and sometimes even efficacious—to appeal to a notion of academic freedom in the sense of positive liberty. That faculty at many universities have voted in favor of OA mandates clearly demonstrates the appeal of *freedom to* open up our scholarship. Like the disciplinary standards we impose on ourselves, certain limitations on academic freedom (in the negative sense) are justifiable on the grounds that the limits are *self-imposed*. The notion of giving oneself limits, in other words, is compatible with a notion of positive academic freedom (which might better be termed *autonomy*).

The fourth lesson to be learned from OA mandates is that this notion of positive academic freedom is best addressed on the level of *disciplinary autonomy*. Academics within a discipline defer to the standards of their own discipline, or they violate them at their own risk. Academics from different disciplines tend to defer to the standards of the other's discipline, provided that the territories staked out by those disciplines do not overlap. That the faculty (in the form of the senate) voted to adopt an OA mandate may de jure mean that all disciplines must comply, but few of us scholars would dispute the rights of individual disciplines (such as history) to resist such mandates.

Risk, Reputation, and Revaluation

That a positive notion of academic freedom (autonomy) is compatible with a negative notion of academic freedom (from external constraint) is not sufficient to secure the success of libraries as scholarly publishers. Most of us scholars have uncritically (and largely unconsciously) embraced the negative notion of academic freedom. As I have argued above, this negative notion of academic freedom presents a significant barrier to libraries venturing into the field of scholarly publishing. If a library wishes to venture into the field of scholarly publishing, then what should it do?

If I am right in my preceding analysis, until we scholars adopt and pursue a notion of positive academic autonomy, there is a limit to what libraries *can* do. Pointing to freedom *from* the existing publishers may have some appeal to some of us scholars. But setting things up so that we have the freedom *to* publish through the library cannot succeed until we scholars recognize this (positive) freedom as worthy of pursuit.

As things stand now, any of us scholars who pursue publication outside the venues recognized by our disciplinary peers as exemplary are taking a risk. It is tempting to think that those of us who publish in "alternative" venues do so only at the expense of extra time. In other words, one might think that, as long as we publish the requisite amount (according to tenure and promotion requirements) in the recognized venues, we are also free to publish in alternative venues. The reality, however, is that in pursuing publication outside the accepted disciplinary norms, we run the risk of being misidentified, of being labeled a maverick at best or an outsider at worst. The safe advice for anyone seeking to pass through peer review is not to confuse the reviewers. Publications outside the norm, however, even accompanied by publications that fall well inside normal parameters, risk producing confusion. In publishing outside the recognized venues, we risk our scholarly reputations.

What we need is a revaluation of academic freedom that emphasizes positive liberty—the *freedom to* publish what we want where we want. Libraries as publishers could serve as a means to achieve that end. However, until we scholars realize, and recognize as a problem, that tenure—intended as the *means* to achieve academic freedom—has become the de facto *end* of scholarship, there is a large disincentive to pursue our freedom in a positive sense.

The barrier of tenure requirements is not one that libraries seeking to branch out into publishing can simply avoid. It will not be enough to build the capacity to publish and hope that we scholars will simply come and use it. Libraries, too, must take risks. Libraries must recognize that building tools and making them available is at most only part of what they must do. Resources are of no use unless they are actually used.

It is essential, then, that libraries engage their potential users as co-designers of their attempt to enter into scholarly publishing. This engagement must take place on multiple levels, including working with individual scholars to learn what design elements are essential and what would make their scholarship even better. But engagement must also take place on larger institutional levels, including those of the department, the university, and, ultimately, the disciplines. Although academic departments often hold sway within universities, disciplines are the seat of academic power. Only if *disciplines* see libraries-as-publishers as a means to the end of empowerment will libraries-as-publishers become viable in the eyes of us scholars.

Libraries-as-publishers are facing a crisis of legitimation. For this reason, it would make the most sense for libraries to partner with scholars from particular disciplines, as well as with disciplinary professional organizations, to develop publications designed specifically for those disciplines. It is essential to this design process that these publications be recognized by the disciplines as respectable venues. Peer review (one of the main trump cards held now by traditional scholarly publishers) should also be included as part of the design, whether the publications planned are journals or books.

The idea that libraries-as-publishers ought to engage disciplines suggests a course of action that runs counter to the discourse of replacing traditional scholarly publishers. The group of traditional scholarly publishers ought to be divided into two groups: for-profit publishers on the one hand and not-for-profit publishers on the other. The currently dominant narrative suggests that universities should be run more like businesses, which results in university presses, disciplinary professional organizations that rely on publication subscriptions, and libraries thinking in terms of "business models" for scholarly publication. A better way to approach the issue of scholarly publication, I have suggested, would be in terms of empowering scholars to pursue their scholarship with maximal freedom and creativity. Speaking in such terms ought to appeal to not-for-profit publishers, as well as to individual scholars, while falling on deaf ears of anyone seeking only profit from scholarship. Libraries that engage us scholars in such terms, rather than thinking only in terms of *business models*, stand a real chance of succeeding as scholarly publishers

Works Cited

AAUP (American Association of University Professors). 1990. *1940 Statement of Principles on Academic Freedom and Tenure with 1970 Interpretive Comments*, upd. 1989, 1990. Washington, DC: American Association of University Professors. www.aaup.org/report/1940-statement-principles-academic-freedom-and-tenure.

Berlin, Isaiah. 1958. "Two Concepts of Liberty." Paper presented at the University of Oxford, October 31.

Biagioli, Mario. 2002. "From Book Censorship to Academic Peer Review." *Emergences: Journal for the Study of Media and Composite Cultures* 12, no. 1: 11–45.

Danner, Richard A., and Barbara Bintliff. 2007. "Academic Freedom Issues for Academic Librarians." *Legal Reference Services Quarterly* 25, no. 4: 13–35.

Frodeman, Robert, and J. Britt Holbrook. 2012. "The Promise and Perils of Transformative Research." UNT Digital Library. http://digital.library.unt.edu/ark:/67531/metadc84363.

Fuller, Steve. 1999. *Governance of Science: Ideology and the Future of the Open Society*. New York: McGraw-Hill International.

Harley, Diane. 2013. "Scholarly Communication: Cultural Contexts, Evolving Models." *Science* 4: 80–82.

Holbrook, J. Britt. 2010. "Peer Review." In *The Oxford Handbook of Interdisciplinarity*, edited by Robert Frodeman, Julie Thompson Klein, Carl Mitcham, 321–32. Oxford: Oxford University Press.

Lamont, Michèle, Grégoire Mallard, and Joshua Guetzkow. 2012. "Beyond Blind Faith: Overcoming Obstacles to Interdisciplinary Evaluation." In *Peer Review, Research Integrity, and the Governance of Science: Practice, Theory, and Current Discussions*, edited by Robert Frodeman, J. Britt Holbrook, Carl Mitcham, and Hong Xiaonan, 415–53. Beijing: People's Publishing House, 2012. Originally published in *Research Evaluation* 15, no. 1 (2006): 43–55.

National Research Council. 2012. *For Attribution—Developing Data Attribution and Citation Practices and Standards: Summary of an International Workshop*. Washington, DC: National Academies Press.

SECTION 2

How Libraries Publish

CHAPTER 3

Toward New-Model Scholarly Publishing
Uniting the Skills of Publishers and Libraries

Monica McCormick

This chapter draws from a career spent among scholars, publishers, and librarians as a bookseller, an acquisitions editor, and now as a librarian/publisher working at a research library and a university press to develop digital publishing services and projects. The challenges of this hybrid position have led me to consider what university-based digital scholarly publishing may become and how the skills available in presses and libraries can be harnessed so that we move forward collectively. The strengths of research libraries and university presses are distinct and not easy to meld, but they offer much. This essay is, in the true sense of that word, an attempt to imagine how we might build from our strengths to construct effective forms of digital scholarly publishing that serve our shared missions.

This work is licensed under the Creative Commons Attribution License 4.0 (CC-BY 4.0).

In what follows, I first sketch out a vision for the future of scholarly publishing. Second, I outline the skills existing among university publishers, librarians, and technologists that can enable it. Finally, I offer examples of existing practices and tools that may be developed further to reach that vision.

A few caveats: I recognize that many research institutions do not have a scholarly press. For those, I hope to suggest how publishing practices may be used in a library setting. Furthermore, I will not investigate costs of achieving this vision, mainly because it could be accomplished in many different ways with widely varying costs. Costs will surely have to be understood to support sustainable publishing, but specifying them is beyond my scope here. I am more concerned in this essay with the benefits of a new model for digital scholarly publishing—an efficient set of ways to produce scholarly work that is rigorous, readily discovered, and in an array of forms that support reading, sharing, engagement, and long-term preservation.

A Vision for Digital Scholarly Publishing

I propose this vision not as a utopia but as a model toward which to build. Scholarly communication is in a long period of transition characterized by an abundance of information and rapid dissemination after centuries of relative scarcity and inefficient distribution. Scholars are now sharing their ideas in an ever-increasing variety of forms and venues. Some take advantage of digital platforms for immediate widespread distribution, even while most continue to rely on traditional practices and venues to publish their conclusions. Eventually most scholars will likely do both, using both print and digital media for what each medium does best. Those of us whose mission is to support the creation, discovery, and preservation of scholarship face an enormous challenge to select among the options and do our work in sustainable ways. As our traditional and well-understood practices become increasingly challenged by technological and economic shifts, we need to adapt and innovate. This section outlines the criteria and characteristics of vibrant scholarly publishing as it may be in the near future. I describe it in the present tense, as if my vision were already real.

Most broadly, I imagine university-supported digital publishing that is multiformat and multimedia, taking advantage of the Internet's capabilities for discovery, sharing, and connection. Such new-model scholarly publications are produced, distributed, and preserved efficiently, using scalable and sustainable practices.[1] The quality of the work relies, as it always has, on scholars' expertise. Scholars not only create the works, but also evaluate them in peer-review practices that may occur before or after publication, openly or in a blind process, depending on the needs of the work and the norms of the community in which it is produced. Scholarship may be self-published by individuals or groups or published in collaboration with university presses, librarians, scholarly societies, and technologists based in universities and colleges, working as needed with partners outside the university (software developers, print-on-demand vendors, freelance editors and designers, and so on). Some publications are freely available on the open Internet, hosted on stable platforms that enable discovery, sharing, and preservation. Other publications are available for fees that provide income streams to sustain the publishing processes. Where useful, content may be offered both online and in print. The copyright status of publications is clear so that readers understand their reuse rights (using, for example, Creative Commons licenses) or can easily find from whom they may request permission. Many works invite reader comments or collaborative authoring so that they may be updated and revised, with versions clearly distinguished. New-model scholarship is readily discoverable by machines (via search engines) as well as humans (through scholarly networks, efficient sharing options, and review media). Works may be cited, used, and paid for (where required) both in whole and in part, allowing readers to select what they need. Given the wide discoverability of these works online, audiences may be widespread and varied, so metrics may be employed to understand access, use, and impact. Analysis of which items are most downloaded, which are read

---

1. I follow the definition of new-model scholarly communication put forth by Rumsey (2011, 2): "What is *new-model scholarly communication*? By scholarly communication we mean the authoring, publishing, stewardship, and use of scholarship. *Digital scholarship* is the use of digital evidence and method, digital authoring, digital publishing, digital curation and preservation, and digital use and reuse of scholarship. And *new-model scholarly communication* is what results when we put those digital practices into the processes of production, publishing, curation, and use of scholarship." (Italics in the original.)

in combination, and which are shared and cited most frequently leads to decisions about further investment to develop selected works for particular audiences or markets. Scholarly publishing is characterized by continuum: from self-published to thoroughly vetted prior to publication; from single-authored to collaboratively created; from openly available to paid content; from ideas in nascent form to heavily revised archival works. Transparency about authoring and review processes is in place so that readers have confidence in the sources of the work and the processes by which it was produced.

This imagined future has considerable variety. There is no requirement that publishing be all digital or all print. Instead, there is a menu of options so that institutions, collectives, and individuals may make choices about which practices work best for their purposes and their capacities.

Publishing Skills at University Presses and Libraries
Processes of New-Model Scholarly Publishing

In this essay, I use *publishing* broadly, to mean the act of making public. It may include many distinct processes. For new-model scholarly publishing, these activities may include

- authoring
- selection
- evaluation, including peer review
- editing and markup
- design, composition, layout
- production of specific formats (online, e-book, print, multiformat)
- marketing and description
- distribution and sales

If we consider publishing a continuum of activities, then not all works demand all these processes, nor could their costs be borne by every publisher. In my imagined future, library and university publishers will choose among these processes according to the needs of their authors, collections, or other content sources, the audiences they wish to reach, and the strengths and capabilities of their own staff. In making such choices, we will need to consider scalability and sustainability. In addition, the practices for digital-only work may differ from those used to produce print works. It took many years to develop the codex, for example, with its table of contents, chapters, sections, pages, footnotes, index, and practices of citation. All those features have analogs in digital publications, but we are still developing them. Traditional practices to ensure accuracy and quality may need to be reimagined for new-model publishing and new workflows created for new forms and their audiences. The many stakeholders in scholarly communication will have, as we do now, distinct and evolving roles to play.

What Do Libraries and Publishers Have to Offer for These Processes?

The staff in university presses and libraries bring a wide range of skills to bear on these publishing processes. Collaboration has its challenges (economic, structural, and cultural), as Watkinson discusses in the next chapter. My experience suggests that a better understanding of each partner's expertise can help to clarify roles and expand opportunities when presses and libraries work together. Here I provide a brief overview of some of the most important skills that will contribute to new-model publishing. The following section will describe how they may be—and are being—put into practice.

University publishers' strengths derive from the combination of their engagement with scholars and their experience gauging the marketplace for scholarly ideas. As the consultant Joseph J. Esposito (2007) has put it, publishers "make an investment in a book or journal, which then starts an entire process. It is a complex process; it took many decades to evolve, it takes years to learn, and it requires talent to master."

University press skills include

- list development: acquiring editors' recognition of new developments in disciplines and the emergence of inter-disciplines
- peer review as way of improving argument and strengthening work

- effective processes for selecting what to publish, based on well-understood criteria
- expertise in editing, design, and production to create high-quality archival products
- repeatable production workflows with understanding of their costs
- the ability to assess potential markets and invest accordingly
- marketing that clearly and concisely articulates a work's contribution to scholarship
- promotion via networks of bookstore buyers, traditional review media, and social media
- distribution through efficient channels to libraries, chain stores, independent bookstores, and online vendors
- broad networks among scholars, reviewers, booksellers, and readers beyond the presses' home institutions[2]

These skills enable university presses to publish hundreds of books and journals each year with predictable costs and schedules in forms that have proven their durability and usefulness. University presses specialize in particular disciplines and genres not only for efficiency but also to build strong intellectual coherence in their lists. Good publishers add value, discovering important new work, shaping it effectively for its audience, and getting it to its markets. That the markets have been changing for decades, challenging scholarly publishers' ability to break even, does not indicate that these skills are not valuable—it suggests, rather, that the business models need to shift.

University presses are surely challenged by the changes in the marketplace, with revenue flat or shrinking and scholars both producing and consuming work in multiple formats, which may be complex and expensive to produce. Publishers were once the only efficient source of marketing and distribution. Now, anyone with a blog and a social media account can publish and promote their work at very low cost. As the market for scholarly content has shifted dramatically, with library budgets heavily skewed toward journals and monograph sales inexorably declining, university presses have had to find ways to cut costs. These pressures have

---

2. Many of these are mentioned in Brown, Griffiths, and Roscoff 2007.

lessened their ability to invest in all the skills listed above. So while the value of these skills has not declined, the conditions in which they may be deployed are changing. Books with the potential for a bigger audience may receive more investment in some of these skill areas, while specialized works with a narrow audience may not. Publishers will specialize in some skills (design, developmental editing, marketing) in order to compete for books in certain fields. A key value for traditional publishing is focus: knowing the disciplines, formats, and markets in which you work is critical to success.

The common assumption that all-digital publishing would save university presses is a canard: up to 80 percent of publishers' costs come *before* printing, binding, warehousing, and shipping (Withey et al. 2011, sec. 1, para. 6). Digital publishing bears its own costs to meet the ever-changing requirements of vendors and readers—format conversions, digital asset management, and distribution in new channels. Nonprofit university presses do not have capital to invest in rapid conversion of their workflows. University presses with journals made the shift to digital earliest, generally by paying vendors (e.g., HighWire, Atypon) to create and distribute their digital content. But for books, print revenue is still the mainstay of university publishers' income—between 80 and 90 percent for most university presses—and e-book revenue appears to be flattening. Online distributors and booksellers (particularly Amazon) are aggressive negotiators, making it expensive to do business with them. For existing publishers, a move to all-digital publishing is not a realistic option in the short term. Instead, university publishers need strategies that support our revenue while enabling us to innovate.

University publishers' efficiencies rely on consistency and repeatability. This may appear to be rigidity and a resistance to change. But through many shifts over the past decades, publishers have continually adjusted. In response to declines in monograph revenue, university presses began in the 1980s to acquire books suitable for teaching, for regional audiences, and for general readers. They have learned to sell and distribute books to the large chains and online vendors, partners that each require specific metadata and publication formats. They have lowered costs by printing fewer copies, using short-run digital printing, and using print on demand. Many have converted to an XML-first workflow for more efficient production of the multiple file types needed for print and digital distribution. The past five years have seen the emergence of several collaborative ventures for distributing e-books to libraries (for example, Project MUSE's University Press Content Consortium, Books at JSTOR, Oxford's University Press Scholarship Online). Such adjustments vary among publishers and may not be sufficient to address ongoing changes, but consistent workflows and predictable costs are a requirement for cost recovery, even in a nonprofit business.

And what do library publishers bring to the table? Their skills emerge from libraries' mission to collect and preserve cultural artifacts for long-term and widespread access and to provide service. Library publishing is a relatively new service, emerging over the past decade or so in response both to new technology (the possibility of digitizing works for wider access) and to economic challenges (rising prices for scholarly publications and a wish to respond by offering open access to scholarly work). I am defining publishing activities and skills broadly here to include the work of encoding texts and making digital collections available, along with producing, hosting, and distributing digital articles and books. And traditional library skills—collection, description, organization, and preservation—are certainly relevant to digital publishing. Many of these deep strengths may take on a different value when considered as part of a publishing program. Preservation is a good example: in print, if publishers use acid-free paper and durable bindings, they have done their part. But for digital publishing, the preservation expertise of libraries may be a critical skill to ensure sustainability.

Library skills that may support publishing include

- content selection, curation, collection development
- management and conversion of structured metadata
- implementation of technical standards for content discovery
- management of hardware and software
- digital text markup and encoding
- digital preservation to ensure permanent access to born-digital material
- software development and programming skills
- repository development to support content hosting
- experience creating and delivering digital collections via the Web
- deep networks the libraries' their home institutions

Library publishing practices cover a wide range (Lippincott 2013). Library publishers produce primarily digital formats, with print as a secondary option. I see two general models for library publishing. On the one hand, many lib-pub programs emphasize hosting, providing access to and preserving digital content via institutional repositories and journal publishing platforms such as Open Journal Systems. This approach requires maintenance and upgrades of the technology platforms and backup and preservation of digital content. Selection and peer review may be left to scholars and editing and design may be minimal or limited to basic templates. The hosting model can scale well, enabling effective online access to large amounts of scholarship with relatively low investment. This IT infrastructure of much library publishing is a parallel to the vendors that many university presses rely upon for digital infrastructure. The other general model of library publishing provides access to digitized content that may originate in the library's collections or from its faculty. Such collections may require digitization and encoding and the creation of formats and metadata to support both preservation and access. The practices of selection, editing, and design in this model are analogous to those in university presses, but with emphasis on transforming content to digital forms for further scholarly work rather than on developing content to reach a specific set of audiences or markets. In both models, metadata to support discovery is a critical component in lieu of common university press marketing practices like advertising, publicity, or exhibiting at conferences. Good metadata can be a very efficient way to ensure that potential readers discover the highly specialized content of many institutional repositories (technical reports, conference proceedings, etc.). Reaching those readers would be cost-prohibitive with traditional marketing methods.

Library publishing practices vary from the broadly scalable to the labor-intensive. One obvious contrast to university presses is that library publishing is not usually required to cover its operating costs by finding revenue streams. This may enable library publishing to have great flexibility in responding to emerging needs, but it can also result in publishing operations whose overall costs are not easy to specify and whose priorities are not clear. Experimentation has implications for efficiency: staff may be pulled part-time from other activities or not well connected to libraries' core service requirements, so publishing programs can have difficulty gaining traction and having clear goals. Hosting platforms often rely on open-source software, which has no up-front price tag but does need upgrades and maintenance with hard-to-calculate staff investment. Grants are available for many digitization projects, but that funding model can encourage one-off efforts whose workflows are not always integrated into other activities. Some library digital collections built in years past rely on technology that is no longer easy to maintain, and the costs of transferring these legacy collections to newer platforms may be prohibitive. Timeframes for new projects may be hard to predict if technology development is required. These examples suggest that library publishing does not have the same critical dependence on predictable workflows and costs that is required for university presses to stay in business. This means that library publishers may be more flexible, taking on new types of projects and publishing forms.

At the risk of oversimplifying these distinctions, I would suggest that university presses are more predictable and less flexible than library publishers, with a discipline-based focus on what they publish (for efficiencies in both acquiring and marketing) and better understanding of their costs, but less ability to innovate rapidly. Library publishers are more experimental and also better at hosting and distributing large amounts of content for low cost. Library publishers' selection emphasizes institutional affiliation rather than disciplines, and their publishing goals may also support traditional library activities such as collection building, providing space, and instruction, in alignment with the institutional mission. Library publishers have less clarity on what it may cost to sustain their publishing services over time. The primary distinction is between the university press emphasis on niche publishing for business efficiency and on library publishing as a service. Underlying all these distinctions, then, are different funding models and different spending models, which lead to very different work practices and priorities.

Despite these differences, there are many analogies between these two lists of skills. For example, acquisitions editors' work in building lists in existing or emerging areas of scholarship has strong similarities to that of archivists and librarians who develop unique collections. Both processes seek quality, create intellectual coherence, and add value to the work they gather by creating a context for it. Marketing staff share with library cataloguers a common concern in describing and highlighting unique collections so that readers may discover, find, and use precisely what they need. Press production and editing staff, as well as developers, emphasize efficient, repeatable processes to generate polished publications. Identifying those analogous methods can provide a shared ground for collaboration.

New Models from Existing Practices

How might our strengths complement and inform each other to make our work more efficient and effective? We might combine the scalability of libraries' digital content management with university presses' predictable costs and workflows for producing new works. We may benefit from blending librarians' depth of understanding of their collections with editors' breadth of knowledge about scholarly work across the disciplines. We may join university presses' skill at targeted marketing to reach specific readers and audiences with library technologists' knowledge of Web discoverability to share the richness of library collections with far-flung audiences. We need not all follow the same path but may select from the options only those that work for us, along with the partners and skills that support our goals. Following are examples of existing practices, on which our shared skills may build.

Selection and Peer Review

Scholarly publishing is distinguished from other forms of publishing most particularly by peer review—subject experts critically vet works prior to publication to verify their quality and adherence to disciplinary norms. Traditionally, journal publishing relies on author submission through scholar/editors, followed by peer review, with final selection by editorial boards. University presses acquire books in a similar manner, but often with the active engagement of professional editors who may commission work from their extensive networks of scholars and work with authors to develop the ideas. Library journal publishing tends to follow this same model, with most journals being peer-reviewed. Evaluation, in all these cases, precedes publication.

The scholar Clay Shirky (2009, 81) has argued that we are now able to follow a different process—publish then filter: "The media landscape is transformed because personal communication and publishing, previously separate functions, now shade into one another. One result is to break the older pattern of professional filtering of the good from the mediocre before publication; now such filtering is increasingly social, and happens after the fact." Blogs are the most common example of this; Twitter and other social media also enable instant widespread dispersal of ideas without editorial intervention. There are many such efforts in the scholarly world.

Open Peer Review

The idea that scholarly publishing might be driven by "personal communication practices" could be alarming, suggesting to some that it will result in mediocrity or popularity contests. Traditional peer review is of course designed to ensure scholarly value, but it is important to note that much scholarship is already made public without such review. In addition to institutional repositories, there are large disciplinary repositories where scholars post their work prior to traditional publication. For example, arXiv.org accepts preprints in physics, mathematics, computer science, and other quantitative sciences on a platform supported by the Cornell University Library. The Social Science Research Network (www.ssrn.com) hosts working papers in a wide range of disciplines. These venues allow scholars to share their initial findings rapidly, without the bottleneck of peer review. Although prepublication sharing of articles is not as widespread in the humanities, it is beginning to emerge. The Modern Language Association and the Center for Digital Research and Scholarship at Columbia University Library are developing Humanities Commons Open Repository Exchange, or Humanities CORE, which will "connect a library-quality repository for sharing, discovering, retrieving, and archiving digital work with Humanities Commons, a platform for scholarly societies and related groups across the humanities" (Williams 2014). Many of the works first shared in repositories (institutional and disciplinary) are ultimately published in traditional peer-reviewed venues. All of these might be considered extensions of the long-standing practice of sharing work early in its development at scholarly conferences. In this sense, the "publish then filter" model for scholarship has long been occurring.

But Shirky describes filtering as an "increasingly social" practice. How might readers who are not expert peer reviewers be brought into the publication process? This, too, is already happening. Digital repositories host and distribute content but generally do not allow readers to comment on it. Technologies are being developed that support reader assessment of online publications. Scholarly blogs are of course a starting point. Beyond those, tools such as CommentPress and Digress.it, which both rely on the open-source WordPress platform, were created to allow readers' comments at the paragraph level, in parallel with the text (rather than underneath it), enabling more granular analysis and showing the author/reader dialog in a less hierarchical display.

Several university presses—Harvard, MIT, and NYU, to name a few—have published books that were reviewed using such tools, either previous to or simultaneous with the traditional peer review.[3] Similarly, two special issues of the journal *Shakespeare Quarterly* were openly reviewed on MediaCommons Press before being published. The *SQ* editors explained their process in an FAQ—peer review in public, with readers' identities known, and final selection at the discretion of the journal editor (*Shakespeare Quarterly* 2010). In a somewhat different process, the edited collection *Debates in the Digital Humanities* (Gold 2012) received traditional peer review, while the volume's authors were each asked to critique two essays in the work using a CommentPress site open only to the contributors. This process, though not public, let the authors engage with each other, strengthen connections, and highlight distinctions among their arguments. In all these cases, the authors benefited from the critique of a much wider community than the usual two or three anonymous peer reviewers. In none of them did the publishers sponsor or technically support the open peer review—that work was managed by other organizations (the Institute for the Future of the Book; MediaCommons Press with technical support of NYU Libraries; and staff at the CUNY Grad Center under the leadership of the *Debates in Digital Humanities* editor Matt Gold). Libraries, publishers, and technologists collaborated with scholars to implement new peer-review methods.

---

3. Wark 2007 was first published for reader commentary online at the Institute for the Future of the Book; Wardrip-Fruin 2012 was first reviewed on the blog *Grand Text Auto* in 2008; the penultimate version of Fitzpatrick 2011 simultaneously received traditional peer review from the publisher and open review on MediaCommons Press; Mittell 2011 (forthcoming from NYU Press) was reviewed on MediaCommons Press as each chapter was completed. Traditional peer review followed.

One challenge of such new methods is to ensure that readers are confident in the sources of scholarly work and the process of its selection. In a white paper on open review written for MediaCommons, Kathleen Fitzpatrick and Avi Santo (2012) argue that peer review may occur in many ways but needs to be transparent and appropriate for the community in which works are produced. Criteria and standards for review must be discussed and shared. Traditionally, journal and book publishers provide peer reviewers with a specific set of questions to address in their blind reports. In open communities, other practices may be used. In January 2004, arXiv.org "began requiring some users to be *endorsed* by another user before submitting their first paper to a category or subject class.... The new endorsement system will verify that arXiv contributors belong [in] the scientific community in a fair and sustainable way that will scale with arXiv's future growth" (arXiv.org 2014; emphasis in the original). Endorsers must have authored a number of works within the relevant field. *PLOS ONE*, a journal with a broad scope in the biological and medical sciences, has standards that are explicitly different from those of many science journals. It shares these criteria on its site, specifying that works must be previously unpublished, based on primary research, and "technically sound and worthy of inclusion in the scientific record. Once the work is published in *PLOS ONE*, the broader community is then able to discuss and evaluate [its] significance (through the number of citations it attracts; the downloads it achieves; the media and blog coverage it receives; and the post-publication Notes, Comments and Ratings that it receives on *PLOS ONE* etc)" (PLOS 2014). The goal is not, as with many journals, to publish only work that will dramatically change the field. Rather, for *PLOS ONE*, it is to publish good science relatively quickly and at scale and then allow the community to continue evaluating it. *PLOS ONE* is very large: in 2013 it published more than 30,000 articles, though the pace has slowed in 2014 (Davis 2014a, 2014b).

An open annotation data model has been proposed to the W3C (Sanderson, Ciccarese, and Van de Sompel 2013), and various groups are working to develop tools that will allow readers even more ways to engage with online works. For open peer review to be widely accepted, scholarly communities and organizations that employ it must share their criteria, norms, and expectations. The scrupulousness with which they establish and uphold those norms will help readers to assess the quality of the work that they publish (Fitzpatrick and Santo 2012, 4). Such practices will continue to evolve and may be combined effectively with traditional peer review to support new-model scholarly publishing.

Selection and New Technology

Content selection is also being supported with new technology in other ways. PressForward is an example of how the publish-then-filter model can be implemented in a way that combines technology with editorial acumen. Developed by the Roy Rosenzweig Center for History and New Media, it is "a tool for aggregating and curating content from the web from within a WordPress dashboard… designed to support bloggers and editorial teams who wish to aggregate and share content from a variety of sources" (PressForward 2013). In a multistage process, the tool first captures RSS feeds from targeted sites that are relevant to a community's interests and identifies posts and topics that generated most commentary or interest in social media. Next, editors select items from those feeds to aggregate on their own site, gathering content that was first published in a wide array of locations. In a final stage, selected blog posts may be peer-reviewed and revised into conventional article form. PressForward thus combines machine-based selection with human editing and review to support a refined form of the publish-then-filter model.

The tool is being used by several journals to select some of their content. The Alliance of Digital Humanities Organizations uses it for the blog *Digital Humanities Now* and works with some authors to further refine *DH_Now* posts into journal articles in *Digital Humanities Quarterly* (ADHO 2014a, 2014b). The *Public Philosophy Journal* plans to use PressForward in combination with traditional methods (submission by authors, invitation by editors) to develop content: "The process of expert curation and crowd sourced evaluation of material from algorithmically generated sets of links will enable the editors to produce weekly and then monthly feeds that further amplify increasingly relevant and timely online discussions. Editors of the PPJ will select promising work from those curated writings to undergo peer review and, if necessary, collaborative developmental re-writing" (*PPJ* 2014). The journal *dh+lib* sponsored by the Digital Humanities interest group of the Association of College and Research Libraries, uses PressForward to select content, along with invited blog posts (ACRL 2014).

How do these practices apply to library publishing and university presses? They demonstrate the range of possibilities for selecting and refining scholarly works. They also suggest the need for partnership. All of these examples required collaboration or coordination between traditional publishers and scholarly innovators, often with the support of libraries and their technologists. The arXiv.org site, on which thousands of scholars share their work, is hosted and maintained at Cornell University Libraries. MediaCommons Press, part of the MediaCommons network of scholars, is supported by NYU Libraries. The publishers who use PressForward recruit volunteers to help curate their content under the guidance of the ongoing journal editors. The journals and university presses that publish works first appearing on such sites are benefiting not only from the technical teams that support them but also from the scholarly communities that contribute their research and commentary.

Metrics to Support Selection

There are other ways that university presses and libraries might take advantage of their strengths, uniting technology with human selection. One way could begin with the large bodies of scholarly material hosted in institutional repositories or libraries' online collections: working papers, theses and dissertations, research and technical reports, and data, along with digitized manuscripts, rare books, images, and other archival material. This wealth of material could become a source of potential new publications by employing tools to measure its use. Alt-metrics such as downloads, numbers of unique visitors, and sharing on social media, as well as citations, can indicate impact and interest. We could also track which items are used in combination with each other. Editorial scrutiny of the content revealed to be of most interest would enable further review, selection, and investment, allowing development of some works into newly elaborated forms.

Such metrics are widely available now—most repositories already track downloads, for example, and website analytics can capture unique visitors, views, and more. The relatively new open-access journal *PeerJ* (https://peerj.com) displays visitors, views, and downloads with each article, and includes "social referrals" (to Twitter, Facebook, LinkedIn, Reddit, etc.), and referrals (from a bookmark or typed URL) by a unique visitor.[4] Impactstory (https://impactstory.org) describes itself as "an open-source, web-based tool that helps researchers explore and share the diverse impacts of all their research products—from traditional ones like journal articles, to emerging products like blog posts, datasets, and software" (Impactstory 2014). Impactstory captures downloads, citations, mentions in social media; it is building tools to help scholars demonstrate their impact with those data.

A more low-tech example of how this can work is the University of North Carolina's Documenting the American South (http://docsouth.unc.edu). This rich collection of materials began as a project to digitize the library's collection of slave narratives, which were heavily used and at risk of damage. Over the years, many more kinds of material were added. The site was created for browser-based reading in years before e-books were commonplace. Members of the public who discovered these materials occasionally requested hard copies, objecting to the need to print out pages not formatted for that purpose. Eventually the library joined forces with the University of North Carolina Press on DocSouth Books (UNC Press 2014) to bring selected works into other reader-friendly formats, such as downloadable e-books and print-on-demand books.

These examples suggest a model that might be widely applicable. Library hosting platforms could offer detailed metrics, which could be combined with editors' and curators' expertise to determine publishing priorities. The results of machine and human intelligence could select, from large amounts of content, the content that would merit an investment in editorial development or conversion into new forms.

Serial Publishing

Related to all these topics—open review, technology, and metrics to guide selection and decisions about investment—is a concept that suggests how new-model publishing may be built upon traditional and emerging practices. That concept is serial (or sequential) publishing, by which work that appears first in one form and venue and is then refined and revised before being published in another. A typical example would be the works of

---

4. For an example (chosen at random) see Bustamante, Vargas-Caro, and Bennett 2014.

Charles Dickens, which were serialized in newspapers before being issued as novels. More recent examples are blogs that become books. Scholarly publishing has long followed this practice, with special issues of journals that are marketed as books, conference talks or articles as the source of book chapters, and dissertations that are revised into books. Despite these long-standing ways of creating new products, many publishers perceive scholars' self-publishing and the widespread distribution of dissertations and preprints online as a threat. The prior existence of such works may suggest that there is no market for that work in another form. But as Douglas Armato (2013) has pointed out, "Our question considering works that have appeared serially online isn't… so much 'have people already read it?' but rather 'how many more readers can we find?' and 'can we make more of it editorially?'" Armato goes on to propose an ecological metaphor to describe how ideas move from one form to another:

> For me, the current place of the individual book in this emerging ecosystem is as an area of highly concentrated, unitary scholarship amid a flow of less concentrated expression, with a membrane (let's dub that membrane "peer review," though it is more than that) regulating the passage between those environments as a form of osmosis. That flow of blog posts, social media interactions, conference papers, online discussions coalesces into the highly concentrated monograph or scholarly book (endosmosis) and then flows out again (exosmosis) in the form of other scholars' blog posts, social media comments, conference discussion, reviews and articles.

For good publishers, that "membrane" is indeed more than peer review: it includes selection, refinement, production, marketing, dissemination—all the traditional scholarly publishing skills.

Armato directs the University of Minnesota Press, which in 2013 announced a book series that combines serial publishing, publish-then-filter models, and new technology (UMP 2013). In the series Forerunners: Ideas First, the press plans to publish short books drawn from other forms—blog posts, articles, plenary talks, or social media. They "think of it as gray literature publishing: where intense thinking, change, and speculation happens in scholarship." The publisher will ask authors for a limited license (for e-books and print only), rather than the more usual all-formats/all-rights contract, and will pay higher-than-usual royalties of 25 percent. Books will be CC-licensed and published with expedited peer review, professional copyediting and proofreading, and a twelve-week production schedule. It will use the platform PressBooks (http://pressbooks.com), which enables books to be edited, designed, and published online and then exported into formats suitable for print and e-books.

What makes Forerunners intriguing is not only that it embraces online and self-published works as a source of good scholarship and offers a more nimble way of producing revised works, but also that it will surely rely for its success upon traditional strengths in acquisitions and marketing. Forerunners is of course only a single example. But it suggests one way of moving past the plaints of the death of the monograph caused by the now decades-old "crisis" in scholarly publishing into a more creative approach. This combination of new modes of publishing with the most fundamental of traditional skills is a model worth exploring.

Collaboration Opportunities

In this final section, I will briefly sketch out other areas of potential collaboration for new-model scholarly publishing, emphasizing its digital nature: that it may be multiformat and easily discoverable in the network. These are places where the combined skills of publishers and librarians can be deployed to build new ways of working together.

Multimedia Publications

One of the obvious advantages of digital publishing is the ability to include images, video, audio, and other formats along with text. This clearly benefits scholars of art, music, cinema, and other media studies, as well as those who wish to incorporate maps, data, and visualizations in their finished work. Readily available content management systems such as WordPress or Drupal make this fairly straightforward. The tool Scalar not only supports multimodal publishing but also lets writers create multiple paths for reading.

These tools are all open-source so that anyone with the skills and inclination can use them without licensing fees and develop the code. As publishers, librarians, and scholars evolve new methods, open-source tools let us add the functionality we need for publishing them. Several of those mentioned above (CommentPress, PressBooks, PressForward) demonstrate this as they were built upon the widely used WordPress platform. Library staffs are more likely to have developers and systems administrators needed to provide the infrastructure for such projects, but the presses have a wealth of content and other expertise to offer.

University presses and libraries are taking advantage of these tools in multiple ways, from supplementing print works with online data, to presenting digital collections online, and publishing original scholarship in digital forms. Challenges will include creating repeatable workflows, which may require limiting unique functionality. The one-off project may be tempting to create, but will be difficult and expensive to maintain. An alternative is to build first-of-a-kind, rather than one-of-a-kind, projects. This is not easily accomplished, given the manifold possibilities of digital publishing and the hopes and expectations of scholars who wish to develop them. Selecting tools and standard practices and establishing guidelines for updates and innovations can help to balance between rigid processes and endless, never-completed experimentation.

Marketing and Discovery

Another opportunity for collaboration will be the multiple activities that enable readers to find published works. In new-model publishing, these should be designed effectively for both humans and machines. We might call human-focused activities marketing; these may include advertising, publicity, exhibits at academic conferences, and social media. Authors whose blogs are a forum for developing their ideas can be seen as engaging in a form of publicity. Social media can be a method not only for announcing the availability of new work but also for starting a conversation, debating ideas, or sharing early results. To support machine discovery, provision of metadata that adheres to standards is critical. For example, ONIX metadata (https://www.bisg.org/onix-books) is used throughout the book distribution business to share information, while libraries continue to rely on MARC (www.loc.gov/marc/faq.html). Resource Description Framework (RDF, www.w3schools.com/webservices/ws_rdf_intro.asp) is a standard for describing Web content, and Schema.org provides a standard for HTML markup for better search engine discovery of webpages. Well-designed repository platforms create metadata that can be discovered via Web searches so that highly specialized works, described with the right keywords, may be made visible to far-flung readers at very low cost.

Offering good metadata via multiple channels (for example, Bowker, OCLC, in webpages, and library catalogs), as well as engaging networks of book reviewers, bookstore buyers, and online readers, would help readers find the content they seek wherever they may be looking. It may be a challenge for collaborators to adopt the standards needed in different channels. Not all the partners may be familiar with the range of appropriate formats, nor have the established workflows to produce them. Scholars who work in innovative online forms may still want their work to be discovered through more traditional channels such as bibliographic references and indexes, and such services may not accept forms other than books or journal articles. New-model publishing will require adopting the approach best suited to the content and its audience.

Distribution and Sales

Distribution was a primary strength of good print publishers: moving books through wholesale and retail channels to customers in different market segments (libraries, chains, independent booksellers, university textbook stores) required multiple relationships and expertise in sales, order fulfillment, and warehousing. Such expertise is still required for the distribution of e-books, with both new and traditional trading partners. (Though many publishers sell e-books direct to consumers, it is hard to ignore Amazon, by far the largest e-book seller, and therefore few publishers opt out of doing business with them.) In the journal world, distribution shifted almost entirely online over the past decades, and service providers such as Atypon and HighWire have developed the technical infrastructure that publishers may not have had the funds or expertise to build themselves, including the provision of authorization and pay wall services. Library publishers may provide distribution via hosting platforms such as Open Journal Systems or institutional repositories.

New-model publishing that is primarily distributed in web browsers may not eliminate the wish to distribute the content in particular forms that readers prefer. In the simplest example, we can make it easy to print and download our content. We may also wish to offer print-on-demand options in combination with open-access reading. This is already being done by Michigan Publishing's Digital Culture Books (www.digitalculture.org), Open Book Publishers (www.openbookpublishers.com), the Australian National University Press (http://press.anu.edu.au), and others. University presses have relationships with print-on-demand vendors that libraries may be able to share. Small printer-binders such as the Espresso Book Machine (see www.ondemandbooks.com) may also be useful for local printing. More complex options would offer large suites of hosted content to readers, who can select the portions they want for their own needs. Book and journal aggregators (Project MUSE, JSTOR, EBSCO, ProQuest, etc.) that license content to libraries are already doing this. But we have yet to fully develop the business terms and functionality to enable, for example, readers to assemble a print-on-demand volume of chapters from multiple books by multiple authors or to offer more financial reward to publishers whose works are most frequently downloaded in licensed aggregations.

Publishing for the Network

A more far-reaching goal for new-model publishing is to create publications that are not only well-crafted scholarship but also a form of data. This is an extension of the idea that our discovery efforts should be designed for humans and for machine. Not only our metadata but our publications too may be both human- and machine-readable, making it easier for readers to discover the people, places, and concepts within them (McGuire 2013).

For example, at NYU, the press and the libraries are collaborating with colleagues at the Institute for the Study of the Ancient World (ISAW) to publish archeological reports, among other things. These reports are rich with data such as photographs, drawings, geographical references, and more. ISAW makes its reports available freely online in XHTML form, richly tagged with digital identifiers for their data (see, e.g., Bagnall and Ruffini 2012), ready for search engines as well as scholars to find and use. NYU

Press publishes the works in print for sale to libraries. This collaboration takes advantage of each partner's skills: ISAW's digital publications expert produces the XHTML and converts it into print-ready PDFs; the libraries' Digital Library Technology Services group supports the infrastructure for online publication and digital preservation; and NYU Press distributes print and e-book versions of these works.

I hope that libraries and university presses will explore ways to enrich our publications so that they operate as structured data in the Web. We can begin by investigating W3C Semantic Web standards (W3C 2014), including Linked Data, defined as "a recommended best practice for exposing, sharing, and connecting pieces of data, information, and knowledge on the Semantic Web using URIs and RDF" (Linked Data 2014). Organizations such as the *New York Times*, the British Broadcasting Corporation, and the US Data.gov site all use these approaches to make their content more easily discovered and shared.[5]

Challenges to Collaboration

As we develop our collaborations, it will be important to recognize that our authors and our readers want content in multiple forms: large suites of digital content for efficient searching, plus works in specific formats for easy engagement, annotation, commenting, and reading. It will be complex and expensive to offer all these options for every publication. To make the best choices, we'll need to balance our own capabilities with the needs of our stakeholders.

We may also need to learn how to communicate better with each other. It will be important to get past hidden assumptions and overstatements. Among those I have heard: that open access is the enemy of cost-recovery publishing; that libraries' funding models enable library publishers to ignore costs; that grant funding is not a business model; that publishers are too focused on their business models to be creative. We all work in contexts with competing interests, powerful stakeholders, and particular cultures, all of which drive how we do our work. Exploring those drivers may help to reveal causes of confusion or conflict.

---

5. For examples, see "Linked Open Data" (http://data.nytimes.com), Feigenbaum 2012, and www.data.gov.

It can be tricky to find the common ground where very busy people with considerably different approaches to their work can meet to be nimble and experimental together. As the person responsible for coordinating efforts between press and libraries publishing at NYU, I have seen (and felt) confusion and frustration emerge from both distinct communication styles and unvoiced expectations about what the other partner could do. We have all had to be willing to work through the discomfort of those feelings, ask more questions, acknowledge our ignorance, be candid about our limitations (of time, staff, expertise), look for support outside the organization, and generally find ways to move forward, often by aiming for a simpler goal. Collaboration challenges us to recognize the way we have adapted to particular working conditions and expectations and provides us with a wealth of (sometimes humbling) opportunities for growth.

Conclusion

As I hope this essay has shown, we are in a time of rich opportunities and big challenges for building the future of scholarly publishing. I encourage all of us with a stake in the future of scholarly publishing to recognize our different strengths, value our distinct skills, and work together to build a sustainable model of publishing that contributes to the development of new forms of scholarship, new models of publishing, and new knowledge

Works Cited

ACRL (Association of College and Research Libraries). 2014. *dh+lib* (blog). Accessed August 20. http://acrl.ala.org/dh.

ADHO (Alliance of Digital Humanities Organizations). 2014a. *Digital Humanities Now* (blog). Accessed August 20. http://digitalhumanitiesnow.org.

———. 2014b. *Digital Humanities Quarterly*. Accessed August 20. www.digitalhumanities.org/dhq.

Armato, Doug. 2013. "From MLA 2013: Considering Serial Scholarship and the Future of Scholarly Publishing." *University of Minnesota Press* (blog), January 7. www.uminnpressblog.com/2013/01/from-mla-2013-considering-serial.html.

arXiv.org. 2014. "The arXiv Endorsement System." Accessed August 20. http://arxiv.org/help/endorsement.

Bagnall, Roger S., and Giovanni R. Ruffini. 2012. *Amheida I: Ostraka from Trimithis, Volume 1, Texts from the 2004–2007 Seasons*. New York: Institute for the Study of the

Ancient World and NYU Press, http://dlib.nyu.edu/awdl/isaw/amheida-i-otrim-1. Also available in print and e-book form.

Brown, Laura, Rebecca Griffiths, and Matthew Roscoff. 2007. *University Publishing in a Digital Age*, Ithaka Report. New York: Ithaka, July 26. http://www.sr.ithaka.org/sites/default/files/reports/4.13.1.pdf.

Bustamante, Carlos, Carolina Vargas-Caro, and Michael B. Bennett. 2014. "Biogeographic Patterns in the Cartilaginous Fauna (Pisces: Elasmobranchii and Holocephali) in the Southeast Pacific Ocean. *PeerJ* 2, e416 (May 29). doi:10.7717/peerj.416.

Davis, Phil. 2014a. "PLOS ONE Output Falls Following Impact Factor Decline." *The Scholarly Kitchen* (blog), Society for Scholarly Publishing, March 7. http://scholarlykitchen.sspnet.org/2014/03/07/plos-one-output-falls-following-impact-factor-decline.

———. 2014b. "PLOS ONE Output Falls 25 Percent." *The Scholarly Kitchen* (blog), Society for Scholarly Publishing, June 3. http://scholarlykitchen.sspnet.org/2014/06/03/plos-one-output-falls-25-percent.

Esposito, Joseph J. 2007. "The Wisdom of Oz: The Role of the University Press in Scholarly Communications." *Journal of Electronic Publishing* 10, no. 1 (Winter). doi:10.3998/3336451.0010.103.

Feigenbaum, Lee. 2012. "BBC's Adoption of Semantic Web Technologies: An Interview." CMS Wire, October 29. www.cmswire.com/cms/information-management/bbcs-adoption-of-semantic-web-technologies-an-interview-017981.php

Fitzpatrick, Kathleen. 2011. *Planned Obsolescence: Publishing, Technology, and the Future of the Academy*. New York: NYU Press. First published by MediaCommons Press, 2009, http://mcpress.media-commons.org/plannedobsolescence.

Fitzpatrick, Kathleen, and Avi Santo. 2012. "Open Review: A Study of Contexts and Practices." White paper, Andrew W. Mellon Foundation. MediaCommons Press, December. http://mcpress.media-commons.org/open-review/files/2012/06/MediaCommons_Open_Review_White_Paper_final.pdf.

Gold, Matthew K. 2012. *Debates in the Digital Humanities*. Minneapolis: University of Minnesota Press.

Impactstory. 2014. "FAQ." Accessed August 20. https://impactstory.org/faq.

Linked Data. 2014. Linked Data home page. Accessed August 20. http://linkeddata.org.

Lippincott, Sarah K., ed. 2013. *Library Publishing Directory*. Atlanta: Library Publishing Coalition. www.librarypublishing.org/sites/librarypublishing.org/files/documents/LPC_LPDirectory2014.pdf. Also available in print form.

McGuire, Hugh. 2013. "A Publisher's Job Is to Provide a Good API for Books." *O'Reilly Tools of Change for Publishing* (blog), February 1. http://toc.oreilly.com/2013/02/a-publishers-job-is-to-provide-a-good-api-for-books.html.

Mittell, Jason. 2011. *Complex TV: The Poetics of Contemporary Television Storytelling*. MediaCommons Press. http://mcpress.media-commons.org/complextelevision. Forthcoming from NYU Press.

PLOS (Public Library of Science). 2014. "*PLOS ONE* Guidelines for Reviewers." Accessed August 20. www.plosone.org/static/reviewerGuidelines.

PPJ (*Public Philosophy Journal*). 2014. "Submissions." Accessed August 20. http://publicphilosophyjournal.org/submissions.

PressForward. 2013. "Plugin Beta Now Available." PressForward website, June 18. http://pressforward.org/plugin-beta-now-available.

Rumsey, Abby Smith. 2011. "New-Model Scholarly Communication: Roadmap for Change." Report, Scholarly Communication Institute 9, University of Virginia

Library, Charlottesville, VA, July 13–15. http://libra.virginia.edu/catalog/libra-oa:3260.

Sanderson, Robert, Paolo Ciccarese, and Herbert Van de Sompel. 2013. "Open Annotation Data Model." W3C, February 8. www.openannotation.org/spec/core.

Shakespeare Quarterly. 2010. "FAQs about the SQ Open Review." MediaCommons Press. http://mcpress.media-commons.org/ShakespeareQuarterly_NewMedia/about/faqs-about-the-sq-open-review.

Shirky, Clay. 2009. *Here Comes Everybody: The Power of Organizing without Organizations.* New York: Penguin.

UMP (University of Minnesota Press). 2013. "Announcing Forerunners: Ideas First: Original E-works to Spark the Spread of New Scholarship." News release, November 14. www.upress.umn.edu/press/press-releases/announcing-forerunners-ideas-first.

UNC (University of North Carolina) Press. 2014. "Announcing DocSouth Books." Accessed August 20. www.uncpress.unc.edu/browse/page/758.

Wardrip-Fruin, Noah. 2012. *Expressive Processing: Digital Fictions, Computer Games, and Software Studies.* Cambridge, MA: MIT Press. First published as *"Expressive Processing*: An Experiment in Blog-Based Peer Review," *Grand Text Auto* (blog), January 22, 2008, http://grandtextauto.org/2008/01/22/expressive-processing-an-experiment-in-blog-based-peer-review.

Wark, McKenzie. 2007. *Gamer Theory.* Cambridge, MA: Harvard University Press. First published by the Institute for the Future of the Book, May 2006, http://futureofthebook.org/mckenziewark.

Williams, Leyla. 2014. "Grant Awarded for the Development of Humanities CORE." *Center for Digital Research and Scholarship* (blog), March 27. http://cdrs.columbia.edu/cdrsmain/2014/03/grant-awarded-for-the-development-of-humanities-core.

Withey, Lynne, et al. 2011. "Sustaining Scholarly Publishing: New Business Models for University Presses," A Report of the AAUP Task Force on Economic Models for Scholarly Publishing. Media Commons Press, March. http://mcpress.media-commons.org/sustaining/ensuring-a-robust-scholarly-ecosystem.

W3C (World Wide Web Consortium). 2014. "Standards: Semantic Web." Accessed July 25. www.w3.org/standards/semanticweb.

CHAPTER 4

From Collaboration to Integration
University Presses and Libraries

Charles Watkinson

University presses and academic libraries should be natural allies in the quest to create a more equitable scholarly publishing system. Expert in scholarly information management, situated on university and college campuses, supported to a varying degree by the same funding sources, and sharing many philosophical ideals, librarians and university press publishers seem to be logical partners. However, until very recently, examples of successful press/library collaboration in the production of knowledge have been lacking. This chapter surveys such collaboration initiatives and proposes a taxonomy of types, identifies some of the challenges that exist for institutions wishing to forge closer alliances, and explores the opportunities that such campus publishing partnerships are

This work is licensed under the Creative Commons Attribution License 4.0 (CC-BY 4.0).

presenting for the respective partners, for their parent institutions, and for the scholars and other publics they ultimately exist to serve.

While the opportunities for publishing collaborations had been a topic of low-level discussion for many years (e.g., Day 1995), a particular focus on this issue arose in the late 2000s. Between 2007 and 2009, several important reports (Brown, Griffiths, and Rascoff 2007; Crow 2009; Hahn 2008) examined the opportunities for campus publishing partnerships, highlighting a few major initiatives that had started to emerge, particularly at the University of California, at the University of Michigan, at New York University, and at Penn State University Press. These early experiments did not immediately appear to stimulate emulation, and a period of relatively little apparent activity ensued.[1] Beyond the most commonly cited examples, the collaborations that did emerge were generally one-off, low risk, and strategically unexciting, with the most common type of collaborative endeavor being digitization and hosting of low-selling backlist titles (offered either completely open-access or just within the parent institution), accounting for one-fifth of all collaborations in Raym Crow's analysis (Crow 2009, 6).

Early proponents of the collaboration model became disillusioned to such an extent that part of the 2011 Sustainable Scholarship conference organized by Ithaka, the sponsor of the 2007 Brown, Griffiths, and Rascoff report, was devoted to an evaluation of the reasons for the perceived lack of receptiveness to the report's recommendations. A survey of library publishing activity across a wide range of North American institutions conducted in 2010 found that fewer than 50 percent of the responding libraries that had access to a potential university press partner within their parent institutions were engaged in any form of collaboration (Mullins et al. 2012, 16), a number that had changed little from a similar survey three years earlier (Hahn 2008, 35).

This chapter proposes that we are now, however, seeing a resurgence of interest in the idea of library/press collaboration and that this time the movement is more sustainable since it is much more broadly based in character, with a diverse group of institutions involved. In 2014, twenty out

---

1. As Mike Furlough (2010, 192) points out, this may at least partly have been due to the 2008 financial crisis, the effects of which were spread over several years of retrenchment in higher education—a bad time for experimental collaborations.

Table 4.1. Presses Reporting to Libraries
Data from AAUP Biennial Press Reporting Structure Survey.

2008/9	2010	2012	2014
Alberta	Alberta	Alberta	Alberta
	Arizona	Arizona	Arizona
Calgary	Calgary	Calgary	Calgary
	Georgia	Georgia	Georgia
			Kentucky
Marquette	Marquette	Marquette	Marquette
	Michigan	Michigan	Michigan
MIT	MIT	MIT	MIT
Nebraska			
New York	New York	New York	New York
		North Texas	North Texas
Northwestern	Northwestern	Northwestern	Northwestern
Oregon State	Oregon State	Oregon State	Oregon State
Penn State	Penn State	Penn State	Penn State
Purdue	Purdue	Purdue	Purdue
Stanford	Stanford	Stanford	Stanford
Syracuse	Syracuse	Syracuse	Syracuse
	Temple	Temple	Temple
Texas Christian	Texas Christian	Texas Christian	Texas Christian
Utah	Utah	Utah	Utah
	Utah State	Utah State	

of one hundred thirty (15 percent) members of Association of American University Presses (AAUP) responding to the organization's biennial Reporting Structure Survey reported to libraries, up from only 11 percent a few years before (see table 4.1).[2] The formal data may underrepresent the shift due to the fact that not all university presses are members of AAUP and that some presses are part of larger consortial entities and would not be counted

---

2. My thanks to Regan Colestock of AAUP for supplying the historical results of the AAUP Biennial Press Reporting Structure Survey Report. The number of actual respondents in 2012 was 112.

separately. An example of undercounting due to consortium membership is Brandeis University Press, part of the University Press of New England, where reporting moved to the dean of libraries during the first half of 2013 (John Unsworth, pers. comm., June 20, 2013). The percentage also may seem low since AAUP also includes some learned society, museum, and public policy publishers among its membership; Peter Berkery, the current executive director of AAUP, estimates that 27 percent of the members of AAUP that describe themselves as university presses report to libraries.

With some exceptions, the AAUP data also do not include most university presses outside North America. While this chapter mostly focuses on the situation in the United States (and, to a lesser extent, Canada) where the government funding context for higher education allows comparison, examples of library/press collaboration from other parts of the world may suggest models and scenarios for the future. In Australia, for example, a highly networked group of six library-based university presses (at the universities of Sydney, Adelaide, Monash, Swinburne, Australian National University, and the University of Technology, Sydney) has a long track record of library/press collaboration and was recently engaged in forming its own member organization, the Australian Universities Publishers Group (Coleman 2006; Missingham and Kannelopoulos 2013). These "new" presses, with full or hybrid open-access models, published significantly more academic books in 2012 than the four established Australian university presses (at the universities of Melbourne, New South Wales, Queensland, and Western Australia; Steele 2013, 285). While presses in the United Kingdom tend to be organized as independent companies (albeit subsidiary or linked to their universities), and continental European university presses have a rather different tradition of institutionally focused publishing, the University of Göttingen Press in Germany (Bargheer and Schmidt 2008) and University of Firenze Press in Italy are both examples of university presses in the American tradition that are institutionally embedded in the library.

From Collaboration to Integration

With the number of university press/library collaborations increasing, it could be suggested that a taxonomy of relationship types is starting to emerge:

- Type 1, little evidence of currently active relationships between press and library (e.g., Columbia, Ohio State, California)
- Type 2, good relationships between the press and one or more libraries, but no reporting (e.g., Cornell, Duke, Florida, UNC, Wayne State, Fordham, Tennessee)
- Type 3, reporting and joint projects, but relative autonomy and no physical collocation (e.g., Penn State, Syracuse, MIT, Temple, NYU)
- Type 4, physical collocation, reporting, but relative autonomy (e.g., Georgia, Arizona, Utah, North Texas, Kentucky, Indiana)[3]
- Type 5, more integrated, shared vision approaches (e.g., Michigan, Oregon State, Utah State, Purdue)

To examine the nature of these different types of relationship, some illustrations may be useful, and it is fortunate that an increasing number of case studies have been published recently, especially as part of the Library Publishing Toolkit, a project of the SUNY Geneseo Libraries that has been made available as a print book but also as an open-access online resource at www.publishingtoolkit.org. An older compilation, but no less useful, is the themed issue of *Against the Grain* (volume 20, number 6, December 2008–January 2009), edited by Michael Furlough and Patrick Alexander. A selection of "case studies in campus-based publishing" (www.sparc.arl.org/resources/publishing/case-studies) hosted by SPARC as part of a broader range of resources on collaboration, is rather out-of-date.

Examples of type 1 relationships are the most poorly documented partly because there is little to report and partly because there may be historical, personal, philosophical reasons that the partners would rather not publicize. The relationships at Columbia University and the University of California are interesting because highly publicized examples of collaboration between library and press organizations were so radically scaled back. The UC Publishing Services (UCPubS) partnership established in 2008, which offered a range of hosting and marketing services to

---

3. Although the executive director of the Office of Scholarly Publishing at Indiana University, to which the press reports, was in 2013 a librarian, Carolyn Walters, the office itself was established by the provost. Due to the physical collocation, the extent of dialog between press and library, and joint strategic planning exercise underway, however, I have chosen to include Indiana University Press in the type 4 category.

the publishing programs maintained by research units throughout ten University of California campuses, was abandoned in 2011, apparently after strategic review by a new press director (Withey et al. 2011, 25). Similarly the Electronic Publishing Initiative at Columbia (EPIC) program at Columbia University, in which researchers from the press, library, and academic information systems with the university collaborated to explore new potential scholarly communication partnerships, announced in 2001, was shut down in 2008. While some products of collaboration, such as the Columbia International Affairs Online (CIAO), persist, press and library now pursue separate strategies (Wittenberg 2001). The closure of EPIC and Fathom, an early online learning venture, represented the library's move away from outward-facing content production programs. They were replaced by the more inward-facing Center for Digital Research and Scholarship (CDRS), which provides scholarly communication services to the university's faculty and students (Furlough and Reid 2012) but sometimes will engage in collaborations with other presses publishing Columbia faculty work. Notable is the interesting, if one-off, publication by CDRS at Columbia University Libraries of an enriched online supplement to the Fordham University Press monograph *Dangerous Citizens*, an account of the Greek left, rich with possibilities for reference to digitized primary sources (Kennison, Panourgiá, and Tartar 2010). In both these cases, changing leadership may have played a role in retrenchment, but it is also worth noting the large scale of the relevant partners and the extremely commercial orientation of the presses at both Columbia and California, the latter also operating in the context of a state university system with many budgetary issues.

Examples of type 2 relationships are the collaboration between Wayne State University Press, reporting to the provost, and the libraries in making several journals available online using the libraries' Digital Commons repository platform (Neds-Fox, Crocker, and Vonderharr 2013); the major collaboration between Cornell University Libraries and Duke University Press to support the publication of a number of important mathematics journals through Project Euclid (Ehling and Staib 2008–2009; Koltay and Hickerson 2002); the collaboration between university press, libraries, and two major academic centers at the University of North Carolina in publishing the Long Civil Rights Movement (Miller 2008); the arrangement between the University of Tennessee Knoxville Libraries and University of

Tennessee Press to create and distribute printed versions of open-access books published by Newfound Press (http://www.newfoundpress.utk.edu), the library's publishing operation; and the publication of Signale (http://signale.cornell.edu), a book series in German studies supported by the Mellon Foundation as a joint project between Cornell Libraries and the press, which reports to the senior vice provost.

A notable feature of the successful type 2 collaborations when contrasted with type 1 is that the collaborations have been "one-off," and continuing expansion of collaboration has not been assumed. As the collaborators at Wayne State write, "Because the partnership is unforced, the partners avoid the dysfunction that can arise when units are combined by administrative fiat, and are free to expand their activities in any mutually agreeable direction."[4] Another key to the long-running relationship between Duke University Press and Cornell Libraries around Project Euclid and that between Cornell University Press and Libraries around Signale has been the existence of an explicit agreement between the partners about respective roles and responsibilities, perhaps particularly key to relationships between institutions but recommended by the collaborators in both cases.[5] Where ambitious collaborations have been embarked on and then scaled way back, as at Columbia and California, the role of personal chemistry between collaborative individuals and the effect of them leaving organizations are notable. Without a reporting relationship or an explicit cross-institutional agreement in place, long-term efforts at collaboration are particularly vulnerable to the departure of the champion.

Both Penn State and NYU have offered conspicuous examples of type 3 projects, although the systems of organization that underlie the collaborations are interestingly different. At New York University, the link between the press and the libraries is embodied by the shared position of Digital Scholarly Program Officer, in 2013 occupied by Monica

---

4. Neds-Fox, Crocker, and Vonderharr 2013, 159. Wayne State University Press previously did report to the library, as Clement (2011) observes, so the staff there have been able to observe both forms of organization.
5. My thanks to Steve Cohn at Duke and Peter Potter at Cornell for their observations about the importance of formal agreements for these kinds of collaboration. Peter's discussion of the Signale relationship appears in the May 2014 issue of *Choice* (www.cro3.org/content/51/09/1543.full.pdf) as part of the University Press Forum feature.

McCormick, which is responsible for scoping and managing joint projects (Koh 2012; McCormick 2008). At Penn State, the collaboration is organized through the existence of an Office of Digital Scholarly Publishing, jointly directed by the director of NYU Press and the associate dean in charge of scholarly communications in the libraries (Alexander 2008–2009). At Syracuse University, the collaboration, currently focused on the support of two new journals, is much newer, and there is as yet no formal architecture for administering the collaboration (Li, Guiod, and Preate 2013).

In two prominent examples of type 4 collaboration, at the University of Arizona and at the University of Georgia, the university presses have reported to their university librarians only since 2010 and even more recently have moved physically into the library space. At Arizona in particular, it is clear the opportunities for more strategic collaborations are being explored, most recently through commissioning an environmental scan of library/press collaborations conducted by ARL Career Enhancement Fellow Charlotte Roh.[6] The relative autonomy between press and library partners may therefore be a feature of the relative newness of the move. This is certainly the case at Indiana University, where the physical relocation of the press into the main library building on campus took place in the first half of 2013, and strategic planning for a more integrated, type 5 future appears to be underway (see IU 2012). However, at other institutions such as the University of Utah, the relative independence of the press appears to represent a conscious decision by the library administration.[7]

Type 5 collaborations are characterized by adding a shared vision to reporting and collocation. This is often articulated in a joint strategic plan but may also be less formally reflected in joint branding, especially marked at Michigan (formerly M) Publishing (www.publishing.umich.edu), which is the umbrella organization for the press and other library publishing activities.[8] The position of the director of the university press is

---

6. I am grateful to Charlotte Roh for sharing a version of her concluding report with me.
7. The relationship is described by Rick Anderson (2013), at time of writing the interim dean of libraries at University of Utah, in a post on the *Scholarly Kitchen* blog.
8. OSU 2011; Purdue University 2011.The Office of Scholarly Publishing at Indiana University is working on such a plan; see Indiana University 2012.

often, but not necessarily, combined with other functions.[9] While poorly documented in the scholarly literature, Michigan Publishing is widely recognized as the leading experiment in North America in integrating the university press into a broader, campus-based publishing function. The creation of such an organization in 2009 was motivated by the twin desires to exploit economies of scale in production and business functions and to support the creation of new types of scholarly publications enabled by advances in digital technologies (Courant 2010). A similar agenda is pursued by the publishing division of Purdue University Libraries, which incorporates the press and is described in more detail below, although the history of development and the organization of leadership are different. At Utah State University, economic forces within the institution have currently led to a reduction in the scope of an ambitious integration agenda, with the press moving in 2012 into a consortial arrangement led by University of Colorado Press, although experiments in the production of open-access monographs made available immediately through the institutional repository and HathiTrust are progressing and are yielding exciting results (Clement 2011; Spooner and Wesolek 2013; Wesolek and Spooner 2013).

Should the taxonomic outline above be understood as snapshots of different stages along a process, where relationships move from collaboration to integration, or as representing different models appropriate in different contexts? Arguments could be made for both suggestions. Some organizational models would make progression beyond the type 2 category, in which collaborations exist but there is a lack of reporting relationship, difficult. A particular example lies in the "system" presses present in Florida, Kansas, and Mississippi, for example, where the presses have extremely positive relationships with libraries but have publishing responsibilities across many different institutions, making integrated relationships with any one campus challenging. Such examples suggest that the taxonomy may reflect different organizational contexts. At Purdue University, however,

---

9. The Director of University of Michigan Press is also Associate University Librarian for Publishing; at Oregon State University, the University Librarian is also director of the university press; the Director of Temple University Press is also Scholarly Communication Officer in the libraries; the head of the Office of Scholarly Publishing at Indiana University is also currently de facto director of the university press; at Purdue, the director of the university press is also head of scholarly publishing services in the libraries.

a process of movement from collaboration to integration can be shown, with the relationship developing from type 3 to type 5 between 2008 and 2012. The Purdue example also highlights the importance of reporting, physical collocation, and shared strategic planning as the main taxonomic delineators and deserves further examination.

The Path from Collaboration to Integration at Purdue University

The predecessor to Purdue University Press, Purdue University Studies, was established in 1960 after the English department had lamented the lack of publishing venues in the humanities. Unlike university presses founded earlier in the century, whose original mission was often directly related to the publication of work by the parent institution's faculty, the Studies series published the work of scholars from outside Purdue from the start. In 1974, Purdue University Studies became Purdue University Press and moved to offices in South Campus Courts, an area of low-status post–World War II office space on the outskirts of campus, positioned near other units involved in the movement of physical inventory.

In 1992, responsibility for the press was transferred to the dean of libraries, mainly as an administrative convenience during a period of structural change. In 1993, Purdue University Press was admitted to membership of the Association of American University Presses. Over the next decade, the number of books produced each year increased from six in 1990 to thirty-five in 2002, and several journals were taken on. Prior to the arrival of a new dean of libraries, James L. Mullins, from MIT in 2004, the director of the press's relationship with the dean had consisted of no more than occasional meetings. But Mullins strengthened the relationship, inviting the press director to participate in the Dean's Council, which brought together the library's associate deans with other senior staff responsible for support roles such as the Business Office and Advancement/Fundraising. However, other staff in the press had little contact with their library colleagues, the press's physical location was still at the periphery of campus, and there was little attempt at strategic alignment, although some small experiments in open-access journal publishing through Purdue e-Pubs, the institutional repository software licensed by the libraries in 2005, were initiated.

The physical relocation of the press in 2008, from South Campus Courts to offices in Stewart Center, immediately above the dean's office and behind the main humanities and social science library, marked a crucial step toward greater integration. Back in 2001, the press had outsourced its physical distribution, and the challenges of moving inventory in and out of a more central location had been removed. The timing of the move was related to greater interest with the libraries in the potential role of the university as publisher, linked with the appearance of the three major reports described above, and a desire for more cautious business oversight of the press. However, it also had a catalytic effect on the staff members who were immediately brought into greater contact and familiarity with their libraries colleagues, notably the manager of the digital repository, who was interested in expanding its role as a publishing platform. When a new director of the press was hired in 2009, preference was given to a candidate who showed knowledge of the three reports and interest in exploring possible synergies.

The next major change came in 2010, when several press staff members were actively involved in the creation of a new strategic plan for the libraries. Published as the *Strategic Plan 2011–2016, The Faculty of Library, Archival and Information Sciences, Purdue University Libraries, Purdue University Press, University Copyright Office* (Purdue University 2011), this document includes a number of specific objectives, such as the "Develop and promote new publishing models," which relate to the publishing function. However, it gives latitude to the libraries' various units and committees to develop their own strategies to accomplish these objectives. This means, for example, that while a preference for open-access strategies is strongly expressed in the strategic plan, the press is free to still charge for access for most of its publications. The implementation of the strategic plan also required reorganization of existing library councils and committees and the creation of several new entities. Representatives from the press were added to several of these, notably the Information Resources Council (IRC), which makes decisions related to bought and licensed information resources; the Digital Scholarship Council (DSC), which coordinates the creation of original information resources; and the Planning and Operations Council (POC), which oversees the implementation of the strategic plan across all spheres of the libraries' operations.

In 2013 the press published around twenty-five books a year, and fifteen journals, a number of them in electronic-only, open-access format in collaboration with Purdue University Libraries. It has particularly focused in recent years in aligning the subject focuses of its publishing program more with the strengths of Purdue University, publishing new books and journals in fields such as science and engineering education, building construction management, aviation and astronautics, and information science. At the same time, in April 2012 the director of the university press was also put in charge of the institutional repository platform, Purdue e-Pubs, recognizing that an area of particular growth in usage lay not in the deposit of versions of previously published articles but in the informal publication of original faculty, staff, and student scholarship traditionally distributed as technical reports, conference proceedings, and white papers. This change in duties was reflected in the new title of Director of Purdue University Press and Head of Scholarly Publishing Services in Purdue Libraries, and efforts are currently underway to better integrate the activities of the staff involved in the publishing division of the libraries and articulate the range of products they produce in a way that makes sense to authors, customers, and administrators.[10]

As the case study from Purdue illustrates, while the move from reporting and loose collaboration to a more integrated organization was neither entirely planned nor grounded entirely in long-term strategy, several key decisions had a substantial impact. The first was the decision to collocate the press within the libraries in 2008, which not only positioned the staff in a much more visible and accessible location on campus but also opened the door to more interaction with library colleagues, both organized and serendipitous.[11] The second was the involvement of senior staff of the press in a libraries' strategic planning exercise during which they were constantly treated as full partners and after which they were integrated into the various committee and councils charged with implementing the

---

10. A new website, Purdue Libraries Publishing (www.lib.purdue.edu/publishing), aims to reflect the relationship between Purdue University Press and Scholarly Publishing Services, and a consolidated catalog was issued for the first time in 2013.
11. Several interesting discussions of the role of proximity and serendipity in stimulating innovation are summarized in a recent *New Yorker* article, "Face Time" (Surowiecki 2013).

plan. Both physically moving the press and involving press staff in the core governance mechanisms of the libraries were acts that raised some concerns, among both press staff and library administrators. Would these changes obscure the distinctive, outward-facing identity of the press? Would press staff share the values of the rest of the library, especially around issues such as open access? But three years later, the results for both partners appear to have been positive. The implications of these changes and the new types of publishing the press has been able to engage in are discussed in the second part of this case study, below. The decision to make the press director responsible for the institutional repository and the types of informal, service-driven publishing more generally associated with the sorts of library publishing described elsewhere in this volume was another key decision, recognizing that the repository could be a publishing platform, not just a compliance tool, preservation service, or branding mechanism. While some of the opportunities this raises are discussed later in this chapter, the full impact is not yet apparent.

Challenges

There are three main areas of challenge that library/press collaborations face. These are economic, cultural, and structural in nature.

In the economic sphere, much emphasis has been placed on the different business models under which presses and libraries operate, with presses predominantly relying on cost recovery and libraries on subsidy. As Raym Crow notes, "a typical breakdown of an institutional library's funding sources would include about 75–85% from university appropriations and about 5–15% from designated funds, with the balance coming from sponsored programs and endowments," while "on average, university presses operate on a combination of earned income (80–90%) and institutional subsidies (5–15%), supplemented by title subsidies and endowment income (5%)" (Crow 2009, 21). The need to cover the majority of its costs from earned revenue limits the opportunity for the press to engage in uncertain and experimental collaborative projects (especially those involving open access) unless financial requirements can be met, for example through grant funding or other subsidies. The "on average" is important, however, because cost-recovery expectations are by no means uniform across presses. The smaller operations that account for almost half of the AAUP membership (designated Group 1 presses in a AAUP stats) rely substantially on subsidies. When direct cash payments from the parent institution are combined with indirect support such as rent-free space or gratis IT support, many of the smaller presses may be receiving almost half of their income from institutional subsidies.

Cultural differences between librarians and publishers that make collaborating on joint projects challenging have sometimes been exemplified by the idea that "libraries are service organizations whose funding comes in part from their success in anticipating needs, they tend to say yes" while "publishers, working to break even in a highly competitive business, evaluating many potential projects, and with quantifiable limits on their productivity, tend to say no" (McCormick 2008, 30). Another common observation is that while libraries and publishers may work with the same faculty numbers, the attitudes to scholarly communication issues that these individuals have are very different depending on whether they are speaking as "authors" or "users" of information. One example is in faculty attitudes to sharing information with others and thus by extension open access. As users of such information they may be enthusiastic, but as authors of information they are cautious, especially if the information shared goes beyond their narrow audience of peers. This has been well-expressed as the "Dr. Jekyll and Dr. Hyde" problem (Mabe and Amin 2002). Because librarians and publishers understand the needs of their constituents differently, the argument goes, it is difficult to agree on the design of an initiative to serve them. It can be argued that, in the last few years, the changing roles librarians are assuming in supporting scholars as authors as well as users of information have removed some of these challenges. "Embedded librarians" are appreciating the diversity of disciplinary needs and focusing on constructing unique and distinctive collections of content, roles familiar to publishers (Garritano and Carlson 2009).

Related to cultural challenges are issues concerning mutual respect and understanding. For example, on the library side, there is a lack of understanding of the value that publishers add. For rhetorical effect, open-access advocates have downplayed the role of the publisher as either simply managing the peer-review process or at the most also adding some grammatical copyediting and template design. In this narrative, peer review is performed by volunteers and the processes of production are commodities, most frequently outsourced to overseas vendors. Not only does this misrepresent the level of commitment that most university presses have to labor-intensive practices such as developmental editing, but the larger picture of publishing as a process of "investment" and "organization" and part of a "value chain" is ignored. Presses complain that the acquisitions editorial and marketing activities they engage in are particularly poorly understood by libraries, and the lack of a publishing certification equivalent to the MLS/MLIS, still held by most exempt-status librarians, leads their staff to sometimes be perceived as amateurs within a professionalized environment.

Libraries also do not always appreciate that publishing is not a unified activity and consists of many different "publishing fields" with their own values, business models, and ways of doing things; university presses have very different missions and incentives from those of shareholder-driven commercial academic publishers (Thompson 2005, 21). That lack of understanding also extends to underestimating diversity within the community of university presses; not perceiving their very different sizes and funding models and the wide spread of different types of monographs, journals, and digital products published. The need to pursue business strategies that cover most costs through earned revenue and the razor-thin margins most university presses operate on are often overlooked by libraries, and university press directors often feel unfairly picked upon when libraries accuse them of dragging their feet on open access or being "disconnected from the academic values of their parent institutions," a common refrain in debate around the Georgia State University lawsuit (e.g., Smith 2012).

On the press side, the major misunderstanding that exists lies in a failure to appreciate the different roles libraries play as advocates for mission-driven publishing versus the pragmatic decisions libraries need to take as stewards of their budgets on behalf of stakeholders. While they have some leeway with operating budgets and special discretionary funds, librarians cannot simply shift materials budgets to subsidize university press publications, especially at institutions where the focus is on science and technology areas where university presses rarely publish. Presses also do not generally understand the major changes that are taking place, especially in larger libraries, from serving the needs of scholars as users of information to helping them throughout the research process as authors. In trying to serve scholars at all stages of the research cycle, it is natural that librarians should become more interested in publishing as they have in the provision of data management and curation services. Much of the development of library publishing programs is motivated by the unmet campus demand that librarians are discovering as they interact with scholars in these new ways (Hahn 2008, 7). These are publishing needs that generally fall outside the editorially intensive, formally peer-reviewed products that university presses traditionally produce, but they are no less real.

Structural challenges to press/library collaboration emerge as perhaps the most problematic, at both the system and institutional levels. Across the United States, it remains the case that only around 100 university presses serve a system of over 2,500 four-year colleges.[12] Of US research universities, only a third have university presses (Clement 2011). Collaboration between a university press and a library on a single campus is often not an option, one of the motivators of the growth in library-based publishing. In some cases, university presses that represent institutional systems may have difficulty collaborating with libraries that are based on individual campuses (Hahn 2008, 35). Cross-institutional collaboration remains a rarity, with some exceptions as at Duke and Fordham University Presses (Ehling and Staib 2008–2009; Kennison, Panourgiá, and Tartar 2010).

Within universities where the press reports to an officer other than the head of libraries, budgeting practices such as Responsibility Center Management and personal animosities or territoriality between top administrators can severely hamper the development of collaborations. Even when the press reports to the dean or director of libraries, it will usually remain classified as an "auxiliary" unit, while the library is a base-funded service unit of the university, a differentiation that can cause challenges to collaboration and even more so to the integration of a press into a library. Auxiliary units within universities are expected to be independent and self-supporting (ideally generating a surplus). Success is mainly defined by financial performance rather than achievement of

---

12. Not all the members of the Association of American University Presses are based on university campuses since the organization also includes presses based in contexts such as museums, public policy and research centers. The National Center for Education Statistics listed 2,774 four year colleges in the United States for 2009–10 (NCES 2014).

mission. The resulting focus on where the next dollar is coming from makes the sort of experimental publishing that library/press collaborations often wish to pursue difficult.

A related "structural" issue (perhaps also a cultural one) lies in the concern that presses have about editorial independence. The period after World War II, argues Rick Clement (2011, 511), marked a change from earlier eras where the idea of the university press as an outlet for the institution's own faculty gave way to a focus on disciplines where publishing one's own faculty become not only less common but in fact a black mark, raising concerns about "vanity publishing." Today, he suggests, presses publish their own faculty members at levels of between 5 percent and 25 percent, although the situation may be changing. In this context, maintaining a separation between other institutional departments and an "arm's-length" relationship with imbedded units such as the library can be seen as a point of pride. Such concern about loss of editorial independence can, however, be confused with vaguer worries about "loss of identity," which may lead to attempts by presses to "fly beneath the radar," a strategy for relationships with a parent institution that has little long-term potential in an age of administrative scrutiny.

Opportunities

Immediate benefits and future opportunities exist for presses, libraries, and their host institutions in greater collaboration and possible library/press integration. Most immediately, the benefits are economic and operational, related to the better leveraging of university resources at a time when institutions are under increased financial pressure and "new synergies" are popular with administrators. Beyond such pragmatic choices, however, lie opportunities for both libraries and presses to better serve the scholarly communication needs of institutional faculty, staff, and students and to develop powerful solutions for particular disciplinary communities whose subject interests align with the strategic strengths of the parent university—an idea strongly focused on in the recommendations of the 2007 Ithaka report on *University Publishing in a Digital Age* (Brown, Griffiths, and Rascoff 2007).

In the economic sphere, the reasons why a university press could benefit from closer relationships with the library are clearer than the advantages for libraries. As described in a number of reports, university presses have long been suffering from the declining market for scholarly books and increased financial scrutiny from their institutions (Thompson 2005, 108-9). Finding new sources of financial support is a clear priority, and opportunities to share overhead costs with campus partners are obviously beneficial. As libraries increasingly either de-accession or remove print materials to remote storage, physical space is often becoming available that may be suitable for press occupancy, although where that space could be turned into classrooms, student needs always win out. Historically situated in areas where it can be easily accessed by faculty and students, library space is often particularly desirable for presses because it can allow them to move from the outskirts of campus to a more convenient and prestigious central location.[13] The libraries also benefit by being able to show to administrations that the vacated space is being occupied by a worthy tenant. The proximity between library and press colleagues is also mutually advantageous in that it can allow more contact to happen at all staffing levels between information professionals with diverse skills, backgrounds, and opinions.

While subsidized or free space is perhaps the most common, other opportunities for synergy frequently come in the areas of IT services, combined human resource and business office support, and shared legal counsel. In a survey conducted by AAUP in 2012, 11 percent of libraries provided some form of cash subsidy to university presses, while 53 percent of libraries provided some other kinds of service. This includes rent-free space but also support for basic office functions, digitization, metadata enrichment, and preservation services.[14] Both libraries and presses share

---

13. While noting the pressure for space on most campuses, Mike Furlough (pers. comm.) has pointed out that because the library is usually such a huge tenant on campus, it may be better connected politically to negotiate for prime space for the press. Of course, occupying library space may not always correlate with a central location—Michigan Publishing, for example, is housed in industrial space at the edge of campus along with some remote storage and administrative operations.
14. These figures were reported in the Press and Library Collaboration Survey of ARL deans and directors and AAUP directors conducted by the AAUP Library Relations Committee (2013) in a report made available on the AAUP website in January 2014, but based on a survey conducted in 2012.

specific needs in these areas that would not be well accommodated by other campus partners. For example, IT specialists in the library tend to understand the metadata standards needed for bibliographic information, HR recruiters are often advertising in similar venues for library and press staff, and legal expertise in areas such as intellectual property is desirable for both partners (even if they may sometimes approach the law from different angles). While many of the business office functions needed by the partners are similar, some challenges can emerge in this area. These are related to handling a revenue-generating unit whose income and expenditure fluctuate over a multiyear cycle (e.g., expenses incurred on a book in one financial year may not be recouped until the following financial year) rather than a library, which spends down an annually renewed budget over a single financial year.

A less tangible area of economic opportunity for both presses and libraries is in developing a better mutual understanding of the economic challenges facing the scholarly communication ecosystem in order to develop more informed strategies for intervention. One example of this lies in the area of open-access publishing, where questions about the "real cost" of publishing both journal articles and, increasingly, books are at the center of library strategies to support this emerging field. Librarians are often vexed by the extremely disparate costs that different publishers charge for open-access journal article publication, ranging from around $500 to over $3,000.[15] University presses, over 50 percent of which publish journals, can help untangle the issues and inform an understanding of what might constitute a fair level of subsidy. With the growing interest in open-access monographs, questions of what constitutes a reasonable first copy cost are again coming to the fore, and the opportunities to work through cost components in an environment of mutual trust are invaluable.

Where university press staff are involved in discussions about collections development (as at Purdue, where the director of the press is a member of the Information Resources Council, which guides collection development activities, or at Michigan, where the assistant director sits on the library Electronic Resources Committee), presses gain insights

---

15. King and Alvarado-Albertorio 2008. In 2012, sixty-two AAUP members published journals, representing almost half of the membership. Libraries often perceive university presses as being almost predominantly book publishers and lacking an understanding of journals. This is not entirely true.

into the processes by which libraries choose what and what not to buy. These are valuable for decision making locally and may give a library-based university press a competitive advantage, but there are also ripple effects as informed press directors and staff spread an understanding of the constraints libraries are operating under within the publishing community more broadly.

Beyond economic and operational convenience, collaboration with a university press gives librarians new insights into the behavior and needs of scholars as authors and greater credibility on campus should the collaboration evolve into a publishing partnership. By combining complementary skills and understanding the needs of both authors and users of scholarly information, partners in an effective press/library collaboration gain enhanced capacity to better serve the changing needs of the scholars who are their key clients and advance the reputation of the institution that pays their salaries. At the same time, libraries are able to advance both information literacy and scholarly communication goals through working with their press partners to create more equitable author agreements and teach ethical publication practices to younger scholars.[16]

The evidence-based 2007 study by the Ithaka organization on university publishing in the digital age identified four emerging needs for scholars whose modes of information production and consumption are increasingly electronic. These are that everything must be electronic, that scholars will rely on deeply integrated electronic research/publishing environments, that multimedia and multi-format delivery will become increasingly important, and that new forms of content will enable different economic models (Brown, Griffiths, and Rascoff 2007, 13–15). Press/library collaborations have the capacity to effectively meet these needs by not only harnessing the complementary skills of publishers and librarians but also enabling university presses to connect peer-reviewed scholarship with less formally produced material, the idea of publishing "across the continuum" described by Daniel Greenstein (2010). The inclination to experiment, which at many university presses has been suppressed by the

---

16. University press author agreement, often originally drafted by risk-averse university counsels, can have a tendency to be unduly restrictive for authors. A recent initiative at Michigan Publishing substantially revised the agreements of University of Michigan Press authors to make them more author-friendly (Kahn 2013).

need to constantly look to the bottom line, can be released in exploring new opportunities: monograph publishers can explore the creation of affordable textbooks (as at Oregon State University), traditional book publishers can dip a toe in journal publishing (as at the University of Pittsburgh), and the publishers of previously discrete content bundles can explore the networked world of digital humanities projects (as at the University of North Carolina). In the next section, we return to the case study of Purdue University to explore some examples of these opportunities in more detail.

The End Products of Collaboration at Purdue University

Like most other university presses, the initial products of Purdue University Press's collaboration with its parent library were open-access digital versions of backlist books and new, online peer-reviewed journals produced using the lightweight workflows imbedded in the library's digital repository software. Many other examples of such collaborations are described above and in reports on collaboration (Crow 2009, 11–14; Withey et al. 2011). Several of the initial journals continue to thrive, notably *CLCWeb: Comparative Literature and Culture*, the *Interdisciplinary Journal of Problem-Based Learning*, and the *Journal of Problem Solving*, and several new journals have been started more recently in disciplinary areas that the press is keen to build book programs in, engineering education (*Journal of Pre-College Engineering Education Research*) and aviation (*Journal of Aviation Technology and Engineering*). All of the open-access journals receive funding either from the editors' institutions or from author article charges. In the case of press books, additional multimedia objects are starting to be made available through the university's institutional and data repositories. In one case, the autobiography of Purdue astronaut Jerry L. Ross, a joint project with the university archives, led to the creation of an iPad app that links the press publication with videos, images, and additional materials from Dr. Ross's papers.[17]

---

17. The various components of this project are showcased at http://www.jerrylross.com, a website the press built for the author with assistance from the libraries' IT department.

More recently, however, Purdue University Press has been able to initiate several more experimental projects that apply the expertise of its publishing staff to scholarly research and teaching needs that extend far beyond the usual purview of a university press. In these cases, "the press becomes more of a research center that plays a role in leading innovation in a scholarly discipline, in addition to serving as a production and dissemination organization" (Wittenberg 2010).

While the *Journal of Purdue Undergraduate Research* (*JPUR*; www.jpur.org) is not formally branded as a university press publication, Purdue University Press is understood by all stakeholders with the university to be the main initiator of the project. Working with faculty members enthusiastic about undergraduate research, the press created the proposal to the provost's office for recurring financial support that established the journal in 2010, and it remains the holder of the budget, administered through the business office it shares with the libraries. Under the supervision of press staff, a paid student intern administers the manuscript management system, part of the libraries' Purdue e-Pubs repository, through which over eighty proposals a year are peer-reviewed. Library faculty members assist with the selection of manuscripts for publication, then take the lead in coaching undergraduate authors in writing, enhancing the students' information-literacy skills and understanding of scholarly communication issues in the process (Davis-Kahl and Hensley 2013, 115–18).

Press staff members are responsible for overseeing the copyediting, performing quality assurance of the design, and managing the distribution of the publication. Print copies are prominently displayed in the various campus libraries, and in the first two years, the libraries organized a celebratory dinner for authors and their faculty advisors at which the provost has spoken. An annual assessment is also conducted by the Wayne Booker Professor of Information Literacy, which measures learning gains by the students and reassures the provost's office that university resources are being well spent (Weiner and Watkinson 2014). While *JPUR* is a project that could theoretically have been handled by the press alone, the partnership with the libraries enhances the pedagogical opportunities the journal offers students. The press is also able to "white label" the journal, not undermining its brand, while still using the experience of working with faculty members and students across all disciplines to open new relationships with disciplinary faculty in science, engineering, and agriculture—fields where university presses traditionally have few connections and can rely on few supporters.[18]

Technical report series often present important scholarly information long before it appears in formal journal or book form. At Purdue University, the Joint Transportation Research Program's (JTRP) technical report series has been a major source of information for infrastructure professionals since it was initiated as a College of Engineering publication in the 1950s. The transition from print to digital publication has disrupted the traditional indexing and dissemination system, and the effective dissemination of the research in which it invests millions of dollars annually has become a major concern for the federal government. In 2009, the libraries initiated a project to digitize and make available online the 1,500 or so JTRP reports originally produced. The press, as a unit of the libraries, then contracted in 2010 to hire a new production editor, to be funded 50 percent by JTRP and 50 percent by the Libraries. A lightweight publication workflow was put in place, and the production editor now administers the publication of around thirty reports a year as well as copyediting and typesetting some of the more technical books published by the press.

In this initiative, the press was able to hire a new staff member to a full-time position and increase its exposure in the area of transportation, a disciplinary area that is not only strategically important to the university but also has a tradition of book as well as journal publication that maps well with the press's skills. The libraries, meanwhile, have been able to gain credibility in their research support activities within civil engineering and are now working on several data and open-access projects in the department. Since the JTRP program is entirely funded by the Indiana Department of Transportation, the collaboration has also received positive attention at the state and federal levels (Newton et al. 2012).

For over a decade, Purdue University Press has published a series in the field of human/animal interaction studies, most commonly reflected in the interaction between pets and people. Covering topics ranging from animal-assisted therapy to animal hoarding, the series reflects the

---

18. The concept of "white labeling" is used in consumer goods manufacturing when a name-brand company manufactures products that are then sold with a reseller's mark on them. This allows the name-brand company to make some extra money while not undermining the value of its own products.

interdisciplinarity of a field that draws in scholars from human and animal health, law and public policy, philosophy, and literature. The book series has been profitable, and the injection of new funding into the field by the National Institutes of Health in the late 2000s stimulated even more research and interest from practitioners. The opportunity not only to support this emerging field but also to position Purdue as a dominant force in it led to a proposal from the press and libraries, collaborating with the College of Veterinary Medicine, to the Human-Animal Bond Research Initiative (HABRI) Foundation to establish an integrated research environment online. The application to the foundation, which represents a coalition of commercial and not-for-profit organizations concerned with the welfare of companion animals, was accompanied by both a financial feasibility analysis and a market research report.

Incorporating a comprehensive bibliography, licensed full-text resources, and a platform for original publication, HABRI Central (www.habricentral.org) debuted in March 2012 and has already received substantial use and acceptance. The press is substantially involved in the project management of the site, which sits on the HUBzero platform for scientific collaboration, and also responsible for original publishing components of the project, which include a new open-access book series, Pets and People. Two library faculty members are responsible for the bibliography (which now includes almost 20,000 entries) and the taxonomic organization of the site, while a library staff member acts as digital repository specialist, in charge of metadata and context upload. Without the complementary skills of publishing and library staff together, the project would not have been possible (Stephens and Yatcilla 2013).

In these three case studies many of the complementary attributes of the press and library, as set out in Crow's (2009, 28) valuable "campus-based publishing core competency table" are demonstrated. Furlough (2010, 195) groups these skills under the broader headings of "strategy development and resource management," "outreach and recruitment," "production and content management," and "distribution and marketing." For the press staff at Purdue, the opportunity to work with colleagues expert in managing, organizing, and preserving digital materials has been even more valuable than having access to additional information technology hardware and software. For the libraries, the press has provided valuable expertise in market analysis and product design, as well as access to a whole information supply chain that enables, for example, the print-on-demand distribution of JTRP technical reports through a range of national and international vendors. By being relieved of some of the financial overheads (the libraries provide free business office, legal, and IT services as well as rent-free space including utilities), the press has been able to experiment with new forms of scholarly communication. Working on such projects, university press and library staff members each build new relationships and forms of expertise.

Where Next for Press/Library Collaboration?

The prior discussion of university press/library collaboration has mainly focused on collaboration between individual libraries and individual university presses. In this final section, we examine two trends that may affect the existing ecosystem in transformative ways. These are the emergence of library publishing services as potential competitors to university presses and the development of multi-institutional press/library collaborations at scale.

As described elsewhere in this book, the last five years have seen a dramatic increase in library-based publishing, with 55 percent of North American academic libraries of all sizes either developing or implementing publishing programs when surveyed in 2010 (Mullins et al. 2012). Within larger research libraries (members of ARL), the percentage increased to 79 percent, up from 65 percent only three years earlier (Hahn 2008). Such activity is currently being formalized in the creation of a Library Publishing Coalition, which in its initial directory numbers 115 library publishers, 60 of them contributing or founding members of the coalition (Lippincott and Skinner 2013). This growth in library publishing has implications that university presses cannot ignore—most especially whether library publishers should be regarded as complementary or competitive.

Most conversations on this topic currently focus on the complementarity of the relationship between university presses and the emerging library publishers. They note the institutional orientation of most library publishing and the disciplinary orientation of university presses. They also contrast the formal nature of monograph publication with the informal, lightweight nature of the products of library publishing, noting library publishers' particular focuses on gray literature, student scholarship, and niche open-access journals that may be important but challenging to sustain through a full cost-recovery model. The recent emergence of several library-based monograph publishers with no links to university presses, most publicly at Amherst College (https://www.amherst.edu/library/press), but also at the University of Nebraska–Lincoln (http://digitalcommons.unl.edu/zea), illustrates that there are exceptions to this picture. While he is not specific about whether he sees them emerging out of libraries, Clifford Lynch (2010) has anticipated a future where many new competitors vie for scholars' attention:

> In the future I envision, every research university, and a number of higher education institutions, have university presses; there are many more than exist today—indeed we see announcements of launches rather than shutterings of presses. Particularly for research universities, the lack of a university press is something that results in some questioning and discussion during the accreditation process for the university. In this future, most university presses are relatively small organizations, some almost cottage industry participants... and operate in much closer alignment with the academic programs of their institutions.

It does not, therefore, seem impossible that some library publishers may become competitors with traditional university presses in recruiting the best authors or in dominating certain disciplines.

Even if the institution-based versus discipline based/informal versus formal characterization remains the norm and the new university presses that Lynch predicts are not connected to libraries, the dichotomy conceals a potential hazard to university presses of becoming "boxed in," both on their own campuses and in the publishing system more generally. At the University of Pittsburgh, for example, the press publishes only books and the library publishes journals, some employing the press brand, but on terms set out by the library publishing unit. As a recent article explains, "The press continues to focus on monographic print publications whereas all material and technical support for e-journal publishing is provided by the University Library System" (Deliyannides and Gabler 2013, 82). There is a real danger for university presses that such stereotyping as a "peer-reviewed book publisher" may limit their ability to expand into new publishing product lines. Potentially, for example, a press interested in entering the business of publishing the proceedings of conferences happening on campus may find itself competing with a library publisher that has already developed a comprehensive solution for local conference organizers.

While some collaborative projects that are characterized as larger scale library/press partnerships exist, the initiators are generally single libraries partnering with multiple presses. Examples are Project MUSE, founded by Johns Hopkins University Press and the Milton S. Eisenhower Library, which serves more than 200 libraries, and Highwire Press, the publishing platform of Stanford University Libraries, which serves over 130 publishers (and also provides the backbone to Project MUSE from 2014 onward).[19] In 2007, the president of the Ithaka organization, Kevin Guthrie, suggested "that it would be beneficial for the community if there were a powerful technology, service and marketing platform that would serve as a catalyst for collaboration and shared investment capital in university-based publishing" (Brown, Griffiths, and Rascoff 2007, 1). Raym Crow (2009, 47) identifies several opportunities to craft multi-institutional initiatives not only to develop shared platforms but also to address social issues such as the challenge that young humanists pursuing tenure apparently encounter in publishing their first books.

While such large "alliance networks" as Crow and Guthrie described have not yet emerged, it is clear that collaboration between university presses and libraries may be close to reaching the critical scale at which such opportunities may be possible to accomplish. While challenges exist to creating firm partnerships, it is increasingly clear from case study after case study that the capacity of library/press collaborations to advance scholarship is an opportunity worth persevering toward. It is hoped that this chapter may play a small role in that movement.

---

19. Duke University Press and Utah State University Press both partner with HathiTrust, which is a coalition of multiple libraries, to preserve digitized books and other cultural artifacts and make them openly accessible where possible.

Works Cited

AAUP Library Relations Committee. *Press and Library Collaboration Survey.* 2013. New York: Association of American University Presses. <In orig MS as Dixon 2014 pp. 34>

Alexander, Patrick H. 2008–2009. "Publisher-Library Relations: What Assets Does a University Press Bring to the Partnership?" *Against the Grain* 20, no. 6 (December–January): 40–44.

Anderson, Rick. "Another Perspective on Library-Press 'Partnerships.'" *The Scholarly Kitchen* (blog), July 23. http://scholarlykitchen.sspnet.org/2013/07/23/another-perspective-on-library-press-partnerships.

Bargheer, Margo, and Brigit Schmidt. 2008. "Göttingen University Press: Publishing Services in an Open Access Environment." *Information Services and Use* 28, no. 2 (January): 133–39.

Brown, Allison P., ed. 2013. *Library Publishing Toolkit.* Geneseo, NY: IDS Project Press.

Brown, Laura, Rebecca J. Griffiths, and Matthew Rascoff. 2007. *University Publishing in a Digital Age.* New York: Ithaka, July 26.

Clement, Richard W. 2011. "Library and University Press Integration: A New Vision for University Publishing." *Journal of Library Administration* 51, no. 5–6: 507–28. doi:10.1080/01930826.2011.589330.

Coleman, Ross. 2006. "Sydney University Press: Publication, Business, and the Digital Library." Paper presented at Connecting with Users: 13th Biennial Conference and Exhibition, Melbourne, Australia, February 8–10. http://ses.library.usyd.edu.au/handle/2123/1426.

Courant, Paul N. 2010. "What Might Be in Store for Universities' Presses." *Journal of Electronic Publishing* 13, no. 2 (Fall). doi:10.3998/3336451.0013.206.

Crow, Raym. 2009. *Campus-Based Publishing Partnerships: A Guide to the Critical Issues.* Washington, DC: SPARC, January.

Davis-Kahl, Stephanie, and Merinda Kaye Hensley, eds. 2013. *Common Ground at the Nexus of Information Literacy and Scholarly Communication.* Chicago: Association of College and Research Libraries.

Day, Colin. 1995. "The Need for Library and University Press Collaboration." *Collection Management* 19, no. 3–4: 107–15. doi:10.1300/J105v19n03_10.

Deliyannides, Timothy S., and Vanessa E. Gabler. 2013. "The University Library System, University of Pittsburgh: How and Why We Publish." In Brown 2013, 79–87.

Ehling, Terry, and Erich Staib. 2008–2009. "The Coefficient Partnership: Project Euclid, Cornell University Library, and Duke University Press." *Against the Grain* 20, no. 6 (December–January): 32–36.

Furlough, Michael J. 2010. "The Publisher in the Library." In *The Expert Library: Staffing, Sustaining, and Advancing the Academic Library in the 21st Century,* edited by Scott Walker and Karen Williams, 190–233. Washington, DC: Association of College and Research Libraries.

Furlough, Michael J., and Michele Reid. 2012. "Business Planning for Research Support Services: Case Studies." Paper presented at the Digital Library Federation Forum, Denver, CO, November 4–5. www.diglib.org/forums/2012forum/business-planning-for-research-support-services-case-studies.

Garritano, Jeremy R., and Jake R. Carlson. 2009. "A Subject Librarian's Guide to Collaborating on E-science Projects." *Issues in Science and Technology Librarianship,* no. 57

(Spring). doi:10.5062/F42B8VZ3.
Greenstein, Daniel. 2010. "Next-Generation University Publishing: A Perspective from California." *Journal of Electronic Publishing* 13, no. 2 (Fall). doi:10.3998/3336451.0013.205.
Hahn, Karla L. 2008. *Research Library Publishing Services: New Options for University Publishing*. Washington, DC: Association of Research Libraries.
IU (Indiana University). 2012. "IU to Establish New Office of Scholarly Publishing." News release, IU News Room, June 29. http://newsinfo.iu.edu/news/page/normal/22724.html.
Kahn, Meredith. 2013. "New Author's Agreement from Michigan Publishing." *Michigan Publishing/University of Michigan Press Blog*, June 7. http://blog.press.umich.edu/2013/06/new-authors-agreement.
Kennison, Rebecca, Neni Panourgiá, and Helen Tartar. 2010. "*Dangerous Citizens* Online: A Case Study of an Author–Press–Library Partnership." *Serials* 23, no. 2 (July)": 145–49. doi:10.1629/231456.
King, Donald W., and Frances M. Alvarado-Albertorio. 2008. "Pricing and Other Means of Charging for Scholarly Journals: A Literature Review and Commentary." *Learned Publishing* 21, no. 4 (October): 248–72. doi:10.1087/095315108x356680.
Koh, Adeline. 2012. "Are You a Press or Are You a Library? An Interview with NYU's Monica McCormick." *ProfHacker* (blog), *Chronicle of Higher Education*, March 27. http://chronicle.com/blogs/profhacker/press-or-library/39216.
Koltay, Zsuzsa, and H. Thomas Hickerson. 2002. "Project Euclid and the Role of Research Libraries in Scholarly Publishing." *Journal of Library Administration* 35, no. 1–2: 83–98. doi:10.1300/J111v35n01_06.
Li, Yuan, Suzanne E. Guiod, and Suzanne Preate. 2013. "A Case Study in Open Access Publishing at Syracuse University: Library and University Press Partnership Furthers Scholarly Communications." In Brown 2013, 215–22.
Lippincott, Sarah, and Katherine Skinner. 2013. "Building a Community-Driven Organization to Advance Library Publishing." In Brown 2013, 367–73.
Lynch, Clifford. 2010. "Imagining a University Press System to Support Scholarship in the Digital Age." *Journal of Electronic Publishing* 13, no. 2 (Fall). doi:10.3998/3336451.0013.207.
Mabe, Michael A., and Mayur Amin. 2002. "Dr Jekyll and Dr Hyde: Author–Reader Asymmetries in Scholarly Publishing." *Aslib Proceedings* 54, no. 3: 149–57.
McCormick, Monica. 2008. "Learning to Say Maybe: Building NYU's Press/Library Collaboration." *Against the Grain* 20, no. 6: 28–30.
Miller, Sylvia. 2008. "Publishing the Long Civil Rights Movement at the University of North Carolina at Chapel Hill." *Against the Grain* 20, no. 6: 36–40.
Missingham, Roxanne, and Lorena Kannelopoulos. 2013. "A Decade of Running a University E-Press." In Brown 2013, 121–26.
Mullins, James L., Catherine Murray Rust, Joyce L. Ogburn, Raym Crow, October Ivins, Allyson Mower, Daureen Nesdill, Mark P. Newton, Julie Speer, and Charles Watkinson. 2012. *Library Publishing Services: Strategies for Success*. Final Research Report. Washington, DC: SPARC, March. http://wp.sparc.arl.org/lps.
NCES (National Center for Education Statistics). 2014. "Fast Facts: Number of Educational Institutions, by Level and Control of Institution: Selected Years, 2980–81 through 2010–11)." Accessed August 25. http://nces.ed.gov/fastfacts/display.asp?id=84.
Neds-Fox, Joshua, Lauren Crocker, and Alicia Vonderharr. 2013. "Wayne State University

Press and Libraries: A Case Study of a Library and University Press Journal Publishing Program." In Brown 2013, 153–60.

Newton, Mark P., Darcy M. Bullock, Charles Watkinson, Paul J. Bracke, and Deborah K. Horton. 2012. "Engaging New Partners in Transportation Research.". *Transportation Research Record* 2291, no. 1: 111–23.

OSU (Ohio State University). 2011. "2011–12 Strategic Plan of OSU Libraries and OSU Press." OSU Libraries. http://osulibrary.oregonstate.edu/files/2011%20Strategic%20 Plan.pdf.

Purdue University. 2011. *Strategic Plan 2011–2016, The Faculty of Library, Archival and Information Sciences, Purdue University Libraries, Purdue University Press, University Copyright Office.* West Lafayette, IN: Purdue University, July 1. https://www.lib.purdue.edu/sites/default/files/admin/plan2016.pdf.

Smith, Kevin. 2012. "GSU and University Presses." *Scholarly Communications @ Duke* (blog), September 17. http://blogs.library.duke.edu/scholcomm/2012/09/17/gsu-and-university-presses.

Spooner, Michael, and Andrew Wesolek. 2013. "Content and Collaboration I: A Case Study of Bringing an Institutional Repository and a University Press Together." In Brown 2013, 171–78.

Steele, Colin. 2013. "Open Access in Australia: An Odyssey of Sorts?" *Insights* (UKSG) 26, no. 3 (November): 282–89.

Stephens, Gretchen, and Jane Kinkus Yatcilla. 2013. "Creating HABRI Central: Librarians in Partnership with Researchers, Software Developers, and Publishers." Presentation at International Congress on Medical Librarianship (ICML), Boston, MA, May 3–8.

Surowiecki, James. 2013. "Face Time." *New Yorker*, March 18. www.newyorker.com/magazine/2013/03/18/face-time.

Thompson, John B. 2005. *Books in the Digital Age: The Transformation of Academic and Higher Education Publishing in Britain and the United States* Cambridge: Polity Press.

Weiner, Sharon A., and Charles Watkinson. 2014. "What Do Students Learn from Participation in an Undergraduate Research Journal? Results of an Assessment." *Journal of Librarianship and Scholarly Communication* 2, no. 2: eP1125. doi:10.7710/2162-3309.1125.

Wesolek, Andrew, and Michael Spooner. 2013. "Content and Collaboration II: Opportunities to Host, Opportunities to Publish." In Brown 2013, 275–80.

Withey, Lynne, Steve Cohn, Ellen Faran, Michael Jensen, Garrett Kiely, Will Underwood, Bruce Wilcox, Richard Brown, Peter Giveler, Alex Holzman, and Kathleen Keane. 2011. *Sustaining Scholarly Publishing: New Business Models for University Presses.* New York: Association of American University Presses, March.

Wittenberg, Kate. 2001. "The Electronic Publishing Initiative at Columbia (EPIC): A University-Based Collaboration in Digital Scholarly Communication." *Learned Publishing* 14, no. 1 (January): 29–32. doi:10.1087/09531510125100241.

———. 2010. "Reimagining the University Press." *Journal of Electronic Publishing* 13, no. 2 (Fall). doi:10.3998/3336451.0013.203.

CHAPTER 5

The Evolution of Publishing Agreements at the University of Michigan Library

Kevin S. Hawkins

One of the main reasons library-based publishing operations have been formed is in response to dissatisfaction with traditional publishers, which are frequently vilified for obtaining nearly exclusive rights to scholars' work and producing expensive products, thereby hindering authors' use of their own work and impeding broad and affordable access by readers. In response, library-based publishers have aimed to publish more cost-effectively and provide fairer terms to authors than traditional publishers, especially by allowing authors to retain copyright, granting to the publisher only those rights necessary for publication. This grant of rights or *license* sometimes happens using a click-through agreement when submitting a manuscript

---

This work is licensed under the Creative Commons Attribution License 4.0 (CC-BY 4.0).

through software like Open Journal Systems (OJS) and sometimes happens by signing a contract. This license is often *non-exclusive*, meaning the author can grant similar rights to another party besides the library-based publisher.

The University of Michigan Library's publishing operation obtains agreements in writing. As the publishing operation grew from a few staff members (the Scholarly Publishing Office) to a multi-department staff (MPublishing) and later an operation fully integrated with the University of Michigan Press (Michigan Publishing), the approach to rights management with authors and editors has evolved along with the organization's thinking about these questions. Taking as an example an open-access journal with a single editor, this chapter discusses the various configurations of rights agreements used by the U-M Library throughout the evolution of the publishing operation, the advantages of the various models, and the reasons for moving from one to another.

First Generation: Memoranda of Understanding

When the Scholarly Publishing Office was first created, journals, bibliographies, and other material were accepted for online publication as opportunities arose. Many had already been published in print, and some of the journals continued to publish in print even after partnering with the library. Each project had unique features, and no standard publication types had yet emerged. What was especially unclear was the division of labor between the library and the publishing partner—in the case of a journal, the editor.

To clarify this relationship, a memorandum of understanding was drawn up. It included a description of what files the editor would provide to the library and what the library would do in return. It was usually written as a letter from the head of the Scholarly Publishing Office to the editor but not signed by either party. SPO staff did not have these reviewed by staff of the university's general counsel, seeing them, incorrectly, as nonbinding agreements.

The library accommodated such journals' production workflow and file formats where possible in digitizing back issues and publishing new issues online. Since these journals already used agreements with their authors, the library's publishing operation sought only a single agreement with the journal editor, not with each author. The standard author agreement was perhaps reviewed to verify that it included rights to publish online, but the responsibility for collecting these agreements lay with the editor. Furthermore, the single agreement with the editor was always non-exclusive: editors were free to make their content available through other channels, both during and after any relationship with the library. Given this arrangement, it didn't make sense for the library to enter into an agreement with each author just for the version published online by the library.

Second Generation: Agreements between the Library and the Editor

As standard publication types emerged, the library's publishing operation (which by then was rebranded as MPublishing) needed boilerplate agreements that included the best clauses from past agreements to ensure the rights of authors, the journal editor, and the library. Furthermore, library staff wanted to ensure that important clauses not previously included in agreements—notably, an explicit granting of publishing rights by the journal to the library—were included as well.

The practice of the library entering into an agreement only with the journal editor continued. The journal editor warranted that he or she had the right to authorize the library to publish the articles in the journal—that is, that the editor had secured author agreements from all contributors. Since the library increasingly took on journals that had not previously been published in print or electronically, it became increasingly important to offer guidance to the editor on author agreements. The library provided two variants of a model agreement for use by the editor: one in which the author retained the copyright but granted to the editor a non-exclusive license to publish and to grant others (such as the library) the right to publish, and another in which the author transferred the copyright in the article to the journal. The latter was originally devised out of concern that, if the author kept the copyright, the library would exacerbate the orphan works problem by making it harder for readers to track down authors in order to republish the work; however, publishing staff eventually decided that the former agreement was indeed sufficient to cover future uses.

In addition to a warranty that the editor had secured the right to publish all content, the single agreement also included a clause, standard in publishing contracts, that guaranteed that the journal contained no defamatory or libelous material. Furthermore, the editor indemnified the library for any breach of the agreement, meaning the editor would be completely liable for any content published by the library as part of the journal that could lead to a lawsuit. This was a problem for journals bringing back issues for migration to the library's site, for which author agreements could not always be secured. It also left the editor personally liable for actions undertaken in the course of editing the journal. The library recommended that agreements be signed not by the editor personally but by a representative of an organization sponsoring the journal (if one existed). Alternatively, editors were encouraged to incorporate as an S corporation or an LLC and sign as this corporate entity.

Past agreements were gradually revisited to move to the new standard agreements. While Creative Commons had emerged as the preferred method for sharing open-access content, the focus for the publishing operation had always been simply on making content available to read online, without insistence on attaching a CC license. While the first-generation arrangements predated Creative Commons as an organization, once use of CC licenses became common, they were incorporated into the model agreements and single agreement with the journal editor. Originally the Attribution license (CC BY) was used for journals, though as one editor after another balked at such permissive licensing, the default was changed to the Attribution-NonCommerical-NoDerivs license (CC BY-NC-ND). However, as major players in open-access publishing such as Elementa, PeerJ, Wiley Open Access, and OASPA began using CC BY (in accordance with the definition of open access from the Budapest Open Access Initiative), the default was changed back to CC BY, with an understanding that this might lead to a productive discussion with the editor and, if necessary, a modification of the terms of the agreement.

Third Generation: Agreements with Editors and Directly with Authors

As the library's publishing operation was fully integrated with that of the University of Michigan Press (with the combined operation rebranded as Michigan Publishing), it made sense to reconcile the different rights agreements in use. The press, as a publisher of monographs, had always made agreements directly with authors. In the case of an anthology, the press would make an agreement with the editor of the anthology, with a brief contributor agreement signed by each author. All of these agreements were kept on file at the press.

The press anthology model will be used as the basis for the third generation of agreements for journals. A single agreement will be signed by the editor and a representative of the university covering the journal as a whole, but the library will also require a signed agreement from every author of a journal article granting a license to publish to the university. This agreement could be consulted in case of a dispute instead of having to rely on the editor's word that the necessary rights had been secured as in previous generations of agreements. More important for the editor, he or she—or the journal's sponsoring organization—would not be liable in case of such a dispute.

However, the story of the evolution of the U-M Library's publishing operation isn't just one of increasing formality and conformance to the model used by the press. The integration of publishing operations and creation of Michigan Publishing also led to an examination of the author agreement used for University of Michigan Press titles. In a new standard author agreement for press titles that debuted in 2013, authors are allowed to keep copyright while granting publishing rights to the press, allowed to deposit the work in an institutional repository after three years, and offered the opportunity to license their work with a Creative Commons license, either immediately or after three years. If they choose the immediate option for a CC license, they receive an advance on royalties. Why do this? Michigan Publishing is committed to taking a leadership role in the expansion of the open-access philosophy to monograph publishing but understands that one of the impediments to author adoption of open access is the risk of losing royalty revenue. The incentive program is designed to nullify this particular concern. While Michigan Publishing believes that, in many cases, open access to monographs will stimulate sales, the advance against royalties serves as a kind of "insurance policy" to authors who would are interested in going OA but don't feel enough data yet exist to persuade them that doing so won't undercut their sales.

As someone who has been involved in the writing and rewriting of these publishing agreements, it's tempting to think that the library has finally settled on the optimal language in these agreements, but I know better since I have so often found language in need of improvement when looking at any agreement with fresh eyes. Michigan Publishing's contracts will surely continue to evolve in tandem with author expectations and publishing practice. As the library's associate university librarian for publishing wrote in the announcement of the new standard author agreement for press titles, "We will continue to work to align our publishing practices with the needs of the scholarly community, increasing the accessibility and viability of the scholarly record while removing obstacles from use and reuse of publications by our authors and other scholars" (Kahn 2013).

Author's Note

I am grateful to Melanie Schlosser, Rebecca Welzenbach, Maria Bonn, Mike Furlough, and especially Kevin L. Smith for providing comments on drafts of this chapter, and to Aaron McCollough for providing the rationale for the advance on author royalties in the rewritten standard author agreement for press titles.

Work Cited

Kahn, Meredith. 2013. "New Author's Agreement from Michigan Publishing." *Michigan Publishing/University of Michigan Press Blog*, June 7. http://blog.press.umich.edu/2013/06/new-authors-agreement.

CHAPTER 6

Library-as-Publisher
Capacity Building for the Library Publishing Subfield

Katherine Skinner, Sarah Lippincott, Julie Speer, and Tyler Walters

Introduction

The role of publisher is increasingly assumed by academic and research libraries, usually inspired by campus-based demands for digital publishing platforms to support e-journals, conference proceedings, technical reports, and database-driven websites. Although publishing is compatible with librarians' traditional strengths, there are additional skill sets that library publishers must master in order to provide robust publishing services to their academic communities.

To help library publishing services mature into a consistent field of practice, practitioners in this growing publishing subfield increasingly cite their need for specialized training

This work is licensed under the Creative Commons Attribution License 4.0 (CC-BY 4.0).

and professional development opportunities. For example, the authors' conversations with participants in the Library Publishing Coalition (LPC), a collaborative network of 60 North American academic libraries involved in publishing, have revealed that no existing graduate-level training program adequately prepares practitioners for the full range of theoretical, practical, and organizational issues involved in publishing. LPC participants have also noted the relative lack of continuing education opportunities targeted toward those who are engaging in publishing—whether in a library, university press, or commercial publishing environment.

This essay provides a brief history of publisher training and uses this context to think about how and where library publishers may engage in capacity building to inform and train this growing publishing subfield. Throughout the essay, we integrate findings from a series of interviews conducted by the authors with 11 industry leaders from several publishing sectors, including university presses, library publishers, and commercial publishers (see Appendix 6.1). We conclude with recommendations for pathways forward, focusing on seven key areas in which library publishers need additional training opportunities. This essay focuses primarily on North American activities.

What Is "Library Publishing"?

"Library publishing" is a growing subfield of publishing. It has been defined (broadly) as "the set of activities led by college and university libraries to support the creation, dissemination, and curation of scholarly, creative, and/or educational works."[1] Using formal production processes, more than 100 North American libraries currently publish original works by scholars, researchers, and students.[2] These publications include journals, monographs, Electronic Theses and Dissertations (ETDs), gray literature, conference proceedings, data, textbooks, and websites.

Library publishing is differentiated from the work of other publishers—including commercial, society, academic, and trade—in large part by its business model, which often relies heavily on being subsidized through the library budget, rather than operating primarily as a cost-recovery or profit-driven activity. Libraries are relative newcomers to the field, largely beginning this work in a digital environment over the last 20 years.

As Karla Hahn noted in 2008, "library-based publishing programs are pragmatic responses to evident needs, not services in search of clients."[3] Many libraries first became involved in publishing because their local faculty and students approached the library for assistance in producing digital scholarly works. In some cases, these are new, born-digital journals, books, or multimedia projects. In other instances, as October Ivins remarked in an interview with the authors, the library may "revive canceled print journals or assist in making other publications viable that would have been dropped by their creators."

These publishing experiments have matured into programmatic channels for a variety of curatorial and economic reasons. From the economic angle, libraries have found that the cost of producing scholarly works within the library is reasonable. Even if libraries only publish a subset of the scholarly record, some libraries argue that this investment could serve both to increase access to scholarship (via open access models, largely preferred by library publishers) and decrease the library's expenditures over time. And libraries have been further motivated to publish content because of their curatorial charge. Licensing and intellectual property constraints often prohibit libraries from managing and preserving today's digital scholarly publications that are produced by external publishers. By publishing digital scholarship themselves, libraries are able to guarantee the persistence of the scholarly record over time.

These distinguishing features provide library publishers with a certain level of freedom from conventional publishing methodologies (particularly those associated with the pre-digital production era). They also motivate libraries to experiment more broadly than many of their counterparts. Their unique position also offers a clear opportunity for collaboration with university presses, in which libraries could "handle less viable titles, or support supplemental materials that could not be included in a printed monograph," Ivins explained.

Even so, as publishers, libraries engage in the same fundamental production activities as the broader field does, from acquisition to dissemination (including both digital and printed works). As libraries embrace this new role, they have a concurrent need for training opportunities, both for existing library staff/faculty who want to grow their publishing skill sets through continuing education and other professional development activities, and also for the next generation of staff/faculty who are beginning now to pursue this new role through degree programs, internships, and other preparatory steps.

So what opportunities for training currently are available to library publishers? Where and how do librarians learn publishing skills and methods, both theoretical and practical? What gaps and opportunities are there in the current education and training landscape for this rapidly growing subfield of publishing?

History of Publisher Training

> We insist on intensive graduate work for medicine, the law, and university teaching—even for high school instruction—so it seems only logical to insist on advanced and intensive instruction for those who want to enter a profession that is so vital a contributor to the political and cultural life of the nation. —John Tebbel, 1984

Publishing evolved for centuries as what has famously been dubbed "an accidental profession," one intentionally lacking in professional training channels and opportunities. The industry had few agreed-upon roles and rules, and each publishing house had its own practices and definitions, conveyed to new acolytes through apprenticeship and on-the-job training rather than through a classroom experience. Editing in particular was considered more an art than a skill, something best gained through a combination of acumen and experience.

The earliest attempts to provide educational courses, broadly defined, appeared in the 1940s, with a smattering of experiments, including a 1943 course sponsored by the Book Publishers Bureau (now the Association of American Publishers) and the renowned workshop launched at Radcliffe in 1947, then known as the "Summer Publishing Procedures Course."[4] Summer institutes and continuing education departments served as the home for most of these early efforts throughout the 1950s–60s, with key distinctions between these two educational forms. The summer institutes were often driven and taught by publishers; the academic courses more often were designed by educators with little input (or interest) from publishers.[5]

By the 1970s, more than 100 institutions were offering more than 200 academic "courses," as documented in 1976 by the Association of American Publishers (AAP).[6] The AAP's "Committee on Professional Education for Publishing" (also called "Education for Publishing Program") worked to establish curriculum guidelines for these programs, as well as establishing the AAP's Stephen Greene Memorial Library and a number of AAP-based training opportunities. The vast majority of these courses targeted "book to market" processes, including editing, marketing, finance, and management. Most did not focus on such art and trade school processes as printing, layout, and design.

Transformations in the publishing landscape from the 1980s onward moved at a rapid pace, and developments such as industry consolidation and the shift from print to digital production required professionals and educators to learn and deploy new skills. This impacted the educational environment, not least because publishers industry-wide, from entry level to seasoned leaders, needed to build capacity and perform an evolving set of functions. Also during the 1980s and 1990s, numerous educational programs were designed to improve managerial training for women and to increase ethnic and racial diversity throughout the scholarly publishing field.

During the 1990s, education for publishing became more formalized through the rise in bachelor's and master's degrees, and these programs became well established by the early 2000s. These academic programs have had to adapt to an ever-changing publishing landscape. As early as 2000, surveys documented the need for new emphasis on business and information technology in publishing education and training programs, direct results of the industry's consolidation and its shift toward digital production.[7] By 2004, publishing educators and community members identified major forces reshaping publishing, including globalization, consolidation, and increased reader demands for multimedia options.[8]

The last decade's rapid changes have produced friction between those advocating for new skill sets and practices (e.g., content management, digital asset management, rights management, new business models[9]) and those concerned with the retention of traditional values (e.g., "initiating and promoting quality content, constructive and compassionate editing, imaginative design, and courageous gatekeeping"[10]). These factions remain at odds, both within the industry itself and also between the industry and academia regarding how best to train and educate the next generation of publishers.

Publishing Education Today

Current assessments of the educational needs of the publishing industry resemble those of the prior decade; however, they are nuanced by an additional 10 years of evolving practices. Publishing educators and interested industry leaders alike cite that "publishing needs ambitious, positive people for whom technology comes naturally, facility with social media is a given and who have a desire to build all manner of services for writers and readers."[11] New positions are being created and filled in the field, including "social media assistant," "data scientist," and "applications developer." For many leaders in the publishing industry, the focus in this new milieu is on training employees to create better value for authors and readers. One observer notes, "We do need people… who can see ways that technology can help build a different kind of engagement between readers and writers."[12]

Publishing education programs at the undergraduate and graduate levels at a small number of institutions such as New York University are incorporating coursework in book metadata and infrastructure, web architecture and content creation, application creation and development.[13] Pacific University offers a degree program in "editing and publishing" to teach the next generation of authors about current trends and practices in the field and to embed scholarly publishing literacy directly into the undergraduate curriculum.[14] The curriculum is changing, and many programs are growing their base of students.[15] While some speculate that the publishing industry's apprenticeship approach of years past is being replaced by degree programs, the industry struggles with an appropriate balance between the application and management of technology, business practices and models, and creating social and business value via producing and disseminating information.[16] The existence of multiple publishing subfields (trade; academic; STM—scientific, technical, and medical), each requiring a different set of qualifications, presents a challenge for the scalability and sustainability of publishing education programs. The majority of extant programs focus on trade publishing, leaving a gap in training for academic and scholarly publishing.[17]

Notably, publishing education still fulfills no industry requirement for publishing careers, regardless of subfield (academic, trade, etc.). Unlike other professional tracks, which use a graduate degree as a qualification for employment (e.g., teaching, librarianship, law, business, medicine), the publishing industry has not established a specific track or degree as part of a credentialing process.[18] Indeed, many publishers consider apprenticeships the only valid rite of passage that prospective publishers—especially acquisitions editors—pursue. Some eschew entry-level applicants with "publishing" degrees, citing their preferences for applicants they can train themselves.[19] As a result, publisher education and training seem to serve two core purposes: first, to forge connections with others in the industry, and second, to gain knowledge and skill sets that may help to advance one's career.

There are six main categories of publisher education operating in the North American context today: academic degree programs, summer institutes, professional development workshops, distance-learning opportunities, in-house training, and internship programs. Some of these target specific publishing subfields (e.g., trade v. academic) or genres (e.g., journals v. monographs). Each of these addresses different audiences within the publishing community, as briefly described below.

1. **Academic degree programs**. Degree programs are offered at both the undergraduate and graduate levels. Often housed within English and journalism departments, the most comprehensive of these degrees provide a grounding in publishing histories, clear understandings of the business of publishing, and a balance of theory (learned in the classroom) and practice (learned through internships and co-ops). Many of these programs provide a broad-based foundation in publishing, including magazine, book, and "electronic" or "digital media" (e.g., New York University's M.S. in Publishing: Digital and Print Media).

2. **Summer institutes (e.g., Denver Publishing Institute, Columbia Publishing Course)**. Taught by top industry professionals (who reputably do this work *gratis* and in order to forge their own connections and scout for new talent), summer institutes follow the immersion model first implemented at Radcliffe in

1947. They most often are taught on academic campuses and are administered through partnerships with continuing education departments or with industry associations. These residential programs are networking opportunities for emerging professionals, usually within the first few years of their publishing careers. Some of these summer institutes now cover "digital media" as a topic alongside "book" and "magazine" publishing. There are also several institutes oriented toward mid-career professionals, including the Yale Publishing Course.

3. **Professional development workshops.** These run the gamut from short workshops on targeted topics to longer-term courses that help professional publishers advance their careers, usually moving toward management and editorial positions. Most of these offerings come through publisher associations and societies (e.g., Association of American Publishers, Association of American University Presses, Society for Scholarly Publishing, STM—the International Association of Scientific, Technical and Medical Publishers) or through continuing education programs at universities and colleges. Notably, bepress launched a three-day, library-focused "Scholarly Publishing Certification Course: A Training Program for Library-Led Publishing Initiatives" in October 2013.

4. **Online or distance programs.** Often coupled with in-person professional development opportunities, there are a number of online programs today. Some offer degrees or certificates through continuing education departments of universities and colleges, and others provide short, targeted training or self-paced opportunities (see, e.g., the Association of Learned and Professional Society Publishers [ALPSP] series of webinars for publishing professionals). One of the most intriguing new ventures in this space is the Public Knowledge Project's PKP School (http://pkpschool.sfu.ca), a self-described "online, open, self-paced collection of courses designed to help improve the quality of scholarly publishing around the world." Launched in 2013, this curated collection of open courses provides some instruction specific to PKP's own product, Open Journal System (OJS), but it also includes a track designed to help practitioners learn how to be editors and provides the necessary administrative and intellectual infrastructure to support a scholarly journal.

5. **In-house training programs.** Publishing houses, particularly the larger corporate entities, have developed their own corporate training programs to provide continuing education on targeted topics to professionals throughout the company and immersion experiences for new recruits. These are not open opportunities, and there is little available documentation about them accordingly, but these currently comprise an important channel for commercial publishing training.
6. **Internship programs.** Many university presses and commercial publishers provide internship opportunities for new professionals. Some of these are designed for local students of a university; others are offered to broader audiences (e.g., The New Press Internship Program). These opportunities are designed to provide prospective publishers with an immersive experience, sometimes focused on one specific area of publishing and sometimes covering the full arc of the publishing process.

Where Do "Library Publishers" Fit?

Personnel involved in library publishing activities often have grown into these positions. Those that have received formal training often have gone through courses/workshops offered by scholarly publishing societies (Society for Scholarly Publishing, Association of American University Presses, STM) or have participated in technology-specific training (e.g., PKP training courses on online publishing and open access publishing models, bepress scholarly publishing certification course).

Currently, there are no known "library publishing"–specific educational tracks available in the U.S., although at the time of writing, several library schools are beginning to explore the possibility of creating courses, badges, and certificate programs. Interestingly, at the time of writing, none of the publishing education programs described above specifically target librarians as prospective attendees, with the exception of the highly regarded Denver Publishing Institute (DPI), where the website's "Who Should Apply" section includes the following five identified audiences:

- College graduates seeking their first job in publishing

- Career-changers interested in opportunities in the field
- Those presently working in publishing who seek a broader view than a specialized job can provide
- **Librarians interested in knowing more about the industry that provides them with their books** [emphasis added]
- Publishers, or students, from abroad who want to find out how it is done in the United States

Clearly, the idea that librarians might lead publishing programs is still relatively unknown and un-addressed within the traditional publishing education channels. Do these programs provide education and training opportunities that are appropriate for library publishers? Or are the differences great enough between the library publishing subfield and other publishing groups to warrant a different approach to training altogether?

More to the point, in an era defined by quick transitions and changing models, have publishing education programs themselves become outdated? And if so, might information schools and library science programs have an opportunity to provide training opportunities that are better attuned to the experimental, evolving environment in which most digitally driven publishing occurs today?

Publishing Education: Adapting to New Skills and Evolving Roles

Interviews were conducted by the authors in September 2013 with ten thought leaders representing academic, university, and commercial presses as well as libraries and iSchools. Along with environmental scanning, these interviews demonstrated the definitional transformations under way in the concept of "publisher" and also revealed a set of core skills for current and future publishing professionals; the gaps and promising opportunities for training; and productive teaching and learning approaches.

The defining characteristic of today's scholarly communication landscape is change. Traditional publishing models that were primarily focused on producing and disseminating—to an often limited readership—a finished scholarly product are challenged continuously today by changing scholarly communication technologies, open movements, information policies and directives, and experimental, digital-only discourse in fields such as the humanities. Stephen Griffin emphasized that academic "publishing" increasingly means reporting on all stages of the scholarly workflow. In this new paradigm, he explained, "the data, algorithms, computing source codes, intermediate artifacts, and approaches" are published in order to clearly communicate the results. He suggested the need to think about "publication in an altogether new way, and 'documents' in entirely new terms."

All of these changes have had implications both for the library and for the broader ecosystem of academic publishing. Leaders in the field acknowledge that publishers, whether libraries, scholarly societies, university presses, or commercial publishers, are now facing major changes in the field brought on by the proliferation of information technologies. As Raym Crow explained in an interview with the authors, new technologies mean "anyone can be a publisher," and technologies that make production and dissemination easier have transformed the processes and workflows that defined a publisher thirty years ago. Publishers still provide traditional value adds (e.g., copyediting), but processes that are increasingly emphasized are associated with selecting new kinds of publications and projects that, as Charles Watkinson remarked, "transform author created works into something interesting for readers."

Some publishers are further along in supporting a transformed scholarly communication landscape, while others struggle to address the new demands of scholars in different disciplines. Industry leaders in library publishing, for example, argue that more emphasis should be placed on ensuring the "sustainability and conformity to standards and discoverability" of new experimental forms of scholarship, such as digital humanities projects (Watkinson, 2013). Publishers address those same discovery and interoperability issues in the sciences and are increasingly called on to meet the demand for more documentation for reproducible research (Griffin, 2013).

The core functions of a publisher have remained largely the same throughout the 20th century and into the early 21st, but how publishers perform these functions has changed, and experts agree that new skills are needed to do this work well and to take on additional roles to address changes in the field. Judy Luther noted that how we approach training publishing professionals depends on whether or not we are training to redesign publishing. Industry leaders suggest "monitoring trends" (Luther, 2013) and "experimenting with applying traditional skill sets to working with different media" (Watkinson, 2013) as ways to develop professionally and to gain a better understanding of where gaps may exist.

Current strengths in publishing education programs appear to be in traditional areas such as "peer-review, marketing, business models, printing and distribution," areas identified by Rosenblum as important new skills for library publishers.[20] However, the conservatism demonstrated within these programs may not sufficiently address emergent skills needs such as developing scholarly publishing literacy programs for authors and researchers, leveraging networked technologies to support traditional and newer forms of digital publication, and managing complex experimental publishing projects. Opportunities may exist for master's programs in library and information science to address these gaps. One observer suggested a THATCamp style approach to engaged learning may be the way to go if training goals are to change the publishing model completely (Luther, 2013).

Identifying Core Knowledge and Skills for 21st Century Publishers

Specific competencies will continue to be a moving target. However, the following types of knowledge and experience (which encompass both technical and soft, traditional and emerging, entry-level and leadership skill sets) have been identified as having enduring importance for publishing professionals.

Scholarly Publishing Context

Academic publishers need a comprehensive understanding of the scholarly publishing landscape as it exists today and an awareness of challenges and future directions for the industry. Specifically, professionals should enter the field with a grasp of the range of existing publishers (commercial, society, university, etc.); the range of functions within a publishing program; "the ways in which research gets produced, consumed, recycled back into the system" (Watkinson, 2013); the range of traditional and experimental practices and products; the historical background of the field (how publishing got to be the way it is); and the more recent history of the field, including the so-called scholarly communications "crises." Familiarity with this broader context enables professionals to think beyond traditional processes and models and helps them better adapt services to the needs of content producers and consumers. An awareness of how the industry is changing prepares both new and seasoned professionals to lead that change.

Academic Context

Understanding the mission of the academy helps scholarly publishers serve their authors, editors, and audiences. In interviews, Ivins emphasized that publishers need to maintain an outward focus even as they develop the skills and knowledge specific to their line of work. Too often, "publishers develop their narrow, deep, vertical areas of expertise… and wind up divorced from the whole university," she cautioned. Watkinson described "a lack of understanding of authors and how authors behave and what the incentives are for them to do their work."

Bonn emphasized that scholarly publishers need to learn to ask the right questions as they conceive their mission and consider their role in the context of their institution. This includes questions such as "Why do we want to publish scholarship? Are we trying to enhance the reputation of a home institution or trying to improve work in the field or creating a network of scholars? How does publishing help the mission of the institution?" Understanding the academic context also helps publishers better interact with and serve authors. "It comes back to understanding author goals and expectations… Being able to locate goals and expectations within the capacity of your publishing house. Does the request match your goals as a publisher?" she explained.

Scholarly publishers must also possess a fundamental knowledge of the different disciplinary practices and cultures they will encounter when working with authors and editors. This may be particularly relevant for library publishers, who work very closely with faculty, students, or other researchers in the editorial and production processes. This does not necessarily entail deep disciplinary knowledge. As Watkinson explained, "a crucial skill is the ability to assess the needs of a particular discipline and quickly get to grips with its norms and market needs. One of the things about that is that it's an advantage to not be too close, to be outside." Understanding these communities helps publishers serve them better as both authors and audiences.

Soft Skills

A variety of soft skills are both exceedingly important and largely difficult to teach in the classroom. Publishing professionals typically develop soft skills, such as relationship building, creative problem solving, and effective communication, on the job over the course of years. Kevin Stranack described the ability to "develop communities of participation around your area of interest," which entails an understanding of what motivates people and how to maintain their involvement.

Soft skills may be increasingly important as publishers outsource or combine more technical tasks such as copyediting and layout. Relationships, innovation and experimentation, and an exceptional grasp of good editorial work will continue to distinguish publishing programs.

Strong communication and relationship-building skills are important not only for serving authors, but for keeping up with developments in the industry. Publishing professionals rely heavily on their professional networks (conferences, personal correspondence, professional organizations, etc.) to keep abreast of current trends and issues.

Business Planning and Management

Business skills cover a wide range of competencies related to planning, project management, product development, marketing, leadership, copyright knowledge, and other aspects of coordinating a successful and sustainable publishing program.

Planning for sustainability, which includes tasks such as identifying revenue streams and writing a business plan, was frequently cited as a major training gap. Crow emphasized the need for publishers to "understand the actual cost of what's being done and cogently understand resource allocations in a standard budgetary sense." Particularly in libraries, he argued, where an operating budget covers many of the associated costs, publishers are "shielded from resource allocation issues" for the time being. However, he encouraged libraries to begin developing the necessary knowledge to plan for other funding scenarios in the future.

In addition to long-range planning, publishing programs need professionals with strong project management and product development skills. These include identifying and working with partners (e.g., campus units, faculty, vendors, scholarly societies); writing policies and contracts; understanding and addressing intellectual property, copyright issues, and other legal concerns such as antitrust, libel, and trademark law; marketing services and products; keeping pace with rapidly changing technical platforms; and assessing needs of content creators and audiences. Crow summed this up as having the ability to "make conscious decisions… not making decisions without knowing it."

In particular, publishers will increasingly need skills that help them consider non-traditional publications from a business perspective. Crow cited a lack of training that addresses "how publishers deliver value, serve audiences, plan activities, and consider the logic under all of that" in more "disruptive models" of scholarly communication.

Technology and Workflows for Production, Distribution, and Preservation

Scholarly publishers will continue to need staff members who are proficient in traditional production and distribution process such as layout and typesetting and metadata and markup.

In addition to proficiency in traditional publishing workflows, publishers will need staff members who possess both a big-picture understanding of digital publishing and preservation technology and a basic understanding (minimum) of software development.

Familiarity with the current and developing slate of tools for digital publishing and their application is essential. Bonn explained, "Good publishers successfully connect creators and users… they have to be cognizant and educated about the use of digital tools, networked technologies, and the implications of their choices. It's important while you're in the trenches to be able to ask about the best mapping between content, format, and intended use." This will be increasingly important for publishers working with experimental and emerging forms of scholarship. Sandy Thatcher and others predicted a growing need for publishers to manage complex digital humanities projects and other publications that go beyond text to incorporate data and interactive/multimedia elements.

Publishers increasingly need staff with at least elementary software development skills, including coding, design, and usability. Griffin predicted that publishers will "need to hire technology and data professionals who [among other skills] understand the ways in which the journal material can be structured for long-term use in other venues, and develop multiple versions of the same journal that suit different purposes instead. These people aren't data analysts or comp scientists, they're people who understand data markup, data structuring, document models: the type of people iSchools (like those in the iSchool Consortium) are producing."

Editorial and Acquisitions

Sandy Thatcher noted, "the editorial function is the key to all of this: that's what makes this publishing." The editorial functions of publishing were described in several interviews as a soft skill. Paul Courant, for example, explained it as "the thing good editors do. They get with an author and figure out how to make the project good." He elaborated that successful editors know how to work with authors and content to make the most of a project by, among other things, connecting it with the right format and digital technologies.

The acquisitions function was cited as the element most often missing from educational programming. Competition between editors and presses has led to this function being framed as an art, not just a skill set. As Thatcher explains, "people don't want to share trade secrets about how they do their editorial acquisitions. They can teach general skills, but not the tricks of the trade that people pick up along the way. And editors at one press don't want to teach another press." The distinctive set of processes a press and/or editor develops within a press environment often pivot on this acquisitions function, and they are rarely transmitted beyond a limited circle of interaction.

This educational gap around acquisitions takes on an interesting cast in the changing environment, as the acquisitions process itself may be shifting. In the text-based publishing realm, long-established branding in a topical area and relationships within disciplinary specialties have helped define which presses published leading works in a given field. In the current publishing ecosystem, digital scholarship is rising in both prominence and importance. Where text-based acquisition has typically focused around a topical area (e.g., a particular university press becomes renowned for publications in particular disciplinary genres), digital acquisitions may be more powerfully defined by platform and visibility. As the publishing process itself continues to transform, the way that acquisitions editors perform their work may likewise change dramatically. The selection process may begin to focus on identifying works that correspond to platform-specific strengths of a press (e.g., particular types of data visualizations or mapping proficiencies, etc.).

Editorial functions are one of the key areas that newer publishers, like libraries, struggle to define. As Ivins cautions, "A publishing program is a program. It's not passive, it's not just talking to faculty about having them work with us." Having clearly defined specialties is likewise important, as noted by Bonn: "They should have an awareness of selection and acquisition criteria and ability to articulate those criteria."

Recommendations for Productive Pathways

In addition to the essential content that training should cover, interviews revealed four general hallmarks of effective approaches to training in this area: a holistic/broad view, opportunities for cross-fertilization, emphasis on hands-on and interactive learning, and responsiveness to current needs.

Holistic Approach

A holistic approach to learning is desirable (and lacking in the current landscape). While training programs exist for a variety of specific and technical skills, Stranack pointed out that "what's really needed is an entry point into a variety of useful information and learning opportunities." Training should expose professionals to the broader scholarly communications, publishing, and academic contexts and give them at least an overview of major developments and challenges in the field. This holistic approach has a geographical component, specifically around encouraging better alignment of training opportunities and processes globally.

Opportunities for Cross-Fertilization

Effective training will bring together professionals across sectors and at different levels within organizations. Without exposure to the practices and priorities of the broader field, publishers risk the creation of silos and tunnel vision. Griffin pointed to the reluctance of publishers to engage with libraries outside of the customer/vendor relationship. "There's a gap between these cultures; no one's come up with [an] idea on how to gracefully merge and give these two cultures the chance to reconcile their differences and forge long-term strategies that will benefit both of them."[21]

Hands-on Experiences

Publishing has traditionally been an apprenticeship profession. New staff members learn on the job through hands-on training. Watkinson explained that "publishing is still something that probably needs to be learned in an experiential way." Effective training will emphasize project-based learning that requires students to consider context, work through processes to see how they add value, and learn from case study examples.

Timeliness and Modularity

Developing relevant and timely training is critical, given the rapid changes in publishing practices, business models, and technologies. Alice Meadows emphasized that "training should be timely and responsive." Training should be developed proactively to address perceived near-future needs and should be easy to adapt and update in response to new and evolving needs. This can be accomplished by designing training modules that can be added to, exchanged, and eliminated as required. Another promising pathway lies in curating preexisting open resources into a web platform. Just-in-time delivery is important for busy professionals who may lack the time and resources to attend lengthy in-person programs.

Conclusion

The seismic shifts affecting the academic publishing industry are not sector-specific. Indeed, the same challenges are faced by the range of players in this area, including university presses, trade publishers, library publishers, and commercial publishers. What differentiates the fields is their degree of experimentation and their willingness to transgress against long-held publishing conventions, something that the new arrivals (libraries and new commercial entities, including self-publishers) may have in their favor.

Educational needs across these sectors likewise seem to converge, with unmet needs for better training in soft skills (flexibility, relationship handling) and digitally relevant hard skills (from XML coding to altmetrics analysis). Several groups are well poised to address these needs, industry-wide, including master's programs in information science and library science; digital humanities and digital science programs; and a broad range of shorter-term in-person workshops (e.g., AAUP, SSP offerings) and online, self-paced coursework. Another promising trajectory may be that of site-specific training that combines analysis of prospective partnerships (e.g., campus-based, regional, disciplinary, or platform-based groups) with targeted training to address the opportunities available in the quickly changing landscape.

All of these delivery mechanisms must be poised for rapid transformations over the coming years. The field of scholarly publishing (much less the broader fields of publishing) will not be well served by courses that quickly ossify and become outmoded. This critical moment of change may best be addressed by a combined approach that uses short-term, lightweight, and lower investment training mechanisms to teach practices and hard skills, and longer-term, more structured, and higher investment educational programs to teach the soft skills and inculcate values that fluctuate less rapidly.

This essay originally appeared in The Journal of Electronic Publishing, *Volume 17, Issue 2: Education and Training for 21st Century Publishers, Spring 2014 (DOI: http://dx.doi.org/10.3998/3336451.0017.207)*

Appendix 6.1: List of Interviewees

- Maria Bonn, University of Illinois Graduate School of Library and Information Science
- Paul Courant
- Raym Crow, Chain Bridge Group
- Stephen Griffin, University of Pittsburgh School of Information Science
- October Ivins, Ivins eContent Solutions
- Judy Luther, Informed Strategies
- Alice Meadows, Wiley - Global Research
- Kevin Stranack, Public Knowledge Project
- Sanford Thatcher
- Charles Watkinson, Purdue University Press and Purdue University Libraries

Notes

1. Library Publishing Coalition website. (2013) See http://librarypublishing.org/about-us

2. *Library Publishing Directory*. (2013) Sarah Lippincott, ed. (Purdue University Press).

3. Hahn, Karla. (2008) *Research Library Publishing Services: New Options for University Publishing* (ARL: Washington, DC, 2008). http://www.arl.org/storage/documents/publications/research-library-publishing-services-mar08.pdf (last accessed September 2013).

4. Tebbel, John. (1984) Education for Publishing. *Library Trends*, pp. 223-233. Retrieved from http://www.ideals.illinois.edu/bitstream/handle/2142/7371/librarytrends-v33i2_opt.pdf?sequence=3#page=136

5. Ibid.

6. See Eastman, Ann Heidbreder, Lee, Grant, and Scholl, Joyce, Education for Publishing: A Survey Report (Committee on Professional Education for Publishing, Association of American Publishers, 1976), and see also *Guide to Book Publishing Courses* (Peterson's Guides, 1979).

7. The Johnson and Royle survey communicates these findings among many others, including that academia and the industry need to work together more closely. Johnson, I. M., & Royle, J. M. (2000) Education and Training for Publishing in Britain Prepares for the "Information Society." *Publishing Research Quarterly* 16 (3): 10-28. http://dx.doi.org/10.1007/s12109-000-0013-9

8. Baensch, R. E. (2004) Education and Training for the Publishing Industry. *Publishing Research Quarterly* 20 (3): 30-33. http://dx.doi.org/10.1007/s12109-004-0014-1

9. Burks, J. (2004) Publishing Education: Who Needs It? An Anglo-American Survey. *LOGOS: The Journal of the World Book Community* 15 (1): 43-48.

10. Curtain, J. (1997) Contemporary Publishing and the Challenges for Publishing

Education. *Journal of Scholarly Publishing* 28 (4): 187–192. http://dx.doi.org/10.3138/JSP-028-04-187

11. Tagholm, R. (2013) What New Skills Do Publishers Need to Navigate in Publishing? (blog post) *Publishing Perspectives*. Retrieved August 12, 2013, from http://publishingperspectives.com/2013/04/what-new-skills-do-publishers-need-to-navigate-in-publishing/

12. Ibid.

13. Habash, G. (2011) Earning More than an "A": Master's Programs Fill the Needs for a More Complex Industry. *Publishers Weekly*. Retrieved from http://www.publishersweekly.com/pw/by-topic/industry-news/publisher-news/article/49570-earning-more-than-an-a-master-s-programs-fill-the-needs-for-a-more-complex-industry.html

14. Gilman, I. (2013) Scholarly Communication for Credit: Integrating Publishing Education into Undergraduate Curriculum. In Davis-Kahl, S., & Hensley, M. K. (eds.), *Common Ground of the Nexus of Information Literacy and Scholarly Communication* (pp. 75–83). Published by the Association of College & Research Libraries, Chicago, IL. http://digitalcommons.iwu.edu/bookshelf/36

15. Ibid.

16. Cowan, Ann. (1992) An End to the Accidental Profession. *LOGOS: The Journal of the World Book Community* 3 (4): 170–178.

17. Canty, Nicholas, & Watkinson, Anthony. (2012) Career Development in Academic and Professional Publishing. In *Academic and Professional Publishing*, Robert Campbell, ed. (Oxford: Chandos Publishing, 2012), 458. See also Baverstock, Alison (2010) Where Will the Next Generation of Publishers Come From? Journal of Scholarly Publishing 42 (1): 31–44.

18. Canty &Watkinson, Career Development in Academic and Professional Publishing.

19. Denver University, Denver Publishing Institute website: http://www.du.edu/publishinginstitute/index.html (last accessed October 24, 2013).

20. Rosenblum, B. (2008) Developing New Skills and Expertise to Support Digital Scholarship and Scholarly Communication. Presented at the 74th IFLA General Conference and Council: World Library and Information Congress, Quebec, Canada. http://www.ifla.org/IV/ifla74/Programme2008.htm

21. In a growing number of institutions, the university press is being reframed as a formal partner of the library, including through the merging of the university press with the library (see, e.g., Purdue University, University of North Texas, Penn State, Utah State, Wayne State, Syracuse, and Oregon State). This trend may help to encourage the creation of long-term strategies that benefit the scholarly publishing field.

CHAPTER 7

Nimble and Oriented towards Teaching and Learning
Publishing Services at Small Academic Libraries

Lisa Spiro

Until recently, library-based publishing has primarily been associated with research libraries, particularly those that partner with university presses. Witness, for example, the visibility of library publishing initiatives at the University of Michigan, Penn State, and University of California. Reports such as Karla Hahn's (2008) *Research Library Publishing Services* and Raym Crow's (2009) *Campus-Based Publishing Partnerships: A Guide to Critical Issues* focus on research libraries. This model can

This work is licensed under the Creative Commons Attribution License 4.0 (CC-BY 4.0).

seem out of reach for institutions that lack university presses with which to partner or budgets to hire full-time publishing staff and deploy (or even develop) open-source publishing platforms. Publishing programs at small academic libraries offer an alternative model. As Charles Watkinson, a member of the Library Publishing Coalition's (www.librarypublishing. org) executive group, notes, "Since much of the innovation within library publishing happens at smaller institutions, it was very important not to exclude a library on the basis of size" (quoted in Schwartz 2013), so the group includes small academic libraries such as the Claremont Colleges, Colby College, Pacific University, and Illinois Wesleyan University, as well as research libraries. Because small academic libraries don't have to navigate the complex bureaucracies of larger institutions and often can build upon strong relationships with faculty and other campus partners,[1] they can be nimble and flexible in experimenting with new services. Small academic library publishing programs distinguish themselves by emphasizing teaching, learning, and undergraduate research, not only publishing undergraduate journals but also training students to run them. Rather than adopting open-source software, small academic libraries typically use hosted solutions, allowing them to focus on services. Constrained by tight budgets, small academic libraries usually lack a full-time position focused on publishing, instead allocating a percentage of staff time to these services.

Method

This chapter offers brief case studies of publishing programs at seven small academic libraries (the Claremont Colleges, Colby College, Gettysburg College, Hamilton College, Illinois Wesleyan University, Macalester College, and Pacific University), and it glances at emerging initiatives from two others (Amherst College and Middlebury College).[2] Some programs

---

1. Of course, small libraries must devote effort to cultivating relationships with faculty.
2. I selected the libraries to include in my analysis by identifying the small academic libraries that are associated with the Library Publishing Coalition, asking for recommendations from interviewees, and searching online. In addition, I found one of the libraries included in the study by determining

have been around since the mid-2000s, while others are quite new. The chapter draws upon semi-structured e-mail and phone interviews with librarians who manage publishing services, as well as with advocates for library-based publishing.[3]

Publishing can describe a range of approaches, from making content available online to applying rigorous peer-review and production processes. Perhaps the most relevant definition of library-based publishing comes from the Library Publishing Coalition, which emphasizes that it typically involves a production process and some kind of review or certification, prefers open access, and is open to experimental approaches (LPC 2013). Further, "Library publishing is very scholar-driven," carried out in close consultation with faculty, graduate students, and in some cases undergraduates (Lippincott and Skinner 2013). As Isaac Gilman (2013b) suggests, libraries should not be too restrictive in conceptualizing what it means to publish, focusing instead on the core goal of making original work available and visible: "Don't be afraid to rethink what it means to offer publishing services, and to explore services all along the continuum (i.e., from distributing ETDs through a repository to overseeing the editorial process and publication of a scholarly monograph that is deposited in the Library of Congress); anything that you can do to help authors share their original work in a public forum should be considered a publishing service." At many small academic libraries, the publishing program grew out of institutional repository services and features content with local significance; for such libraries, digitizing back issues of local journals published through the repository and making available undergraduate theses qualify as publishing, even if traditional peer review typically isn't part of these services.

---

which small college libraries are using bepress for publishing activities. Note that after I conducted my research in the summer of 2013, the Library Publishing Consortium issued *Library Publishing Directory 2014* (www.librarypublishing.org/resources/directory-library-publishing-services), which includes most of the colleges that I discuss here as well as a few other small colleges engaged in publishing activities.

3. While I have tried to be as accurate as possible in transcribing interviews, quotations may include paraphrases.

Defining Publishing Services at Small Academic Libraries

Small colleges are defined not only by their size, but also by their emphasis on teaching and learning.[4] Often small colleges are liberal arts institutions, valuing undergraduate research, an intellectually rigorous curriculum that embraces inquiry across disciplines, rich residential and co-curricular experiences, and intimate classes. To provide faculty and students access to research materials, liberal arts college libraries often participate in consortia and engage in resource sharing, valuing collaboration over competition (Graves 2013). Whereas libraries at Research 1 universities have well over one hundred total staff members, between nineteen and forty-three staff members work at the libraries included in this study. Perhaps because larger libraries have more resources, they are more likely than smaller institutions to address scholarly communications in their strategic plan or mission statement, hire a chief scholarly communication librarian, and offer an institutional repository; likewise, more research libraries (55 percent) offer or are interested in offering publishing services than libraries from the Oberlin Group of selective liberal arts colleges (30 percent; Del Toro, Mandernack, and Zanoni 2011; Mullins et al. 2012).

Yet small academic libraries offer compelling examples of innovative publishing programs that advance teaching and learning. As Diane Graves (2013) argues, liberal arts colleges have a vital interest in scholarly communications because their faculty actively engage in research and because issues such as access to knowledge and authors' rights intersect with their curricula. As libraries collaborate to shape publishing services, it is vital that small academic libraries participate. Some wondered why Colby College Libraries joined the Library Publishing Coalition as a founding institution because it was the only small college library to do so at the time (now the Claremont University Consortium, Illinois Wesleyan University, Macalester College, and Pacific University are also members). But director of libraries Clem Guthro (2013) insists that small schools need to be

---

4. Typically small colleges have less than 3,000 students, although this study also includes a slightly larger university (Pacific University, which has approximately 3,500 students across four campuses) and a consortium of seven small colleges with a total of 6,300 students (Carnegie Foundation 2013).

represented because "unless you're at the table you don't get to express" your needs, such as the importance of being able to "scale up and scale down" to create tools and resources that benefit institutions with different publishing needs and infrastructures. Likewise, Barbara Fister (2013) suggests that small academic libraries should get involved in publishing both to fulfill their mission and to promote diverse approaches: "Leaving it to research libraries would be both an abdication of our values and could result in solutions that don't scale well to our settings. Small libraries could provide small, nimble, and affordable solutions that could benefit a lot of people with limited means." Like many research libraries, small academic libraries publish journals more frequently than monographs or conference papers, embed publishing services in an "emerging program of related services" such as institutional repositories and digitization programs, embrace open access, consult on topics such as metadata and copyright, typically publish electronically, and pay for a significant part of their operations out of library budgets (Hahn 2008, 6). But small academic libraries also offer a publishing model defined by adapting to constraints such as lean staffing and the lack of robust technical support, embracing experimentation and iterative development of services, integrating publishing into the curriculum, and emphasizing locally significant collections, including archival holdings and undergraduate research (Schwartz 2013).

In describing the advantages that small academic libraries enjoy over larger institutions, several interviewees invoked terms such as *nimble* and *flexible*. Rather than navigate "multiple layers of bureaucracy" (Fishel 2013b), small academic libraries can move quickly to establish new initiatives and rework positions (Geffert 2013). At smaller libraries, staff may be able to experiment and learn more quickly than at larger institutions that use more cumbersome planning processes. As Stephanie Davis-Kahl (2013a) suggests, "Liberal arts colleges are so well-positioned to do these projects because they are so nimble and entrepreneurial." Since many small academic libraries work closely with faculty, they often better understand their needs and can build on prior relationships in launching new services (Schwartz 2013). As Zach Coble (2013) noted, "Everyone knows everyone else, so we had no trouble finding a librarian with a close working relationship to each journal's faculty mentor." Since most small colleges do not have a university press, the library can fill an important void by offering publishing services, although such libraries also lack access to the expertise and potential synergies offered by a press (Schwartz 2013).

While small academic libraries may lack the prestige of well-established presses, they serve an important need by publishing works that reflect the institution's mission, pedagogical practices, or faculty research interests (Coble 2013). Many "campus-grown journals" are not well suited for commercial publishers because they may be of local interest, have a small audience, or are "untested," but they provide value to the institution and the larger community (Bankier and Perciali 2008, 24). As Isaac Gilman (2013b) says, "Rather than putting our resources into providing access to knowledge that is readily accessible through other venues (or that is simply overpriced), we are putting our resources and time into providing access—through publication—to knowledge that would otherwise have a limited audience." For example, publications may focus on emerging areas such as STEAM (science, technology, engineering, arts and math); fairly specialized research areas such as communal societies; local interests such as the history of the college; or undergraduate work.

Libraries are taking the lead in experimenting with innovative approaches to scholarly communication, exploring new business models and working with content outside the scope of traditional publishing, such as "digital humanities projects, gray literature, research datasets, and student work" (Lippincott and Skinner 2013). Middlebury College is developing a "skunkworks" to explore "small-scale" publishing services for "ad hoc projects" (Roy 2013). Since the Claremont Colleges are expanding their engagement with digital scholarship and digital humanities support, the Claremont Colleges Library would like to explore new models for scholarly communication that involve data curation or incorporate multimedia, mashups, and other rich, interactive media (Claremont Center for Digital Humanities 2013). In experimenting with alternative publishing models, the Claremont Colleges' library is moving beyond its existing out-of-the-box publishing platforms such as Digital Commons for journals, monographs, and institutional repository materials and CONTENTdm for other digital collections. For example, the library collaborated with faculty and students on a project focused on the Edward S. Curtis Photo Gravure collection, which resulted in a Scalar book featuring five essays by faculty and research by undergraduate students and graduate fellows (Swift 2014a). While mainstream academic presses may see publishing multimedia works as outside their business model or beyond the capabilities of their publishing systems, small academic libraries have some freedom to experiment, even as they cope with changes in technology and with limited staffing. For example, Macalester's DeWitt Wallace Library has just published *Captive Audiences/Captive Performers: Music and Theatre as Strategies for Survival on the Thailand-Burma Railway 1942-1945* (Eldredge 2014), a book that links to audio and video to describe the importance of music and theater to 61,000 prisoners of war. Such experimentation raises challenges such as working out technical issues and determining how to provide services with limited staffing. When the project was initiated around four or five years ago, the technologies to support interactive multimedia reading experiences, such as iPad apps, had not emerged, so the library has had to cope with shifts in technology. Since the library does not have editing expertise in house, it contracted with an outside editor to work with the book manuscript. Experimentation includes not just content and technologies, but also staffing models.

Case Studies of Library Publishing at Small Colleges and Universities

In order to describe why and how small academic libraries provide publishing services, I offer a snapshot of activities at eight small colleges and universities. While each approach reflects a unique mission, history, and publishing focus, several commonalities emerge, including support for teaching and learning, doing much with little, and wanting to make unique local collections more widely available.

Macalester College

As a SPARC member since 1999, Macalester's DeWitt Wallace Library views its publishing program as a manifestation of its long-standing interest in reforming scholarly communication. Its institutional repository and publishing programs are closely intertwined. Through its institutional repository, the library pursues three main goals (Fishel, Faiks, and Digital Assets Management Working Group 2006, 2-3): preservation (including providing access to student publications otherwise accessible only through interlibrary loan and ongoing access to born-digital faculty work), "participation in the new open access publishing model" (including increasing the discoverability and visibility of faculty publications) and providing "new tools for scholarship and teaching" (including improving student/faculty collaborative research and increasing students' understanding of the new publishing environment). In 2005, the library decided to implement an institutional repository in part so that it could meet an immediate need: allowing readers to discover and access students' honors projects online rather than having to make an appointment to use them in the archives (Fishel 2013b). Within a year after launching its Digital Commons platform, the library began expanding into journal publishing through conversations with the philosophy department about digitizing its journal (Fishel, Billings, and Gonzalez 2009).

Now DeWitt Wallace Library publishes scholarly journals (most of which are edited by Macalester faculty), undergraduate research journals, and a multimedia book (Macalester College 2013b). Partners include Macalester's Institute for Global Citizenship and the departments of geography, biology, philosophy, classics, American studies, and physics, as well as the Association for Nepal and Himalayan Studies (ANHS). Macalester provides support not only for publications edited by its own faculty, but also for the interdisciplinary scholarly journal *Himalaya* (http://digitalcommons.macalester.edu/himalaya), which is edited by faculty from Yale and Dartmouth (but was once edited by a faculty member at Macalester). Connecting the library's publishing program with the college's teaching mission, Library Director Terri Fishel co-teaches a course in which students learn about scholarly communications and produce *Tapestries* (http://digitalcommons.macalester.edu/tapestries), an interdisciplinary undergraduate journal hosted by the library. Effective strategies at Macalester include leveraging its expertise in managing content, working with strong partners, beginning with a project that serves a particular audience and meets specific needs rather than getting caught up in "death by planning," and building on successes (Sietmann and Fishel 2008).

Colby College

When Colby Libraries first started its institutional repository program around 2005, it didn't really consider what it was doing as "publishing," according to Director of Libraries Clem Guthro. Instead, it aimed to offer a digital repository for faculty publications. Since that approach didn't get much uptake, the library shifted its focus to archival collections and undergraduate research. To celebrate the college's bicentennial, Colby Libraries digitized six college histories and published them as e-books through the Digital Commons platform, books that can be read online, downloaded as PDFs, or, in some cases, purchased through the college bookstore (Colby College 2013a). Digital Commons also contains digitized back issues of *Colby Quarterly*, a journal about literature and the history of the Maine region that ran from 1943 until 2003. Since the journal is easily discoverable, it gets a high level of use, typically around 20,000 downloads per month (Guthro 2013). Through a partnership with the college's new center for the arts and humanities, Colby Libraries plans to help relaunch *Colby Quarterly* and start an undergraduate research journal in the humanities. Colby Libraries has also partnered with the college's Office of Communications to provide a permanent digital archive for its publications, beginning with *Colby Magazine*. Through the Colby Environmental Assessment Team collection, Colby Libraries publishes annual reports on the ecology of Maine's Belgrade Lakes system (http://digitalcommons.colby.edu/lakesproject), which are produced by undergraduates in a capstone environmental studies course and have become important resources for homeowner and lake associations throughout Maine. By providing online access to undergraduate research, the library contributes to the college's undergraduate research program, one of the strengths of the institution. Colby Libraries thus makes nearly 1,000 honors theses and senior scholar papers available through its Digital Commons platform, both by enabling students to self-archive their work and by digitizing legacy projects (Colby College 2013b).

The Claremont Colleges

The Claremont Colleges Library (CCL) serves seven different institutions with close geographical proximity but unique identities and needs. According to Head of Scholarly Communications and Publishing Allegra Swift (2013), such diversity among institutions produces a "great petri dish" for publishing experiments. Currently Swift is responsible for digital publishing, scholarly communication and Scholarship@Claremont; a digital scholarship librarian will also be hired. CCL's publishing portfolio features five peer-reviewed scholarly journals in music, mathematics, botany, theater and STEAM (science, technology, engineering, art and mathematics) and three student publications, including a one focused on undergraduate academic writing and one on papers for a national undergraduate conference (CCL 2014). Scholarly Communications and Digital Publishing at the CCL provides a range of publishing services, including training and education, scholarly communications consulting, support for the publishing platform, assistance with collection management, advocacy, and marketing. Swift works closely with faculty editors both in transitioning print journals to electronic formats and in launching new journals, making them aware of the possibilities for online publishing and open-access options. Applying their expertise in metadata and discovery services, cataloging staff create DOIs and catalog records for new journals, while Swift signs journals up for registries and works to include them in appropriate disciplinary indexes. For example, Swift collaborated with the *Journal of Humanistic Mathematics* on design, open-access publishing, and negotiating contracts with indexers such as EBSCO. Now Gizem Karaali, the editor and a math professor, has become a strong advocate for open access publishing and recently did a presentation on the topic at an important mathematics conference (Karaali 2013); Karaali and Swift also presented about open-access publishing on a panel at the 2014 Mathematical Association of America MathFest (Swift 2014b).

Illinois Wesleyan University

According to Stephanie Davis-Kahl (2013a), Scholarly Communications Librarian at Illinois Wesleyan's Ames Library, "Publishing is at its foundation an experiential educational activity," one that offers opportunities to bring topics such as peer review, writing, marketing, and graphic design into the curriculum. As a small, private liberal arts college with approximately 1,900 students, Illinois Wesleyan has a library publishing program that builds on its long tradition of undergraduate research, reflected by its tradition of undergraduate publishing dating back to the nineteenth century, annual undergraduate research symposium that started in 1990, endowment for undergraduate summer research, and undergraduate honors program (Davis-Kahl and Seeborg 2013). Indeed, that history informs the library's case for providing publishing services. Two people—the Scholarly

Communications Librarian and the Digital Projects and Reserves Coordinator—run Illinois Wesleyan's scholarly communications program, with assistance from student workers.

The library's publishing program emerged from its institutional repository services. Soon after the library began subscribing to bepress's Digital Commons, the university's website experienced a catastrophic crash, corrupting the webpages for several student journals. Fortunately, Illinois Wesleyan's Ames Library already had copies of the journals in Digital Commons, demonstrating that the platform could be used to publish student publications. The platform also offers the ability to manage the production of academic journals, such as the submission, peer-review, editorial, and communication processes. These capabilities attracted the economics department, which adopted Digital Commons for one of its student journal *Undergraduate Economics Review* (*UER*; http://digitalcommons.iwu.edu/uer). An open-access, born-digital undergraduate research journal, *UER* attracts submissions from around the world, accepting only about 25 percent (Davis-Kahl and Seeborg 2013). Students review submitted manuscripts and oversee the day-to-day operations of the journal, a responsibility they take quite seriously in order to protect the college's credibility. Along with economics professor Michael Seeborg, Davis-Kahl serves as faculty advisor for the journal, providing guidance on editorial guidelines, journal structure, submissions, management, and marketing. Through a capstone economics course connected to *UER,* students gain practical experience in reviewing for a journal and explore issues in scholarly communication (Davis-Kahl 2013a). This program both expands students' understanding of the research and scholarly communication process and "shifts how students may think about libraries from providing access to being an active partner in creating content" (Davis-Kahl 2013a). According to Davis-Kahl (2013a), the collaboration with the economics department has been a "great experiment in how to work together," including how to develop workflows and assess usage data. Illinois Wesleyan has used this partnership to reach out to other journal editors, some of whom are curious about the possibilities of using Digital Commons to disseminate their journals, while others are more resistant. Rather than offering a one-size-fits-all solution, the library is flexible. The library now supports six other undergraduate journals and is investigating whether there is a market to provide publishing services for faculty journals.

Pacific University

At Pacific University, a private university in Oregon with nearly 3,500 students (1,720 undergraduates) and four campuses, the library pursues an active publishing program that includes teaching a course, collaborating on a publishing and editing minor, and supporting both scholarly and undergraduate journals as well as other publications (Pacific University 2013; Gilman and Kunkel 2010). Pacific University's publishing services grew out of its decision to implement an institutional repository. As one of its initial projects in 2009, it transferred the journal *Essays in Philosophy* from its previous institutional home to Pacific's Digital Commons platform (Gilman and Irons 2011). Building on this collaboration, the library partnered with a philosophy faculty member to launch an open-access journal collecting papers presented at an undergraduate philosophy conference, *Res Cogitans*. As a result of its iterative approach to developing publishing services, the library has "been able to experiment and more clearly identify what services we are reasonably able to offer—and where we want to go in the future" (Gilman 2013b). Currently the library publishes three scholarly journals, one professional journal and two publications focused on undergraduate research, as well as exhibit catalogs, technical reports, and other works.[5] In the near future, the library plans to publish monographs, a service similar to those recently launched at Amherst College (Gilman 2013b).

As the library became more involved in publishing activities, in 2010 it launched Local Collections and Publication Services (LCPS), a collaborative team responsible for archives and the institutional repository as well as publishing services (Gilman and Kunkel 2010, 21). Isaac Gilman, Scholarly Communication and Publishing Services Librarian, devotes approximately 35 percent of his time to publishing, receiving occasional assistance from library staff and students with copyediting and related work. Gilman also teaches a course on scholarly journals and is actively involved with the university's publishing minor. Gilman helps editors (Pacific University faculty) with designing their journals' websites and articles, registering ISSNs and digital object identifiers (DOIs), and creating

---

5. The journals are found at http://commons.pacificu.edu/peer_review_list.html. Technical reports are at http://commons.pacificu.edu/mono/4 and http://commons.pacificu.edu/mono/5. Books such as exhibit catalogs are at http://commons.pacificu.edu/mono.

journal policies (Gilman 2013b). To manage the publication process, the library uses bepress's EdiKit, an editorial workflow management tool that can be used as a stand-alone application or as part of Digital Commons (Bepress 2013b). Upon request, it offers editors training and support in using EdiKit and in editorial best practices, and it helps them negotiate contracts with aggregators and indexers. The library also employs the Issuu Reader to provide features such as page turning, social media sharing, and full-screen display.

Gettysburg College

By providing publishing services, Gettysburg College's Musselman Library aims to "support and enrich the scholarly environment on campus" (Coble 2013).[6] The library's support for campus publishing grew out of its decision to implement an institutional repository, which it launched in April 2012 under the name The Cupola: Scholarship at Gettysburg College (http://cupola.gettysburg.edu/). In developing its support for campus publishing, the library performed an environmental scan to discover who on campus was publishing on a regular basis and whether those publications would be a good fit for the Cupola. Out of a number of publications identified, the library picked four journals to target for inclusion in the Cupola. Before soliciting partnerships, a subcommittee developed "Policies and Procedures for Requesting the Start of a New Journal in the Cupola" (Musselman Library 2012) so that everyone would have a shared understanding of support, areas of responsibility, and the end product. As Zach Coble (2013), who was Systems and Emerging Technologies Librarian at Gettysburg College until October of 2013 and is now Digital Scholarship Specialist at NYU Libraries, indicates, "The process of creating this document, which was essentially reviewing other libraries' documents and adapting them to our needs, gave us a better understanding of what's really involved in library publishing and what is expected of the library in order to provide a high-quality publishing service." In the spring of 2013, the library began hosting two undergraduate journals, *Gettysburg Historical Journal* (which focuses on works produced by students at the college) and *Get-*

---

6. The information in the section on Gettysburg College is primarily based on an interview conducted in 2013 and may not be fully up-to-date.

tysburg College Journal of the Civil War Era (which solicits contributions from beyond the college); as of October of 2014, the library host two more undergraduate journals, *The Mercury* (an art and literary journal) and the *Gettysburg Economic Review* (Wertzberger 2014). In addition to hosting the journals through Digital Commons (http://cupola.gettysburg.edu/peer_review_list.html), Musselman Library trains student editors in using the platform, helps with uploading back issues, and applies for an ISSN as necessary (Coble 2013).

Hamilton College

Hamilton College's Couper Press (www.hamilton.edu/library/couperpress) differs from the other library-based publishing programs in this study because it produces print monographs. Founded in 2006 by Randall Ericson, then the director of Hamilton College's Burke Library, the Couper Press aims to increase the visibility of the library's special collections, particularly its strengths in communal societies. It also grew out of the need among scholars of communal societies, including independent researchers, for outlets for their research. In addition to publishing *American Communal Societies Quarterly*, a full-color journal that highlights Hamilton's communal societies collections, the press publishes two to four monographs a year. These include works of original scholarship as well as reprints of unique or hard-to-find documents from Hamilton's special collections. To support the college's publishing needs, the press also published the proceedings of a conference held at Hamilton. In Ericson's (2013) view, the press, which is the college's only publishing enterprise, brings stature to the college and raises awareness of its special collections on and off campus.

Ericson and his collaborators spent about two years planning the press, securing the support of the dean of the college and funding through an endowment fund. Most of the work is done by Ericson as editor (who continues in the role after having retired from Hamilton two years ago), the associate editor (the head of Special Collections), the manuscripts editor, and an archival assistant. An editorial board that includes scholars, librarians, and book dealers provides feedback on submissions for the monograph series, serving in an advisory capacity. However, the editors alone make decisions about what will be published in the quarterly journal. Currently the press issues only print publications, since Ericson (2013) believes that its audience prefers this format. He also notes, however, that scholars have made significant use of digitized versions of the nineteenth-century Shaker journal hosted by Hamilton and that some publications—such as bibliographies—might work better in electronic formats. Hence the press is considering publishing some works online, potentially under Creative Commons licenses. The press targets "small niche markets," reaching many of its readers by attending annual conferences such as the Communal Studies Association, alerting past customers and subscribers to the quarterly journal of new publications through direct mail, and using word of mouth (Ericson 2013). To reduce the risk of unsold inventory, the press prints short runs of its publications, which only slightly increases the price per copy.

Amherst College

Convinced that the current scholarly communication system is "so broken that we have to try radical new things," the Amherst College Librarian Bryn Geffert (2013) has committed the library to launching Amherst College Press, an open-access press that will focus initially on liberal arts disciplines. With the rising costs of serials, libraries have less money to spend on scholarly monographs. University presses look for works that have broad appeal, making it more challenging for scholars to get work in specialized fields published. Despite having a budget larger than most of its peers, even Amherst's library can't give faculty and students everything they need. On a broader level, most of the world lacks access to scholarly literature (Geffert 2011, B13). Instead of paying others to disseminate scholarly literature, Geffert (2011, B13) suggests that libraries can take control of this process themselves, promoting quality and access. Starting an open-access press reflects Amherst's motto, "Terras Irradient," or "Let them give light to the world," an aspiration that also captures the mission of libraries. The Amherst College Press reflects Geffert's larger vision for open-access publishing. Ultimately Geffert hopes that libraries will reach a tipping point where enough institutions publish open-access that libraries can redirect savings from their acquisitions budgets to cover the costs of their own publishing operations. Of course, in order to save money, libraries must be willing to cancel expensive subscriptions and commit to supporting open-access publishing.

Whereas previous open-access publishers, such as the Rice University Press, relied upon sales to cover their part of their costs, the Amherst College Press will pursue a "simple" business model that does not depend on generating revenue (Gilson and Strauch 2013; Boutilier 2013). Amherst College Press's founding director, Mark D. W. Edington, will be responsible for launching the press, planning, management, and strategic focus (Amherst College 2013b). The press will also bring in two editors who will solicit manuscripts, edit, and manage the production process (Gilson and Strauch 2013). In order to pay for the new press, Amherst Library is shifting funds for two staff positions (vacated by retirements) to hire the two editors and is establishing an endowment to cover the director's salary. The library also plans to use some existing endowment funds to cover operating expenses such as copyediting, which will be outsourced. Other campus departments, including public affairs, IT, and advancement, will assist with graphic design, running the platform (yet to be selected), and fundraising. As an open-access, digital press, Amherst College Press can take advantage of certain efficiencies. It doesn't need to pay for a distribution network, bookkeepers, sales agents, or printing and shipping costs. Rather than using expensive traditional forms of marketing such as printed catalogs, the press will make sure that its publications are discoverable through major indexes (e.g., the *MLA International Bibliography*) and catalogs (e.g., WorldCat) and will use search engine optimization (SEO) and social media to attract readers. Ideally the press will publish its books only on the Web and in e-book formats. However, Geffert (2013) acknowledges that readers continue to want print, so the new director will determine whether to also make available publications through print-on-demand. Geffert aims to integrate the press with the campus through activities such as hosting author talks and conferences, providing student internships, and partnering with Amherst's humanities center (Gilson and Strauch 2013).

Although Amherst has confronted challenges in starting up the press, Geffert (2013) says he has been surprised by "how easy the politics have been so far." To date, the biggest challenge has been the amount of time it takes to start a press. Another challenge will be balancing the need for an efficient workflow with the desire to experiment with new forms of publication, such as data-driven works. Geffert also acknowledges that Amherst may struggle to convince authors to publish with a new, "untested" press (Boutilier 2013). However, the press hopes to attract authors through the credibility of the Amherst name, its commitment to quality and to strong editorial support, its power to reach bigger audiences as a result of making works freely available, and its ability to publish multimedia works. The press will take submissions through a rigorous peer-review process and will commit to high editorial standards, providing "thorough" content editing and copy editing for its publications (Amherst College 2013a).

Patterns in Library-Based Publishing at Small Colleges

While each college publishing program is unique in how it works with campus partners, addresses local needs, and supports the academic mission, they take more or less similar approaches to their missions, staffing, technology infrastructure, funding model, and support for teaching and learning. There is some variation depending on whether library publishing programs help to teach students, as well as whether they focus on journals or monographs.

Mission and Motivation

Many librarians see publishing as a logical extension of their mission to disseminate knowledge and as a strategic opportunity both to provide value to the college and to promote changes to the scholarly communication system. As libraries shift from being content providers to supporting the creation, organization, dissemination, and preservation of knowledge, publishing advances those strategic goals (Davis-Kahl 2013a). According to Fishel (2013b), publishing services fit the mandate of the twenty-first-century academic library as well as its expertise: "I firmly believe that a continuing development for academic libraries will be to provide support for enabling faculty and students to develop digital projects, to assist them in providing a place for publishing, and ongoing support to ensure those projects are preserved and continue to exist as new technologies are developed. Our expertise in copyright, intellectual property, and preservation are all strengths that contribute to our role as publishers." Furthermore, moving into publishing gives libraries a way to shape the scholarly communication system and not only advocate for open-access publishing, but also practice it. Even though open access is a powerful advantage that college libraries can offer, not every journal is necessarily drawn to this model; for example, a journal showcasing undergraduate creative writing balked at adopting Creative Commons licenses, fearing that students wouldn't be able to republish their work in other contexts. In order to build local support for open access and confront fears about losing control of intellectual property, small academic libraries often take it as part of their mission to educate faculty and the larger community.

Establishing and Maintaining Publishing Programs

For small academic libraries to offer publishing services, they need to have a compelling vision, administrative support, access to necessary technologies, staff time and expertise, and partnerships with faculty and other collaborators. By starting fresh, libraries have more freedom than established publishers to craft a program that makes sense for the current and future environments rather than dealing with legacy systems, workflows, and expectations (Geffert 2013). However, as new entrants into publishing, libraries may not know what kind of planning is necessary, so they may make avoidable mistakes (Lippincott and Skinner 2013). They may also struggle to establish their credibility on campus and in the broader scholarly publishing community (Lippincott and Skinner 2013). Indeed, most libraries (small and large) do not themselves provide peer review, instead securing it through partnerships with scholars.[7] Building their reputation depends on strong relationships with faculty and the administration, good services, and high standards. Moving toward new publishing models entails significant risks, including the understandable reluctance of some faculty to stake their careers on digital publications that may not carry weight with tenure and promotion committees. To make library-based publishing credible, libraries have to demonstrate that they apply sound policies for developing and reviewing content—otherwise they risk being seen as a

---

7. I draw this point from interviews that Korey Jackson and I have conducted with leaders of library publishing operations as well as of digital humanities centers.

"dump" for unsupported and undeveloped content (Swift 2013). Further, it may be difficult to sustain momentum with some publications. At several of the colleges included in this study, some journals have not published issues on a regular basis. As one interviewee noted, faculty members may get excited about starting a new journal, but then their interest or available time may decline over time, leaving journals languishing. To head off potential problems, libraries are establishing clear policies outlining what is expected of journal editors and what the library can provide, in some cases requiring a memorandum of understanding.

Staffing and Organizational Structure

Typically small college libraries lack the resources to hire new staff for publishing initiatives, so they reallocate the time of existing staff. According to a 2010 survey, Oberlin Group libraries allocate .9 FTE to publishing services, compared to 2.4 FTE in ARL institutions (Mullins et al. 2012). While librarians can leverage existing skills in areas such as metadata creation and digitization, they often need to develop new skills such as design, layout, marketing, business planning, developing contracts, copyediting, and working with publishing technologies (Lippincott and Skinner 2013; Mullins et al. 2012). As publishing services have changed, so have the roles of staff that provide them. For example, Stephanie Davis-Kahl, now Illinois Wesleyan's Scholarly Communications Librarian, began working at the college in 2004 as a public services librarian, but her position has "evolved" to focus first on digital media, then on scholarly communications and the repository (Davis-Kahl 2013a). At both Macalester and Illinois Wesleyan, decreasing demand for electronic reserves meant that staff in these areas could shift their attention to the institutional repository and publishing program, drawing upon their knowledge of copyright and digitization. While some libraries have departments with primary responsibility for digital collections and publishing, others create multi-departmental teams to distribute that responsibility across different library units.

Even if a few people may have primary responsibility for publishing, staff across the library (including student workers) typically support the initiative, whether by promoting publishing services, integrating understanding of scholarly communications into library instruction, or assisting with metadata.

Technology Infrastructure

Since small libraries lack the staff and technical infrastructure to install and maintain publishing platforms, they often turn to hosted solutions. Nearly all of the small academic libraries included in this study use bepress's Digital Commons, a commercially hosted institutional repository and publishing platform. However, other platforms appear to be more common at larger institutions; the recent Library Publishing Services survey showed that more libraries use Open Journal Systems (57 percent) and DSpace (36 percent) than Digital Commons (25 percent; Mullins et al. 2012). Arguing that libraries can reinvigorate their institutional repositories by publishing open-access journals, bepress has both designed its platform to support publishing services and helped to disseminate best practices (Bankier and Smith 2008; Bepress 2013a; Bankier and Perciali 2008). Several colleges selected Digital Commons because it can serve as both an institutional repository and a hosted publishing platform, with support for the editorial workflow provided by EdiKit (Gilman and Irons 2011). By choosing a hosted solution, small colleges such as Gettysburg can "focus on acquiring and publishing content rather than spending time with the technical details" (Coble 2013). Several interviewees praised bepress's technologies and customer support; for example, Stephanie Davis-Kahl (2013a) suggested that the company acts as "partners in the true sense of word," helping with customization and serving as a sounding board for new ideas. The wide adoption of Digital Commons by small colleges demonstrates the intersection of institutional repository and publishing functions as well as many colleges' need for a hosted solution and services such as design and customization.

Funding Models

Sustaining library publishing programs over the long term presents a key challenge to small colleges.[8] The main funding for library publishing services usually comes from the library's regular budget. At some colleges, administrators or journal sponsors also help cover the cost of

---

8. Of course, larger institutions likewise face challenges in securing adequate staffing and funding to support scholarly communications initiatives. See Del Toro, Mandernack, and Zanoni 2011.

the publishing platform. For example, Illinois Wesleyan's library shares the cost for the Digital Commons platform with the Center for Teaching and Learning, the Provost's Office, and the President's Office, since the software is also used for records management and faculty governance documents. Out of all of the publishers examined in this study, only Hamilton's Couper Press charges for its publications (although Colby also sells print versions of some its freely available digital books). As a print publisher, the Couper Press must fund the costs of printing and distribution, and revenues generated through this commercial activity are modest.

In order to sustain and scale up publishing programs, libraries will need to demonstrate clear value and develop sound business models, which may involve partnerships, sponsorships, endowments, or fees for content or services. As Terri Fishel (2013b) remarks, "Finding an economic model that can sustain ongoing digital publishing will be a big piece of the puzzle." While Macalester is committed to open access, it also recognizes the need to provide a stable source of funding for staffing, the publishing platform, and other costs, which can be challenging when works are freely available online. Given limitations in staffing and support, some libraries are reluctant to scale up services because they don't want to promise what they can't necessarily deliver. At the same time, the current model for funding scholarly communications is likewise unsustainable, as journal prices are rising and libraries struggle to cover costs (Lippincott and Skinner 2013). To justify funding for publishing, libraries consciously demonstrate the value of these services to the institution, such as advancing teaching and learning, raising the profile of the college, and assisting with knowledge management. For example, Illinois Wesleyan's library is "very intentional about communicating benefits and areas of growth," including by tracking downloads and geographic reach (Davis-Kahl 2013a). In a successful bid for the Andrew W. Mellon Foundation grant, "Digital Humanities at the Claremont Colleges: Developing Capacity and Community," the Claremont Colleges Library will provide space, technology and staff to support faculty and curricular development for undergraduate teaching and research in digital humanities, as well as explore publishing and archiving support for the created resources.

Integration with Teaching and Learning

Not only do small academic libraries produce undergraduate research journals and collections of papers from undergraduate research conferences, but many also integrate publishing and scholarly communications into the curriculum, helping students learn about key issues and how to produce an academic journal. Since students at elite liberal arts colleges are more likely to receive a PhD than those from other institutions, they need to understand the research process and the scholarly communications system (Graves 2013). As Davis-Kahl (2013a) notes, scholarly communications topics already infuse information literacy programs, but such programs can do more to promote understanding of open access, author rights, and indicators of credibility such as peer review and citations. By engaging students in journal publishing, the library can contribute to "closing the loop of information literacy instruction," integrating theory and practice (Davis-Kahl and Seeborg 2013). For example, an economics capstone course at Illinois Wesleyan fosters skills in critical thinking, writing, research, data literacy, peer review, and knowledge of current issues in scholarly communications. Building on students' prior training in commenting on peers' work, the course exposes students to core criteria for evaluating journal submissions, gives them practice reviewing, and charges them with reviewing a new submission to *Undergraduate Economics Review* so that their work reviewing for a journal informs helps them to become better authors; several students volunteer to continue reviewing for the journal after the course concludes. According to a survey of thirty-two students who reviewed articles for the journal, most agreed that doing so definitely or somewhat exposed them to other research models, was a valuable use of time, and enhanced their understanding of how articles are reviewed and selected for publication by professional journals (Davis-Kahl and Seeborg 2013). Through linked co-curricular activities, students assume much of the responsibility for running the journal, with Stephanie Davis-Kahl and economics professor Michael Seeborg serving as faculty advisors. As a result of their active involvement in peer review, students enhance their own research and writing skills and are motivated to produce better work (Davis-Kahl and Seeborg 2013). While the program faces challenges, including dealing with frequent transitions to new editorial teams, ensuring consistency in reviewing, and attracting the best submissions, it also delivers significant benefits, including promoting critical thinking and leadership skills, building connections with alumni and students at other schools, and tightening the partnership between faculty and the library (Davis-Kahl and Seeborg 2013). Further assessment of student learning through publishing programs is needed, but such a program seems to promote the best practices of liberal education articulated by the AAC&U "High-Impact Educational Practices," including undergraduate research, collaborative assignments, and writing-intensive courses (AAC&U 2014; Davis-Kahl 2013b; Davis-Kahl and Hensley 2013). As a result of her work with *UER*, Stephanie Davis-Kahl has developed a keener understanding of student perspectives on scholarly communication and open access, which has informed how she approaches information literacy training (Davis-Kahl and Seeborg 2013).

As Isaac Gilman (2013c) argues, the best way to raise students' understanding of scholarly communications is to integrate it into for-credit coursework. At Pacific University, the library participates in two linked curricular initiatives focused on scholarly communication. Since 2011, Gilman has taught a two-credit undergraduate course, Journal Editing and Publishing, through the media arts department. The course aims to increase students' understanding of the publishing process, publishing models, legal contexts, and review process. In this two-week winter term course, students produce a research paper that is peer-reviewed by fellow students; participate in a debate about scholarly communications; and create a proposal for a new scholarly journal. This course counts toward a new minor in editing and publishing collaboratively developed by the library and the English department. Integrating liberal arts capacities such as critical thinking with practical skills such as copyediting, the minor brings together courses in English, media art, art, and business. The minor aims to promote students' career prospects in publishing and academic research, provide training in communication, distinguish the institution, and improve student retention (Gilman 2013d). The minor has faced several challenges, including finding appropriate practicum opportunities for students with local organizations (particularly scholarly journals) and developing its book publishing specialization (Gilman 2013a, 2013d). However, the library's involvement in the publishing curriculum has advanced several strategic goals, including increasing students' understanding of scholarly communication and their publishing skills, deepening the library's connections to the curriculum, promoting collaborations with faculty, enabling the library to adopt a leadership role, and demonstrating its value and relevance (Gilman 2013d).

At Macalester College, the undergraduate journal *Tapestries* grew out of a two-credit spring 2010 course team co-taught by Terri Fishel and Jane Rhodes, Dean for the Study of Race and Ethnicity (Fishel and Betsworth 2011). Fishel addressed the economics of scholarly communication, intellectual property, and related issues. The first offering of the course challenged students to generate the idea for a new journal, define its mission, determine how engage various audiences, and develop submission guidelines (Macalester College 2013c). The students formed an editorial collective, aiming for a collaborative, less hierarchical approach to editing. Subsequent student editorial collectives have further developed the journal, which published its first issue in spring 2011.

Recommendations

Even as small academic libraries face challenges such as resource constraints and shifting faculty interest, they seem to agree that publishing provides value to the college and the larger educational community. In the process of developing these services, they have learned important lessons about how to build support and establish sound policies. Drawing upon the collective wisdom of the librarians interviewed for this study, let me offer the following recommendations for libraries considering similar programs:

1. **Understand the local and national environment.** In exploring how to integrate publishing into the undergraduate curriculum, Davis-Kahl (2013b) suggests reflecting on strengths, opportunities, champions, and goals; understanding roles, responsibilities, timelines, and resources; and planning for and implementing assessments to understand what works and what can be improved. Zach Coble (2013) also points to the importance of having a sense of the broader context around scholarly communication system because "it's a huge web with a lot of moving parts, and it's important to understand how a library publishing program fits into this system, and what ripple effects it might have in other places in the system."

2. **Embrace experimentation.** Several interviewees emphasized the need for experimentation. For example, Gilman (2013b) recommends that libraries interested in publishing services experiment with "one or two small projects (and an author or editor who is willing to explore/learn with you), and use them to explore what publishing services are feasible for you to offer and what relevant knowledge you already possess (e.g., knowledge/skills that staff members in other library departments have that could be used to support publishing services) and what you need to learn." By experimenting, libraries can learn what it takes to publish and create a proof of concept demonstrating what it can offer.
3. **Build alliances with faculty and academic units.** To gain faculty interest and support, libraries need to conduct outreach, find advocates (such as the center for teaching and scholarship), and showcase the success of early adopters (Fishel 2013a). Often partnerships with faculty grow out of prior relationships. At Macalester, for example, the library's success with an information fluency program led to a collaborative course.
4. **Develop clear policies.** Even as libraries should be nimble and flexible in recognizing and responding to needs, they also are wise to establish policies setting expectations and limits. These include both internal processes that define the publishing program's objectives, staffing model, budget, services, and target audiences, and external policies that articulate the level of support, expectations for publishing partners such as faculty editors, and approaches to intellectual property (such as takedown requests from students who don't want their work shared online; Mullins et al. 2012). For example, the Claremont Colleges Library insists that each new journal complete a proposal demonstrating that it "is integral to the department" and has long-term support (Swift 2013). Likewise, Macalester developed a set of policies that govern starting up new journals and submitting and withdrawing content to the institutional repository (Macalester College 2013a). Its journal policy states that journals should be "open access compliant" (at minimum, providing open access to back issues no more than two years after publication) and ongoing (sign-off of department chair or department head is required), mandates that peer-reviewed journals have an editorial board,

leaves copyright with authors in most cases, and makes the publishing department responsible for promotion of the journal (Macalester College 2010). In devising these policies, librarians can draw upon models provided by other institutions.

5. **Educate the campus.** In addition to having clear policies, libraries need to educate faculty, administrators, and students (and sometimes their own staff) on scholarly communications issues and build broader understanding of and support for the publishing program. To recruit faculty partners, librarians need to "get out in front of people, helping them understand what you could do for them" (Swift 2013).

6. **Develop strategies to increase visibility of publications.** Raising awareness of new works constitutes a significant challenge, particularly for those dependent on sales revenues. The Couper Press faces difficulty in marketing its books, particularly in reaching libraries in an era of declining budgets. Some libraries have had success with using social media to raise the visibility of scholarly publications. For example, in launching the new *STEAM Journal*, the graduate student editor and Swift made a "concerted effort" to promote it through in-person events, blogs, Twitter, and other social media outlets (Swift 2013). It leapt to the top of Claremont's download statistics.

7. **Demonstrate value.** For the library's publishing program to attain long-term institutional support, its work must be connected to the larger mission of the library and the institution. According to Isaac Gilman (2013b), the greatest challenge facing libraries providing publishing services is "trying to convey the importance of the library being involved in this area," which is essential to garnering financial resources and support from faculty, administrators, and other stakeholders. As his experience at Pacific University has illustrated, faculty and administrators do recognize the importance of such services for education and research and appreciate the library's ability to take a leadership role in scholarly communications.

8. **Collaborate with libraries and other institutions.** Given their resource constraints, small college libraries need to collaborate, both within and beyond their institution. Within the college, libraries partner with faculty, research centers, academic pro-

grams, and student groups to start up and support journals and other publishing ventures. Some small academic libraries also collaborate with campus units such as information technology or the provost's office to secure funding and technical support. As with most collaborations, challenges within publishing-related partnerships include maintaining clear communications, establishing roles and responsibilities, and making partners accountable (Gilman 2013b).

Beyond the campus, libraries can work together to build collective wisdom and share best practices, thus reducing duplication of effort and getting up to speed more quickly. Several interviewees echoed the call in *Library Publishing Services* (Mullins et al. 2012) for greater information sharing about publishing and praised the Library Publishing Coalition (LPC) for helping to advance this goal. By providing core resources and connections, the coalition enables libraries to share knowledge and "band together" rather than "reinventing wheels or starting up in a vacuum" (Swift 2013). Likewise, library publishing can connect to existing cultures of collaboration, such as in the digital humanities (Swift 2013). Such a collaboration could involve developing new publishing models, such as data-driven, multimodal, or interactive, iterative publications.

Libraries could also collaborate to secure access to staffing and technical infrastructure, whether through a consortial model, shared staffing, or collaborative licensing of technology platforms. The LPC is exploring the possibility of coordinating internships or staff exchanges and helping to match institutions interested in shared staffing or services (Lippincott and Skinner 2013). Potential areas for shared services include copyediting, metadata creation, graphic design, and legal counsel. A shared staffing model could allow libraries to get quick access to competent, trustworthy expertise, accomplish more with a relatively small budget, and foster greater collaboration across institutions. Already some grant-funded positions are shared across multiple institutions, although these positions tend to disappear after the duration of the grant (Swift 2013). Likewise, services such as virtual reference rely upon libraries sharing staff time and expertise. Perhaps library publishing units could establish or work with consortia to negotiate collective buying agreements or create a structure for shared services or technical infrastructure such as a publishing platform. For example, the CLIC consortium (www.clic.edu), of which Macalester is a member, purchased consortial access to CONTENTdm. Yet shared staffing may be difficult to accomplish given the unique needs, cultures, resources, and practices of different institutions. In order to share a position across multiple libraries, partners would need to work out agreements regarding the reporting structure, responsibilities, communication, and resources (Lippincott and Skinner 2013). Ultimately collaboration may make the most sense for larger, technically demanding initiatives, such as data curation and preservation (Swift 2013).

Alternatively, libraries can work with trusted vendors to secure access to services they can't bring in house, including coordinating external peer review, copyediting, developmental editing, and technical support. While Colby could contract with a copy editor, it lacks the funds or the institutional support to bring one on staff, and it wouldn't have enough work to justify hiring one anyway. Given the challenges that a small press faces with marketing and distribution, Randy Ericson (2013) sees possibilities for partnerships with larger presses. Other service providers for academic publishing will likely emerge, especially as effective business models are developed.

On a more ambitious level, the Oberlin Group launched the Lever Initiative (http://leverinitiative.wordpress.com) to investigate whether liberal arts college libraries could collectively start up and sustain an open-access press. While most small academic libraries aren't ready to launch a new press as Amherst has done, they may be willing to "make smaller contributions toward a joint effort" (Geffert 2013). Promoting such collaborations involves significant challenges, including confronting the fear of failure, dealing with the free rider problem in which institutions are unwilling to provide resources for what they can get for free, and confronting the "identity problem," in which small libraries see themselves as the consumers rather than producers of information (Roy 2013). But, as Barbara Fister (2013) notes, "We can do a lot more together than we can one at a time." Rather than maintaining a broken system and ceding control to publishers, Fister (2011) argues that libraries should transform the system for the good of scholarship and the public: "Why don't we retool our organizations, built around purchasing stuff, and hire the expertise needed to develop books, complementing their expertise with our established track record of making information accessible and shareable?" Libraries could work together to build an open-access publishing system that promotes much greater access, better quality, more innovation, and lower overall costs (Fister 2011). Consortial publishing offers the advantage of getting more people and institutions involved and promoting publishing as a "common venture for the common good" (Geffert 2013) rather than driven by the bottom line.

During its initial research phase, the Lever Initiative, which is led by a small task force of Oberlin Group members, hired a consultant to oversee the research process and write a landscape review of open-access publishing models. It conducted a series of virtual workshops with library directors, held telephone interviews with people in and outside of the Oberlin Group, convened a task force workshop, and performed a survey of faculty from Oberlin Group institutions and from non–Oberlin Group institutions. According to the survey of faculty from Oberlin Group institutions, 43 percent of respondents said they would consider publishing with a "new innovative, open access press for publishing scholarly books" launched by a group of liberal arts colleges, while 40 percent responded "maybe" (Kenneway 2014c, 35). This work fed into a report examining the feasibility of launching an open access publishing venture for the liberal arts (Kenneway 2014a). According to the report, a new publishing venture would face challenges in developing a sustainable business model and dealing with authors' lack of interest in new publishing models, but it could find a niche by focusing on short-form works and meeting authors' need for excellent peer review, editorial and marketing services. The report outlined four options for moving forward, including creating an open access press, partnering with extant publishers, supporting "unlocking" programs such as KnowledgeUnlatched, and advocating for open access. In September of 2014, the Oberlin Group announced its plans move into Phase 2, with the goals of exploring the logistics of developing a "new publishing venture," creating a business plan, and finding potential partners (Kenneway 2014b).

Conclusion

Even as they deal with a lack of staff, technical support, and funding, small academic libraries can make their small size a strength. Small libraries typically don't have to navigate large, complex bureaucracies and can more easily experiment with new solutions. Moreover, small academic libraries often can work more closely with faculty and connect publishing to the university's teaching and learning mission. Resource constraints can lead to a greater focus on core services, promote collaboration, and foster creativity. Indeed, Fister (2011) sees a special mission for small academic libraries to fulfill in devising flexible solutions that don't require massive resources: "We can make contributions to developing the kind of low-investment high-impact technologies and processes that can make a difference in many settings." Small libraries have leveraged the Digital Commons platform and existing staff expertise to provide publishing services without hiring additional staff, developed policies that allow them to establish limits and expectations, and worked closely with faculty, students, and campus units to advance common goals. Mike Roy (2013) acknowledges that libraries face "risk and uncertainty" in becoming more engaged in publishing, but suggests that there is more risk in doing nothing. Ultimately what's at stake for libraries is the ability to have more influence in the scholarly communications system—"greater agency in determining their path" (Coble 2013).

Author's Note

I would like to extend my sincere thanks to those whom I interviewed; the chapter is much richer as a result of their insights, as well as their helpful feedback in reviewing the chapter.

Works Cited

AAC&U (Association of American Colleges and Universities). 2014. "High-Impact Educational Practices." Accessed October 11. https://www.aacu.org/leap/hips.

Amherst College. 2013a. "Amherst College Press." Accessed July 24. https://www.amherst.edu/library/press.

———. 2013b. "Amherst College Press Names Founding Director." News release, December 6. https://www.amherst.edu/aboutamherst/news/news_releases/2013/12-2013/node/522697.

Bankier, Jean-Gabriel, and Irene Perciali. 2008. "The Institutional Repository Rediscovered: What Can a University Do for Open Access Publishing?" *Serials Review* 34, no. 1 (March): 20–26. http://works.bepress.com/jean_gabriel_bankier/1.

Bankier, Jean-Gabriel, and Courtney Smith. 2008. "Establishing Library Publishing: Best Practices for Creating Successful Journal Editors." In *Open Scholarship: Authority,*

Community, and Sustainability in the Age of Web 2.0: Proceedings of the 12th International Conference on Electronic Publishing held in Toronto, Canada, 25–27 June 2008, edited by Leslie Chan and Susanna Mornati, 68–78. Berkeley, CA: Bepress. http://works.bepress.com/jean_gabriel_bankier/2.

Bepress. 2013a. *DC Telegraph* (blog). Accessed July 24. http://blog.digitalcommons.bepress.com.

———. 2013b. "Publish Professional-Grade Journals with Digital Commons." Accessed July 10. www.bepress.com/editors.html.

Boutilier, Emily Gold. 2013. "Librarians Will Lead the Revolution." *Amherst Magazine*, Winter. https://www.amherst.edu/aboutamherst/magazine/issues/winter_2013/feature_librarians_will_lead_the_revolution.

Carnegie Foundation for the Advancement of Teaching. 2013. "Size and Setting Classification." Carnegie Classifications, accessed July 10. http://classifications.carnegiefoundation.org/descriptions/size_setting.php.

CCL (Claremont Colleges Library). 2014. "Peer-Reviewed Content." Scholarship @ Claremont, accessed October 14. http://scholarship.claremont.edu/peer_review_list.html.

Claremont Center for Digital Humanities. 2013. *Claremont DH* (blog), accessed July 28. http://claremontdh.com/.

Coble, Zach. 2013. E-mail interview by Lisa Spiro, July 16. At the time of the interview, Coble was Systems and Emerging Technologies Librarian at Gettysburg College; he is now Digital Scholarship Specialist at New York University Libraries.

Colby College. 2013a. "Colby E-Books." Digital Commons @ Colby, accessed July 25. http://digitalcommons.colby.edu/colbiana_books.

———. 2013b. "Honors Theses." Digital Commons @ Colby, accessed July 25. http://digitalcommons.colby.edu/honorstheses.

Crow, Raym. 2009. *Campus-Based Publishing Partnerships: A Guide to Critical Issues*. Washington, DC: SPARC, January.

Davis-Kahl, Stephanie. 2013a. Telephone interview by Lisa Spiro, June 12. Davis-Kahl is Scholarly Communications Librarian at Illinois Wesleyan University.

———. 2013b. "The Value of Library Publishing and Undergraduate Education." Paper presented at the ACRL, Indianapolis, IN, April. http://works.bepress.com/stephanie_davis_kahl/39.

Davis-Kahl, Stephanie, and Merinda Kaye Hensley. 2013. *Common Ground at the Nexus of Information Literacy and Scholarly Communication*. Chicago: Association of College and Research Libraries, 2013. http://works.bepress.com/stephanie_davis_kahl/34.

Davis-Kahl, Stephanie, and Michael Seeborg. 2013. "Library Publishing and Undergraduate Education: Strategies for Collaboration." Presentation at the ACRL 2013, Indianapolis, IN, April. http://works.bepress.com/stephanie_davis_kahl/38.

Del Toro, Rosemary, Scott Mandernack, and Jean Zanoni. 2011. "Evolution of Scholarly Communication: How Small and Medium-Sized Libraries Are Adapting." Paper presented at the Association of College and Research Libraries (ACRL) Conference, Philadelphia, PA, March. http://epublications.marquette.edu/lib_fac/11.

Eldredge, Sears A. 2014. *Captive Audiences/Captive Performers: Music and Theatre as Strategies for Survival on the Thailand-Burma Railway 1942–1945*. Saint Paul, MN: DeWitt Wallace Library, Macalester College. http://digitalcommons.macalester.edu/thdabooks/1.

Ericson, Randall. 2013. Telephone interview by Lisa Spiro, July 23. Ericson is the former

Couper Librarian of Burke Library at Hamilton College and current editor of the *American Communal Studies Quarterly and the Couper Press.*

Fishel, Teresa. 2013a. Telephone interview by Lisa Spiro, June 11. Fishel is Library Director at Macalester College.

———. 2013b. Written responses, interview by Lisa Spiro. June 11.

Fishel, Teresa, and Jacquelyn F. Betsworth. 2011. "DeWitt Wallace Library Annual Report, 2010-11," Annual Report—Library and Media Services, Paper 6. http://digitalcommons.macalester.edu/cgi/viewcontent.cgi?article=1005&context=libanreport.

Fishel, Teresa, Marilyn Billings, and Allegra Gonzalez. 2009. "Academic Library as Publishing Agent: Showcasing Student, Faculty, and Campus Scholarship and Publications." Presentation, ACRL 14th National Conference, March 12-15, Seattle, WA. http://works.bepress.com/marilyn_billings/36.

Fishel, Teresa, Angi Faiks, and Digital Assets Management Working Group. 2006. "Digital Collections Master Plan: Content, Systems, Access and Comprehensive Management Framework." DeWitt Wallace Library Reports, Paper 4, September 22. http://digitalcommons.macalester.edu/annrep/4.

Fister, Barbara. 2011. "'Selfless Audacity' Means Creating a Sustainable Not-a-Business Model." *Library Journal,* March 24. www.libraryjournal.com/lj/newslettersnewsletterbucketacademicnewswire/889840-440/selfless_audacity_means_creating_a.html.csp (page not available).

———. 2013. E-mail interview by Lisa Spiro, June 1. Fister is Academic Librarian at Gustavus Adolphus College.

Geffert, Bryn. 2011. "Libraries, Publishers, and a Plea for Shotgun Weddings." *Chronicle of Higher Education* 57, no. 29 (March 25, 2011). http://chronicle.com/article/Libraries-Publishinga/126755.

———. 2013. Telephone interview by Lisa Spiro, June 3. Geffert is Amherst College Librarian.

Gilman, Isaac. 2013a. "Connecting with Curriculum." Presented at the ACRL 2013 Conference, Indianapolis, IN, April 11. http://commons.pacificu.edu/libfac/22.

———. 2013b. E-mail interview by Lisa Spiro, July 1. At the time of the interview, Gilman was Scholarly Communications and Research Services Librarian at Pacific University; he is now Scholarly Communication & Publishing Services Librarian at Pacific.

———. 2013c. "Journal Editing and Publishing." Accessed July 11. https://sites.google.com/site/pub364/home.

———. 2013d. "Scholarly Communication for Credit: Integrating Publishing Education into Undergraduate Curriculum." In *Common Ground at the Nexus of Information Literacy and Scholarly Communication,* edited by Stephanie Davis-Kahl and Merinda Kaye Hensley. Chicago: Association of College and Research Libraries. http://commons.pacificu.edu/libfac/21.

Gilman, Isaac, and Lynda Irons. 2011. "Open Access and Open Lives: The Changing Role of Academic Libraries." In *Internet 2.0: After the Bubble Burst 2000-2010,* edited by Jeffrey Barlow [authors' manuscript]. Forest Grove, OR: Berglund Center for Internet Studies. http://commons.pacificu.edu/libfac/15.

Gilman, Isaac, and Marita Kunkel. 2010. "From Passive to Pervasive: Changing Perceptions of the Library's Role through Intra-Campus Partnerships." *Collaborative Librarianship* 2, no. 1 (January 1, 2010): 20-30. http://commons.pacificu.edu/libfac/7.

Gilson, Tom, and Katina Strauch. 2013. "ATG Interviews Bryn Geffert, Librarian of the College at Amherst College." ATG News Channel, March 12. www.against-the-

grain.com/2013/03/atg-interviews-bryn-geffert-librarian-of-the-college-at-amherst-college.
Graves, Diane J. 2013. "Scholarly Communications and the Role of the Liberal Arts College Library," preprint. In *Reflecting on the Future of Academic and Public Libraries*, edited by Peter Hernon and Joseph R. Matthews. Chicago: ALA Editions. http://digitalcommons.trinity.edu/cgi/viewcontent.cgi?article=1025&context=lib_faculty.
Guthro, Clem. 2013. Telephone interview by Lisa Spiro, July 25. Guthro is Director of Libraries at Colby College.
Hahn, Karla L. 2008. *Research Library Publishing Services: New Options for University Publishing*. Washington, DC: Association of Research Libraries.
Karaali, Gizem. 2013. "The Brave New World of Open Access and Creative Commons: A Humanistic Experiment in Mathematical Publishing." Presentation, Mathematical Association of America and American Mathematical Society Joint Mathematics Meetings, San Diego, CA, January 10. http://scholarship.claremont.edu/pomona_fac_pub/391/
Kenneway, Melinda. 2014a. *Lever Initiative: Investigating the Feasibility of Launching a New Open Access Publishing Venture for the Liberal Arts*. Oberlin Group, March 17.
———. 2014b. "Phase 2 Commences." *The Lever Initiative* (blog), September 22. http://leverinitiative.wordpress.com/2014/09/22/phase-2-commences.
———. 2014c. *Shaping the Future of Monograph Publishing in the Liberal Arts: Results of a Survey to Oberlin Group Faculty*. TBI Communications, January 28. http://leverinitiative.files.wordpress.com/2014/03/survey_results_oberlin_faculty_jan14.pdf.
Lippincott, Sarah, and Katherine Skinner. 2013. Telephone interview by Lisa Spiro, June 11. Lippincott is Program Manager for the Library Publishing Coalition. Skinner is Executive Director of the Educopia Institute.
LPC (Library Publishing Coalition). 2013. "About Us," accessed August 9. www.librarypublishing.org/about-us.
Macalester College. 2010. "Policies and Procedures for Requesting the Start of a New Journal in the DigitalCommons@Macalester." DigitalCommons@Macalester. http://digitalcommons.macalester.edu/newjournal.pdf.
———. 2013a. "DigitalCommons@Macalester College Policies and Procedures." DigitalCommons@Macalester, accessed July 14. http://digitalcommons.macalester.edu/faq.html.
———. 2013b. "Peer-Reviewed Content." DigitalCommons@Macalester, accessed July 11. http://digitalcommons.macalester.edu/peer_review_list.html.
———. 2013c. "Tapestries." Macalester College, accessed July 11. www.macalester.edu/academics/americanstudies/tapestries.
Mullins, James, Catherine Murray-Rust, Joyce Ogburn, Raym Crow, October Ivins, Allyson Mower, Daureen Nesdill, Mark Newton, Julie Speer, and Charles Watkinson. 2012. *Library Publishing Services: Strategies for Success: Final Research Report*. Washington, DC: SPARC. http://docs.lib.purdue.edu/purduepress_ebooks/24.
Musselman Library. 2012. "Policies and Procedures for Requesting the Start of a New Journal in the Cupola." September. http://cupola.gettysburg.edu/newjournal.pdf.
Pacific University. 2013. "Pacific University Facts." Accessed July 10. http://www.pacificu.edu/about-us/who-we-are/pacific-university-facts.
Roy, Michael. 2013. E-mail interview by Lisa Spiro, July 10. Roy is Dean of the Library at Middlebury College.
Schwartz, Meredith. 2013. "Ten Questions with the Library Publishing Coalition." *Library*

Journal, April 2. http://lj.libraryjournal.com/2013/04/library-services/ten-questions-with-the-library-publishing-coalition.

Sietmann, Janet, and Teresa Fishel. 2008. "Showcasing Student, Faculty and Staff Publications: Promoting, Populating and Publishing in a Small Liberal Arts College Institutional Repository." Presentation, SPARC Digital Repositories Meeting, Baltimore, MD, November 18. http://digitalcommons.macalester.edu/lib_pubs/3.

Swift, Allegra. 2013. Telephone interview by Lisa Spiro, June 10. At the time of the interview, Swift was Digital Initiatives Librarian at Claremont Colleges Library, Claremont University Consortium; she is now Head of Scholarly Communications and Publishing there.

———. 2014a. "New Directions for Digital Collections at the Claremont Colleges." Paper 20, Library Staff Publications and Research, Claremont Colleges, Scholarship@Claremont, February 26 (originally given as a presentation in the New Directions for Digital Collections at Academic Libraries Seminar, held online via videoconferencing February 13). http://scholarship.claremont.edu/library_staff/20.

———. 2014b. "Why Open Access?" Paper 28, Library Staff Publications and Research, Claremont Colleges, Scholarship@Claremont, August 9 (originally given as a presentation, MathFest, Mathematical Association of America, Portland, OR, August 9). http://scholarship.claremont.edu/library_staff/28.

Wertzberger, Janelle. 2014. Email to Lisa Spiro, October 16. Wertzberger is Director of Reference & Instruction at Gettysburg College's Musselman Library.

SECTION 3

What Libraries Publish

CHAPTER 8

Textbooks and Educational Resources in Library-Based Publishing

Cyril Oberlander

Introduction

Calls for the transformation of higher education often focus on expanding access and reducing the cost of colleges and universities. Textbooks have long been an integral learning platform in higher education; however, steady price increases have made their use increasingly problematic for students and higher education as a whole. The US Government Accountability Office reported in June 2013 that the cost of college textbooks rose about 6 percent annually from 2002 to 2012, with an overall 82 percent increase (GAO 2013, 6). The 2005 GAO report showed that textbook prices rose 186 percent between 1986 and 2004 (GAO 2005, 9). The rising cost of textbooks now jeopardizes the quality of student learning. The *2012 Florida Student Textbook Survey* of over 22,000 students showed that because of textbook costs, 64 percent of students didn't purchase a required textbook, 45 percent didn't register for a course, 49 percent took fewer courses, and 27 percent dropped a course (Florida Virtual Campus 2012, 8). The current model is clearly too expensive to students, libraries, and the academy in general. As a result, innovative solutions are needed.

Fortunately, college and university libraries are well positioned to address these problems. On January 2009, at the American Library Association Midwinter Conference, the Association of College and Research Libraries (ACRL) and Scholarly Publishing and Academic Resources Coalition (SPARC) held a joint ACRL-SPARC Forum on the Transformative Potential of Open Educational Resources. Open educational resources, or OERs, were described as "a logical extension of what the library community supports in the Open Access movement, and underscore the need for the larger field on which scholarly communication takes place to be made more equitable" (Malenfant 2008). This logical extension can be one of the key strategies formulated by libraries and the academy to address a significant problem of cost and scale. Academic libraries are stepping up to this challenge by reexamining their roles in scholarly communications and, more recently, developing library publishing services. These initiatives are key new strategies that can prove critical in lowering the cost of textbooks. Scholarly communications libraries that focus on developing open-access journals, scholarly monographs, and digital projects have a developed infrastructure well suited to open textbook publishing. Similarly, library instruction programs developing integrative or embedded instruction strategies have developed key pedagogy and resource supports for faculty and students that are extremely well suited for open educational resource development and open textbook publishing.

Academic librarians, at the core of higher education's learning environment, are currently working with faculty to find alternative textbooks that are assembled from library and open-access resources and open textbooks that are free or freely distributed online textbooks. Shaping a combined library strategy with instruction and publishing that can reduce the cost of textbooks and a college education provides tremendous value across the academy. These initiatives are key new strategies that can prove critical in lowering the cost of textbooks and can support open-access goals to provide unrestricted access to scholarship. Open access and open textbooks are essential strategies to support the academy at a time when both the textbook market and higher education are experiencing significant transformation.

The Problem

The steady price increases of textbooks, with the GAO (2013) reporting, as stated earlier, an 82 percent increase between 2002 and 2012, has garnered scrutiny by many federal and state agencies, most attempting to understand why and what strategies could help reduce the cost of textbooks. In fact, from 2006 to 2007, one report lists the thirty-two states that considered legislation on textbooks, of which twelve had passed the legislation (OPPAGA 2008, 6–7). The federal government enacted significant legislation in the 2008 Higher Education Opportunity Act (HEOA; www.gpo.gov/fdsys/pkg/PLAW-110publ315/pdf/PLAW-110publ315.pdf), which required colleges to list the ISBNs of textbooks. Although this requirement was intended to make it easier for students to comparison-shop, it also served as a warning that change was essential. Nevertheless, textbook costs continued to increase steadily by about 6 percent annually (GAO 2013).

Library staff are familiar with the textbook cost problem; students often complain about the cost of textbooks or the short loan periods for textbooks on course reserves; students often go to lengths to borrow the textbooks from other libraries using interlibrary loan and accrue overdue fines because they don't return the books until the end of the semester. If this sounds like a familiar problem, the problem is far more serious. One recent study reported that 37 percent students did not purchase required textbooks and over 23 percent of students indicated that they did not register for a class because of the high cost of textbooks (Morris-Babb and Henderson 2012, 150). Students seeking alternative editions also risk the quality of their learning. Steven J. Bell, ACRL President 2012–2013, recounting the story of a student reading an older edition of a textbook, asks, "What sort of education system are we creating when a science major would prefer to learn with an outdated text?" (Bell 2012).

Textbook cost is not shouldered solely by students and their parents; the cost to libraries is much higher than expected. For instance, at the State University of New York (SUNY) at Geneseo, in addition to purchasing $2,500 in textbooks each year and staffing to support course reserves, Milne Library spends money to borrow textbooks using interlibrary loan. Our textbooks on reserve program covers about 73 percent of the titles required at SUNY Geneseo. These are an extremely high-use and scarce resource: 787 unique titles were checked out 12,561 times last year, a 203 percent increase from the previous year. Although having textbooks on reserve is a much-needed service, it doesn't scale effectively for budgetary reasons, as well as the physical limitations of sharing high-use items and the weightiness of managing overdue fines.

From August 2011 to March 15, 2012, some 3,012 textbook requests were filled, about 15 percent of interlibrary loan requests for returnables. Students requested an average of five textbooks via interlibrary loan, and the total cost of filling those requests was roughly $1,472 in lending charges, not including lost book billing, staff, or delivery costs. It is obvious that the current model is expensive for students and libraries, and as a result, innovative solutions are needed.

Faculty selecting textbooks for courses may not be as familiar with the problem caused by expensive textbooks to access to higher education and to the quality of learning. However, the Student Public Interest Research Groups (Student PIRGs) are trying to change that by providing students with outreach material to promote campus and faculty awareness of the cost of textbooks. Student PIRGs in particular highlight that the average annual cost of textbooks is approximately $1,200, and they suggest a variety of alternative strategies to students and faculty (Senack 2014, 4). Other agencies are also trying to encourage awareness of the issue of costly textbooks. Some states have passed legislation that encourage faculty to reduce textbook costs. However, the challenge of implementing this type of legislation without adequate support or outreach cannot be overlooked. After California passed such legislation, the California State Auditor interviewed some faculty and found few were aware of the law and "many did not understand how their textbook selection decisions and priorities could affect student costs" (Howle 2008, 2). A 2009 survey of Florida faculty and administrators found that only 7 percent of faculty were very familiar with open-access textbooks, and 52 percent were not at all familiar with open-access textbooks (Morris-Babb and Henderson 2012).

Initially, increased awareness and innovation was slow, however, much progress is being made across the academy and country. For example, to promote the discovery of open textbooks, the University of Minnesota recently launched an Open Textbook Library (https://open.umn.edu/opentextbooks) and has incentivized its faculty to write reviews of the titles. OER Commons (www.oercommons.org) and other resources are making it easier to find open educational resources. One of the earliest developments, the Multimedia Educational Resource for Learning and Online Teaching (MERLOT; www.merlot.org/merlot/index.htm), began in 1997, and by the time of the writing of this article, it has some 117,475 members, 42,631 materials and 3,844 peer reviews (MERLOT 2013).

Calls for the transformation of higher education often focus on expanding access and reducing the cost of college and universities. Although many faculty are producing and sharing their works widely on the Internet, open textbooks that lack traditional editorial services, such as peer review and copyediting, are less likely to be widely adopted. Therefore, libraries can lead in developing innovative publishing solutions to support students and faculty, authors and readers. Because textbook costs will likely only increase, libraries have a strategic opportunity to combine the efforts and benefits of library instruction and publishing initiatives to reduce the cost of college education and to support faculty production of high-quality open educational resources.

The Opportunity

Since the cost of textbooks is widely seen as a serious problem by students and has a costly impact on libraries, libraries are supporting the development of open educational resources and open textbooks. Libraries do this also because many support open access, the unrestricted access to scholarship. Open access and open textbooks are essential strategies that support the academy at a time when higher education and the textbook market are being disrupted:

> The textbook market is ripe for economically and technologically disruptive models…. Dysfunctional

> textbook economics, flexible format delivery, integrative course content delivery options, and the growing availability of new technologies associated with electronic textbooks can provide significant opportunities for innovators in the textbook marketplace, including libraries. (Raschke and Shanks 2011, 56)

Greg Raschke and Shelby Shanks identified textbook publishing as a significant opportunity for libraries. They also added an extremely important point about textbook publishing; it is dissimilar to traditional publishing and scholarship because it isn't "integrated so closely with promotion and tenure" (Raschke and Shanks 2011, 52). In other words, textbook publishing is a form of scholarship that may have more flexibility to evolve. Two examples of this evolution are the alternative textbook programs at UMass Amherst and Temple University libraries. In 2011, the University of Massachusetts Amherst Provost's Office and University Libraries launched a program offering faculty $1,000 per course to adopt resources that include open-access and library resources (UMass Amherst Libraries 2011). Temple University Libraries also began their program in 2011, with eleven faculty members granted $1,000 each to develop an online alternative to a textbook (DeSantis 2012).

Solving the textbook cost problem isn't simple and requires a suite of traditional and innovative strategies; however, the components for the development and use of open textbooks will likely involve all of the following:

- **Increased awareness and adoption of open educational resources.** Faculty need a trusted source of high-quality resources that aligns well to their teaching methods and goals. Currently, there is a wide array of directories and information:
  — College Open Textbooks Collaborative (http://collegeopentextbooks.org),
  — OpenStax (http://cnx.org),
  — MERLOT (www.merlot.org),
  — Open Textbook Library (https://open.umn.edu/opentextbooks),
  — OER Commons (www.oercommons.org),
  — Orange Grove (http://florida.theorangegrove.org/og/access/home.do), and

— our own Open SUNY Textbooks (http://opensuny.org). Determining how faculty will become increasingly aware of their choices and how OERs strengthen their curriculum resources requires a local communication strategy, as well as a distributed communication strategy.
- **Increased authoring of open educational resources.**
  — Faculty have options. Posting content to the Web is easier than before; however, faculty may want to author an alternative textbook, relying heavily on the expensive resources the library already subscribes and provides access to. Faculty may also be interested in authoring open educational resources and, specifically, open textbooks.
  — Author strategies vary; authors may develop an alternative textbook and later refine their work as a comprehensive open textbook. They may develop learning objects integrated into their learning management system that can later be combined to build an open textbook. Whichever the process the authors use, service options should be made as clear as possible at any institution. If they can be shared or distributed, the service can scale and leverage a greater set of expertise.
- **Increased support from library publishing services.** Libraries need to pilot their publishing services with projects and move promptly to iterative planning of services and roles required to use various publishing platforms and expertise. The workflow appears simple; however, each process has details to be developed and should be familiar to authors and reviewers: call for authors, selection by an editorial board, format of the reviews, editorial workflow as organized by the publishing platform, communication and marketing strategy, and assessment process.

Cooperative Pilot: Open SUNY Textbooks

Open SUNY Textbooks began as a multi-campus pilot program, funded by the State University of New York Innovative Instruction Technology Grant (IITG) and library funding. The program started with six libraries—College of Brockport, SUNY Environmental Sciences and Forestry,

SUNY Fredonia, SUNY Geneseo, University @ Buffalo Libraries, and Upstate University—interested in developing publishing services that focus on open-access textbooks. The program goals are to reduce textbook costs in higher education and to establish a faculty/librarian publishing program for producing high-quality open textbooks that is both scalable and sustainable. Open SUNY Textbooks' library publishing model is unique because it focuses on open-access textbook publishing and uses a distributed network approach: representatives of participating libraries contributed staff time, often the library directors in setting up the program. From SUNY Geneseo's Milne Library, the author of this chapter served as the principal investigator (PI), and much of the infrastructure was established with Geneseo's publishing team.

The concept for editorial review began with the idea of inviting SUNY Distinguished Faculty members to serve on an editorial board. However, because the grant funding had time constraints, it was clear a one-year timeline could not support both a call for editors and a call for authors. Rather, participating qualified library directors and librarians would serve as the editorial advisory board for the manuscript proposal selection process. The PI and the advisory board developed the guidelines and call for authors, as well as an evaluation rubric for the proposed manuscripts. The program design requirements included peer review and copyediting, essential services to ensuring this pilot program would produce high-quality textbooks.

Each process required developing our own set of guidelines, establishing processes, identifying roles, and assigning tasks. The Open SUNY Textbooks pilot benefitted from periodic consultation with Donna Dixon, co-Director of SUNY Press. They explained their editorial workflow for scholarly monographs and shared example documents from their process.

One of the formidable challenges we faced in the program was accepting proposals from all disciplines. This required a broad base of disciplinary expertise, a role for which librarians are perfectly suited. However, it also meant accepting a variety of manuscript style guides and format types (e.g., Word, LaTeX, etc.). We wanted this program to include all disciplines because the pilot was designed to explore the textbook publishing environment at SUNY. This exploration gave us ample opportunity to develop instruments for editorial workflow and templates for improving the authoring and production workflow.

Call for Authors and Selection

The IITG grant and library funding provided an incentive to authors and reviewers. We compensated selected authors who released their work with a Creative Commons license: CC-BY-SA-NC unported 3.0. The basic author incentive was $3,000; however, if the author incorporated students in the production of the textbooks and assessed their learning, we added another $1,000. This strategy gave us an opportunity to see what students would learn about the authoring process and enabled faculty to test their work with the intended learner audience.

We sent the call for open textbook authors as an e-mail to the SUNY Chief Academic Officer e-mail list, and from there it was sent out to each campus, reaching more than 34,000 faculty members among the sixty-four SUNY campus system. The call for authors was also posted as a PDF using our instance of Open Monograph Press (OMP). Within two weeks, we received thirty-eight excellent proposals for open textbooks; two submissions were received in OMP, the others via e-mail. We soon realized how many exceptional proposals the program received, and because grant funding limited publishing to four textbooks, the College of Brockport, SUNY ESF, SUNY Fredonia, and SUNY Geneseo libraries contributed additional funding, enabling us to approve the development of fifteen textbooks.

During fall 2013, the SUNY Open Textbooks pilot began to publish the fifteen open textbooks by faculty representing nine SUNY schools and many disciplines: anthropology, business, computer science, education, English, geological sciences, mathematics, music education, and physics. In fact, during Open Access Week, October 20-24, 2013, we released the first two: *Literature, the Humanities, and Humanity* by Theodore Steinberg, and *Native Peoples of North America* by Susan Stebbins. One week after publishing the first two of the fifteen open textbooks, our Open SUNY Textbooks catalog had 1,349 new visitors, with 20 percent visiting from outside the United States. The sixteenth open textbook in Open SUNY Textbooks will be about the program, providing all the plans, documents, templates, and information on how this process worked and what lessons were learned.

Editorial Workflow and Design

The program uses Open Monograph Press as the publishing platform and plans to host both PDF and EPUB open textbook editions. The program design involves SUNY faculty authors and faculty reviewers and includes librarians and library staff providing editorial work, serving as managing and acquisition editors, copy editors, and graphic designers. In addition, consultation services are being provided by an instructional designer and SUNY Press.

The basic editorial workflow for the Open SUNY Textbooks pilot was generally as follows:

1. Open SUNY Textbooks issues call for authors.
2. Author sends manuscript proposal.
3. Participating Open SUNY Textbooks team reviews and evaluates proposals using a rubric.
4. Team sends approval and revise/resubmit notification.
5. Author writes manuscript.
6. Author submits manuscripts to editors for peer reviewer feedback.
7. Author accepts or rejects reviewer feedback and revises manuscript.
8. Editor receives manuscript and sends to copy editor (librarian or freelance copy editor).
9. Author accepts or rejects copy editor's feedback and managing editor's comments.
10. Text layout is done.
11. Author and librarian review final proof to approve publication.
12. Libraries market publication.

Instructional design services were offered to the authors, and for those interested, the instructional designer discussed types of interactivity and media authors might want for their textbooks. Although the results are in process, the discussions developed a guide and template of seven interactive devices that are available to the Open SUNY Textbooks program, including multiple-choice quiz with feedback, concept map, images, slideshow, movie, tables, and audio (available at: http://opensuny.org/omp/index.php/SUNYOpenTextbooks/information/authors). One of the planned textbooks, on geological science, will initially be published, like the others, in PDF and EPUB formats, but it will then serve as a proof-of-concept for a completely interactive e-book that includes modular customization and learning analytics.

The program is finalizing the publication of fifteen textbooks and is about to start another call for authors, thanks to IITG renewal of grant funding. This time, the amount is $60,000, and the target is a mix of addressing heavy-enrollment courses and adding to the variety of subjects. This next grant phase will increase our awareness of marketing, which is a critical component for any publishing program. One of the main ideas we are looking forward to testing is a new acquisitions editorial workflow that leverages campus expertise about the market for a textbook. The innovative review will invite campus departments to review blind abstract proposals for the manuscripts in their discipline and, using a rubric and interview, evaluate the strengths and weaknesses and the likelihood that the open textbook would be adopted by that department. Department liaisons and other librarians will be invited to have these conversations with colleagues at various SUNY institutions, enabling an aggregation of proposal review data to better inform which project to select and which project is most likely to be adopted. We also hope that these conversations will reinforce the library instruction and departmental discussions of curriculum and resource needs. These conversations are vital; faculty are increasingly aware of the competition that is making academics vulnerable:

> Publishers do, however, hoard enormous war chests from sales of educational materials, and we should question whether they have taken control of teaching and learning processes that would be more appropriately owned and overseen by academics....
>
> I could self-publish the book online under a Creative Commons license that allows noncommercial use but not remixing. Ultimately, I chose this latter publishing model because it gave me the greatest control over my project and the potential for the greatest impact....
>
> We need to realize our power as authors and publishers. Working collaboratively, we can create dynamic teaching and learning environments. (Moxley 2013)

The most important connections librarians are making with publishing services are ensuring the future of teaching and learning and a friendly academic future for authors and readers. Furthermore, the opportunity to collaborate in the transformation of educational resources from various proprietary learning management systems and expensive packaging toward open educational resources leads toward a sustainable future for the academy.

Conclusion

As libraries develop their publishing services, the potential for solving real-world challenging issues, such as addressing unsustainable high-cost textbooks and lowering the cost of college access, also provides an opportunity to shape the transformation of higher education. Publishing pilots provide an opportunity to test new ideas and develop expertise across the academy; each iteration provides an opportunity to refine the model to improve its efficiency and effectiveness. Without doubt, librarians can effectively serve various roles to support authors with critical services that in turn offer readers high-quality open textbooks. Open textbook production requires a team, and librarians have the interest and expertise for the various roles, whether as editor, copy editor, instructional designer, or person responsible for text layout. By leading the development process and managing the editorial workflow of creating open-access textbooks, libraries provide tremendous value to their institution and to the global community of learners. Collaborating faculty and librarians are creating viable alternatives to textbooks and providing an answer to the call for transformation of higher education to both expand access and reduce education costs.

Appendix 8.1. Various federal and state agencies reviewing cost of textbooks, some strategic responses added for context

Agency/Institution	Year	Documents
US Government Accounting Office (GAO)	2005	*College Textbooks: Enhanced Offerings Appear to Drive Recent Price Increases,* GAO-05-806. Report to Congressional Requesters. Washington, DC, GAO, July. www.gao.gov/products/GAO-05-806.
US Congress (111th)	2009	Learning Opportunities with Creation of Open Source Textbooks (LOW COST) Act of 2009, H.R. 1464, 111th Congress (2009). https://www.govtrack.us/congress/bills/111/hr1464/text. Died.
US Congress (111th)	2010	Open College Textbook Act of 2010, H.R. 4575, 111th Congress (2010). https://www.govtrack.us/congress/bills/111/hr4575. Died.
US Government Accounting Office (GAO)	2013	*College Textbooks: Students Have Greater Access to Textbook Information,* GAO-13-368. Report to Congressional Committees. Washington, DC: GAO, June. www.gao.gov/products/GAO-13-368.
US Department of Education	2008	Higher Education Opportunity Act (HEOA) <link to http://www2.ed.gov/policy/highered/leg/hea08/index.html>
US Congress (110th)	2008	Higher Education Opportunity Act, Pub. L. No. 110-315, 122 Stat. 3078 (2008). www.gpo.gov/fdsys/pkg/PLAW-110publ315/pdf/PLAW-110publ315.pdf.
US Department of Education	2009	"Higher Education Opportunity Act Information Page," http://www2.ed.gov/policy/highered/leg/hea08/index.html.
US Department of Education Advisory Committee on Student Financial Assistance	2007	*Turn the Page: Making College Textbooks More Affordable.* Washington, DC: US Department of Education, May. http://www2.ed.gov/about/bdscomm/list/acsfa/turnthepage.pdf
Illinois Board of Higher Education, Student Advisory Committee	2005	"Textbook Affordability Recommendations." Minutes of the meeting of the Illinois Board of Higher Education, August 2005. www.ibhe.state.il.us/Board/agendas/2005/August/SAC%20textbook%20item.pdf (page now discontinued).

Appendix 8.1. Various federal and state agencies reviewing cost of textbooks, some strategic responses added for context

Agency/Institution	Year	Documents
State Council of Higher Education for Virginia	2006	*A Report on Textbook Purchasing Practices and Costs in the Commonwealth*. Richmond: State Council of Higher Education for Virginia, January 10. http://www.schev.edu/Reportstats/2006TextbookStudy.pdf
Minnesota Office of Higher Education	2007	*Strategies for Reducing Students' Textbook Costs*. St. Paul: Minnesota Office of Higher Education, February. http://archive.leg.state.mn.us/docs/2007/other/070189.pdf.
University of Wisconsin System	2007	Office of Operations Review and Audit. *Textbook Costs in Higher Education: Program Review*. Madison: University of Wisconsin System, April. http://www.uwsa.edu/audit/textbookcosts.pdf.
California State Auditor	2008	Howle, Elaine. *Affordability of College Textbooks: Textbook Prices Have Risen Significantly in the Last Four Years, but Some Strategies May Help to Control These Costs for Students*, Report 2007-116. Sacramento, CA: Bureau of State Audits, August. www.bsa.ca.gov/pdfs/reports/2007-116.pdf.
New York State Comptroller	2008	*Textbook Pricing Disparities*. Albany, NY: Office of the State Comptroller, 2008. http://www.osc.state.ny.us/reports/highered/textbookpricing12-18-08.pdf.
Florida Office of Program Policy Analysis and Government Accountability	2008	*Options Exist to Address the Rising Cost of Textbooks for Florida's College Students*, Report 08-29. Tallahassee, FL: OPPAGA, April. www.oppaga.state.fl.us/Reports/pdf/0829rpt.pdf.
Florida legislature	2009	Created Florida Distance Learning Consortium and tasked to plan development of open-access textbooks.
Florida Distance Learning Consortium (FDLC)	2010	*Open Access Textbook Task Force: Final Report*. Tallahassee: FDLC, February 27. http://www.fldlc.org/pdfFiles/OATTF_Final_Report_All_sections[CORRECTED.pdf

Appendix 8.1. Various federal and state agencies reviewing cost of textbooks, some strategic responses added for context

Agency/Institution	Year	Documents
University of Michigan Library	2010	Nicholls, Natsuko Hayashi. *The Investigation into the Rising Cost of Textbooks: A Background Study of the Context of Michigan Initiatives with an Eye Toward Launching a Library-based College Textbook Publishing Program*. Ann Arbor: University of Michigan Library, April 2009, updated January 2010. http://www.lib.umich.edu/files/SPOTextbookBackground.pdf

Works Cited

Bell, Steven J. 2012. "Coming in the Back Door: Leveraging Open Textbooks to Promote Scholarly Communications on Campus." *Journal of Librarianship and Scholarly Communication* 1, no. 1: eP1040. doi:10.7710/2162-3309.1040.

DeSantis, Nick. 2012. "Temple U. Project Ditches Textbooks for Homemade Digital Alternatives." *Wired Campus* (blog), *Chronicle of Higher Education*, February 7. http://chronicle.com/blogs/wiredcampus/temple-project-ditches-textbooks-for-homemade-digital-alternatives/35247.

Florida Virtual Campus. 2012. *2012 Florida Student Textbook Survey*. Tallahassee, FL: Florida Virtual Campus.

GAO (US Government Accountability Office). 2005. *College Textbooks: Enhanced Offerings Appear to Drive Recent Price Increases*, GAO-05-806. Report to Congressional Requesters. Washington, DC: GAO, July. www.gao.gov/products/GAO-05-806.

———. 2013: *College Textbooks: Students Have Greater Access to Textbook Information*, GAO-13-368. Report to Congressional Committees. Washington, DC: GAO, June. www.gao.gov/products/GAO-13-368.

Howle, Elaine (California State Auditor). 2008. *Affordability of College Textbooks: Textbook Prices Have Risen Significantly in the Last Four Years, but Some Strategies May Help to Control These Costs for Students*, Report 2007-116. Sacramento, CA: Bureau of State Audits, August. www.bsa.ca.gov/pdfs/reports/2007-116.pdf.

Malenfant, Kara. 2008. "ACRL and SPARC Announce Speakers for Forum on Open Educational Resources." *ACRL Insider* (blog), December 16. www.acrl.ala.org/acrlinsider/archives/320.

MERLOT (Multimedia Educational Resource for Learning and Online Teaching). 2013. Member Results search page, www.merlot.org/merlot/members.htm; Material Results search page, www.merlot.org/merlot/materials.htm; Peer Review Results search page, www.merlot.org/merlot/reviews.htm. Accessed September 23, 2014.

Morris-Babb, Meredith, and Susie Henderson. 2012. "An Experiment in Open-Access Textbook Publishing: Changing the World One Textbook at a Time." *Journal of Scholarly Publishing* 43, no. 2 (January): 148–55. doi:10.1353/scp.2012.0002.

Moxley, Joe. 2013. "Open Textbook Publishing." *Bulletin of the American Association of University Professors* 99, no. 5 (September–October). www.aaup.org/article/

open-textbook-publishing#.VAHh7fldXh5.

OPPAGA (Office of Program Policy Analysis and Government Accountability). 2008. *Options Exist to Address the Rising Cost of Textbooks for Florida's College Students*, Report 08-29. Tallahassee, FL: OPPAGA, April. www.oppaga.state.fl.us/Reports/pdf/0829rpt.pdf.

Raschke, Greg, and Shelby Shanks. 2011. "Water on a Hot Skillet: Textbooks, Open Educational Resources, and the Role of the Library." In "No Shelf Required Guide to E-Book Purchasing," special issue, *Library Technology Reports* 47, no. 8: 52–57.

Senack, Ethan. 2014. *Fixing the Broken Textbook Market: How Students Respond to High Textbook Costs and Demand Alternatives*. Washington, DC: Student Public Interest Research Groups. www.studentpirgs.org/reports/sp/fixing-broken-textbook-market. Citing information from College Board. 2014. "Average Estimated Undergraduate Budgets, 2013–14." Trends in College Pricing. http://trends.collegeboard.org/college-pricing/figures-tables/average-estimated-undergraduate-budgets-2013-14.

Stebbins, Susan. 2013. *Native Peoples of North America*. Open SUNY Textbooks. http://opensuny.org/omp/index.php/SUNYOpenTextbooks/catalog/book/75.

Steinberg, Theodore. 2013. *Literature, the Humanities, and Humanity*. Open SUNY Textbooks. http://opensuny.org/omp/index.php/SUNYOpenTextbooks/catalog/book/76.

UMass (University of Massachusetts) Amherst Libraries. 2011. "Taking a Bite Out of Textbook Costs." News release, December 1. www.library.umass.edu/about-the-libraries/news/press-releases-2011/taking-a-bite-out-of-textbook-costs.

CHAPTER 9

More Than Consumers
Students as Content Creators

Amy Buckland

Thinking of our students as future researchers offers libraries many reasons to support those students as creators in the scholarly publishing world. The peer-review process helps students better understand critical discourse. The submission and acceptance process helps them learn about their rights as creators. Their participation in the publishing process develops their presence in the academic world, giving them oh-so-important "street cred" as academics. But other than writing a dissertation and the occasional conference proceeding, college and university students typically participate in the scholarly publishing continuum as consumers. Libraries have long helped students become better consumers by teaching them about authority and authenticity in publishing (be that online or in print) and are key to growing informed graduates. Currently, libraries are able to support a different role for students in this continuum—that of creator. This support can come in many different forms,

This work is licensed under the Creative Commons Attribution License 4.0 (CC-BY 4.0).

from instruction around author rights and the publishing process itself, to launching student-run peer-reviewed journals, to making student work available through a repository.

These opportunities for engagement with our community present libraries as a partner instead of simply a resource. We are central to the education of these junior scholars, whether or not they choose to stay in the research and publishing realm. Partnering with students also helps us keep our services "plugged in" to their needs and better support the teaching and learning mission of the institution.

Both student-run journals and repository deposit are important as library publishing services, but there are even more ways to support students' participation in the scholarly community. A significant amount of outreach, from information literacy workshops, to embedded librarians, to curriculum services, all can, and should, incorporate scholarly publishing issues:

- Understanding the concept of peer review, in all of its variations, and why that has long been the foundation for scholarly publishing, will introduce students to the concepts of critical discourse and public scholarship.
- Author rights are increasingly important in this age of open access, funding mandates, and the growing critique of traditional publishing models. Librarians are all too familiar with the issues around copyright transfer agreements and are well positioned to open the discussion with students. This discussion also opens the door to a discussion about attribution and the difference between copyright infringement and plagiarism.
- Discussions of online privacy can be enhanced through a frank conversation about student's online presence as professionals, which ties in well with creating a public profile as a scholar through publishing.
- Exploring different publishing environments also helps students find their "tribe". Before deciding where to publish, students can evaluate the resources available to them and truly find the right place for their research. This is especially important for graduate students who are looking to continue their career in academia. They want to be well-positioned in their field, and that may mean publishing solely in open-access journals or working with publishers that encourage new forms of publishing.

Incorporating the concepts of critical discourse, evaluation of resources, and participation in the scholarly conversation is what libraries do. Add two of the most frequent ways libraries support student publishing (student-run peer-reviewed journals and making work available through an institutional repository), and we have a solid setting to ensure that future researchers are prepared for public scholarship.

Student Work in Repositories

Libraries have a long history of supporting access to student work by making theses and dissertations available to the public. In the past, indexing and microfilming via third parties like UMI (University Microfilms International) and covering the costs for services like ProQuest's Dissertations and Theses Database (PQDT) positioned students within the scholarly sphere. The transition to in-house digitization services, born-digital workflows, and homegrown repositories is an example of the library's commitment to student success. Be it dissertations, working papers, capstone projects, or honors undergrad work, it can find a home in a repository. There is much debate as to whether making work available through a repository is truly publishing, but it is generally understood that it is publishing insofar as distributing a creator's work to a wider audience is publishing. Making work available via a repository places students within the scholarly community of their institution—offering them a place at the table, helping them create an online presence as researchers.

Theses and dissertations are often easy to collect and make available in a repository because there is no third party (publisher) that must give permission to make the work available. (Institutions may also have other requirements, including deposit in PQDT, various fees, etc.) Some institutions make the work available immediately while others offer students an embargo period for their work, when it is available only on campus, like other licensed resources. Much debate has ensued about whether embargoes are a good idea for students, with groups like the American Historical Association wading in to the debate. The AHA wants to see a six-year embargo for dissertations (AHA 2013), claiming that junior scholars are having difficulty publishing their first monograph as the dissertation, on which it is usually based, is publicly available. This is a spurious argument as there is nothing but anecdotal proof that university presses won't publish worked derived from a dissertation (Patton 2013). University presses put pressure on graduates to buy in completely to the publish-or-perish model of scholarship, creating another generation of scholars who are beholden to institutional tenure and promotion policies instead of seeking new ways of sharing their scholarship.

Inclusion in the repository positions students as part of the institutional community, giving them an online presence for their professional lives. Some institutions have seen push-back on this front from senior academics, concerned that their work would be found alongside student work, and restricted the deposited works to solely PhD dissertations. Including master's theses, and even undergraduate work, however, is a way to prepare students for their future as scholars. Depositing your work in a repository, alongside that of famous alumni and respected scholars, gives another dimension to the value of the work. Students may be more careful and critical of their work. Librarians are well poised to help them evaluate their sources, learn more about attribution, and look at how their work fits within the discipline.

Booth (2012) sees the repository as a pedagogical tool:

> If scholarship thrives on the exchange of ideas in public forums, it is critical to introduce students to the complicated experience of contributing to open discourse and mentor them in the social/academic accountability it entails.

Making student work available via the repository gives librarians the chance to discuss access issues when it comes to research work. Helping students understand the information economy and how institutional membership really is a privilege when it comes to accessing quality information is a discussion that needs to happen more often. Understanding that their work will be publicly available, and that those without institutional affiliation rely on such works, will raise the level of discussion that currently happens only at the faculty level. (Some schools have taken to using events like Open Access Week to teach students how to find scholarly OA resources they will have access to post-graduation, when they no longer have an academic library's resources at their fingertips.

Tying discussions around access to scholarly information to information on depositing in an open-access repository positions students as part of the solution, not the problem.)

In the University of Illinois system, the Ethnography of the University Initiative (www.eui.illinois.edu) integrates original student research into current classes and workshops. Not only does student work find a home in UI's repository, Illinois Digital Environment for Access to Learning and Scholarship (IDEALS), but groups on campus are encouraged to make use of this work in their current teaching and learning. Students are able to watch their work complete the scholarly publishing cycle, from creation, to use, to re-creation. EUI also hosts student conferences, offering yet another opportunity for students to join the conversation as researchers and scholars.

Student-Run Journals

Student-run journals are one of the most obvious examples of a need for publishing support, and another way for students to join the scholarly conversation. In these instances, the library offers varying levels of support (from hosting various publishing software all the way to advising on how to create an editorial board). Learning about peer review and the editorial process helps develop critical thinking and improve writing skills. Developing copyright policies for the journal helps students understand author rights and intellectual property issues. Participation of a faculty member to oversee and advise the journal ensures the library/department liaison model is sustainable and furthers strengthens ties between the two campus units.

As part of their role in the university community, students are familiar with having their work evaluated—be that by a professor distributing grades or by peers when workshopping papers in writing courses. Formalized peer review adds another layer to the process. Instead of being driven solely by grades, students must keep in mind the readability of their writing, authority of their arguments, and clarity of their voice. Peer review also offers students the opportunity to revise their work and address the queries of their colleagues, something that is not found in the typical class-based writing. On top of the review process, the knowledge that this writing will be publicly available increases the importance of proper attribution, solid research, and a grasp of how this work fits in the discourse of the discipline.

Part of the publishing process involves copyright and intellectual property issues. Participating in a student-run journal gives students the chance to explore these rights issues from the viewpoints of both the publisher and the author. Including an image from an article in your term paper requires proper attribution to avoid plagiarism charges. Including an image from one article for inclusion in another that is to be published might require more than just attribution—the student may need to go through the process of getting rights for republication. Here the library can step in to discuss copyright transfer agreements and author rights and begin (or further) discussions around open-access publishing. As publishers, students begin to learn the logistics of scholarly publishing: the importance of copyediting and layout, production timelines, indexing and findability of the journal, and the concept of credibility when it comes to journals (especially student journals).

Many libraries offer journal-hosting services, where the library manages software and contractual agreements (sometimes paired with the repository). This helps lower the barrier for publishing by giving students a platform for making their work available. Libraries also help with ISSN registration, getting the journal listed in sources like DOAJ and Ulrich's and included in aggregators such as EBSCO, increasing the credibility of the journal by making it exist outside of the university URL.

One of the concepts taught to students when they are evaluating a resource is how to determine authority. Part of this authority can stem from the length of time a journal has been published. Continuity is important not just for metrics like impact factor, but also to establish credibility—a journal can't simply exist for a year and then be shuttered. Partnerships with faculties or departments help prevent the fly-by-night publication of journals. These agreements can range from a yearly publication of students' capstone projects to ongoing journals that publish quarterly. The importance is that there is someone in the faculty who will ensure that when the current editors of the journals graduate, there is someone to step into their place. This continuity is useful when discussing the importance of editorial boards, considering the difference between editors and editorial board members, and determining the vision of the journal. Faculty advisors (be they professors or librarians) are a great resources for student-run journals—their familiarity with the publishing process, as well as their direct interest in student success, can help smooth the waters when issues arise.

Many institutions publish an undergraduate research journal. Offering a space that is not discipline-specific can be more welcoming to students who may be hesitant to make their work public. The *Journal of Purdue Undergraduate Research* (http://docs.lib.purdue.edu/jpur) has student authors, editors, and designers, with faculty advisors. The journal has support from the library and Purdue University Press, as well as Purdue Marketing and Media and the Online Writing Lab. Partnering with writing groups on campus can cement the journal as part of the overall learning experience at the institution. Partnering with writing-intensive courses is another opportunity for libraries to support publishing. When students know that their final project of the year will be published in the annual volume of the undergraduate journal, they have more incentive to take advantage of library resources from the start, as opposed to trying to modify a paper for publication later in the process.

Graduate student publications frequently have long histories on campus and are a prime opportunity for library publishing support. As opposed to undergraduates, grad students have taken the next step in their participation in the scholarly community, with many deciding that joining the research or academic life is their goal. Grad students are able to take on more responsibility than their junior colleagues and are more familiar with the state of their discipline.

At UCLA, the library partnered with the Graduate Students Association to digitize the full runs of graduate student journals—increasing access and ensuring preservation by depositing them in the Internet Archive. This practice falls perfectly in line with the mandate of many libraries to digitize and preserve the institution's unique content—be that rare manuscripts or born-digital information. The GSA has also liaised with the library to offer a series of lunchtime workshops looking at issues around scholarly communication and publishing.

The Journal Incubator project (www.journalincubator.org) at the University of Lethbridge is an example of teaching students the skills required for publishing from a purely production angle. At Lethbridge, students learn production skills working on a suite of journals, all funneled through the same production office. In this instance, the focus is on managing the peer-review process, managing revisions, copyediting, doing layout, and ultimately making the work available. All of this work is independent of the content (which is handled by subject specialists). Students learn transferable and sought-after skills while becoming familiar with the scholarly publishing process. From the library's point of view, an incubator-style service could be more nimble and easier to initially manage than rolling out a full-fledged publishing program and help standardize output of community publications. Having a single point of contact on campus for all publishing requests also makes the service much easier to promote. Combining activities like copyediting and layout design also saves resources and production costs for all journals involved in the incubator.

Intersections with Other Library Services

In "Riding the Wave: Open Access, Digital Publishing, and the Undergraduate Thesis," Miller (2013) discusses the required senior thesis seminar at Pomona College. In this article, he highlights another way the library can support student publishing—the seminar is co-taught by three librarians. Students develop a research topic with the ultimate goal of making it available in Claremont Colleges' repository—the students' first foray into publicly sharing their work. Librarians help students craft their research topic, evaluate primary and secondary sources, and craft their thesis—all while thinking about the scholarly publishing world from the start, instead of as an afterthought.

At McGill, librarians are part of the Arts Undergraduate Research Fair, where they present on a number of topics, including student publishing. Jones and Canuel (2013) prepared a workshop discussing the benefits of student publishing. Focusing on building a professional profile and understanding how being a published author can be a competitive advantage when applying to grad school or on the job market, the workshop was well received. Following the first workshop, a number of students approached the library publishing unit on campus with ideas for new student-run journals.

At Pacific University, the library has worked with faculty in the English department to create a minor in editing and publishing for undergraduates. Virtually housed in the Editing and Publishing Center, the courses meet the interests of students looking for opportunities to work on their editing and publishing skills. The library's course, Introduction to Scholarly Journal Publishing, directly connects the library's journal publishing services with students, giving them an opportunity to discuss scholarly publishing for credit. Tying it into other courses already on offer, the university was able to create a cohesive curriculum on the topic of scholarly publishing. The library found this a useful advocacy tool, as well as a chance to present scholarly publishing as more than something that is done solely at the university. Gilman (2013) reports that student evaluations frequently mentioned that students learned things in the course that they probably would not have otherwise.

In the *Library Publishing Directory* (Lippincott 2013), a number of institutions report supporting student-run journals. Of particular note is an initiative at Cal Poly, San Luis Obispo, where there are plans to hire an Endowed Digital Scholarship Services Student Assistant to offer opportunities for students to work on digital publishing issues from within the library. This initiative is one that could be easily replicated and would make a useful practicum for libraries affiliated with LIS programs. Future librarians are both interested and equipped to begin delving in to the scholarly publishing landscape—offering them a place in the library to get real-world experience on these issues, while supporting scholarly publishing, is an appealing way to encourage student involvement.

Is It Really That Easy?

There are, of course, challenges with supporting students as creators. Objections may be raised regarding the quality of student work. Faculty are hesitant to have their names alongside those of students in the repository—as the implication might be they are of equal value. It is true that not all student work is publishable. Many students attend university with no intention of becoming researchers or academics or even going on to a life that requires scholarly writing on a regular basis. Teaching them about the scholarly publishing system, however, has value beyond students-as-authors. Learning to fully understand the system through participation in a student-run journal, by having their work made available in a repository, or even simply learning about how the peer-review process can add an extra level of authority to articles, ensures that students become better information consumers. Their ability to critically evaluate what they read is instantly valuable in all aspects of life, regardless of their profession.

It is true that institutions have students as a captive audience for only a few years, depending on the degree (and how long ABD status can be maintained), so it is doubly important that discussions about scholarly publishing become a standard part of all library outreach. Information literacy cannot happen without evaluating the environment in which information is presented. Discussions around authority on the Internet can use traditional scholarly models as their basis. Libraries are able to participate in growing a more informed community for only a short amount of time; we must take advantage of the opportunity as soon as it presents itself.

Works Cited

AHA (American Historical Association). 2013. "American Historical Association Statement on Policies Regarding the Embargoing of Completed History PhD Dissertations." *AHA Today* (blog), July 22. http://blog.historians.org/2013/07/american-historical-association-statement-on-policies-regarding-the-embargoing-of-completed-history-phd-dissertations.

Booth, Char. 2012. "Project Curve, Part Seven: Open Access Publishing for Learner Engagement (AKA OA FTW)." *info-mational* (blog), April 26. http://infomational.wordpress.com/2012/04/26/oaftw.

Gilman, Isaac. 2013. "Scholarly Communication for Credit: Integrating Publishing Education into Undergraduate Curriculum." In *Common Ground at the Nexus of Information Literacy and Scholarly Communication*, edited by Stephanie Davis-Kahl and Merinda Kate Hensley, 75-92. Chicago: Association of College and Research Libraries.

Jones, Julie, and Robin Canuel. 2013. "Supporting the Dissemination of Undergraduate Research: An Emerging Role for Academic Librarians." In *Imagine, Innovate, Inspire: The Proceedings of the ACRL 2013 Conference*, edited by Dawn M. Mueller, 538–45. Chicago: Association of College and Research Libraries.

Lippincott, Sarah K., ed. 2013. *Library Publishing Directory*. Atlanta: Library Publishing Coalition. www.librarypublishing.org/sites/librarypublishing.org/files/documents/LPC_LPDirectory2014.pdf

Mitchell, Catherine. 2014. "Libraries in the Publishing Game: New Roles from Content to Access." Panel presentation, ALA Annual Conference 2014, Las Vegas, NV, June 28.

Patton, Stacey. 2013. "Embargoes Can Go Only So Far to Help New PhDs Get Published, Experts Say." *Chronicle of Higher Education*, July 30. http://chronicle.com/article/Embargoes-Can-Go-Only-So-Far/140603.

CHAPTER 10

Archival APIs
Humanities Data Publishing and Academic Librarianship

Matt Burton and Korey Jackson

Introduction

Data publishing for humanities scholarship is a relatively new activity within the academic library. But it's becoming increasingly important to the work of humanities scholars, especially those working in the broad field of digital humanities. With the creation and aggregation of material like digital image and sound files, XML and XSLT files for textual markup, GIS data, and CSV and other data formats used for many different kinds of digital projects, humanists are increasingly participating in scholarship that produces digital information in need of organizing, vetting, sharing, and preserving—in other words: publishing.

That said, "publishing" is in no way a monolithic operation: there are any number of services and products that meet at the

This work is licensed under the Creative Commons Attribution License 4.0 (CC-BY 4.0).

intersection of data and publishing.[1] For one, specific data publications have been an expected part of scientific research for some time. And many enterprise-level responses to data publication have come from the public and private science sector.[2] These supplemental venues offer data content analogous to (and often cross-linked with) the typical journal article. Data sets—their collection and development—are discussed in detail by researchers, are vetted by reviewers, have appropriate metadata applied, and have final versions made available (with varying degrees of access) for sharing, reusing, and citing.

Rather than focus solely on these kinds of publications and publishing platforms, however, in this chapter, we are more interested in how the academic library can serve as a space for both "upstream" and final production of humanities data. In this way, the focus of our discussion comes closer to what has been called "data curation" than it does to more traditional data publication. This isn't to say that such publication doesn't have a place within the ecosystem of digital humanities data—it certainly does, as should be evident from our examples below—only that fostering such publishing is not currently in the library's wheelhouse, nor is it a prerequisite to helping scholars productively manage their data.

Data Curation as Data Publishing

Data curation has a long and multidisciplinary past. Palmer et al. (2013) offer a concise history of the rise of curatorial practices and informatics coming out of fields ranging from museum studies to genomics—a past that helps to surface data curation's discipline-agnostic roots and its recognition that all scholarly fields require the ongoing stewardship of research data.

Before we discuss how the humanities in particular can benefit from curatorial services, let's start with a definition of the term itself: *data*

1. The term data *publishing*, like so many terms used to characterize the management and stewardship of research data, is not without its critics. See Parsons and Fox 2013 for more on the general phraseology debate.
2. For examples, see Scientific Data, www.nature.com/scientificdata; Faculty of 1000, http://f1000.com; and the Dryad Digital Repository, http://datadryad.org.

curation is "the active and ongoing management of data through its lifecycle of interest and usefulness to scholarship, science, and education; curation activities enable data discovery and retrieval, maintain quality, add value, and provide for re-use over time" (Cragin et al. 2007). In other words, data curation resembles many of the activities essential to publishing: quality assurance, discovery, and added value through format enhancement.

This overlap between data curation and publishing has been productively examined by scholars like Trevor Muñoz (2013), whose blog post "Data Curation as Publishing for Digital Humanists" explores the ways that a "publishing-minded" approach to data can enable improved data management for humanities scholars. Additionally, Sayeed Choudhury, Joyce Ray, and Mike Furlough (2009), in "Digital Curation and E-Publishing: Libraries Make the Connection," make the case for uniting curatorial and publishing practices as a means of expanding the suite of services (and funding for those services) within the academic library.

We can safely assert, then, that curation of data is essential to new forms of humanities scholarship, and that such curation—in making data more accessible and more usable—constitutes a form of publishing. But the question that still needs to be answered is: what exactly are humanities data? Or, more specifically: what kinds of data are humanist scholars producing and consuming?

With the growing profile of digital humanities scholarship (and the rise in funding and institutional support for this scholarship), such questions have received more recent and widespread attention. In 2006, the American Council of Learned Societies commissioned a report from top scholars and administrators in the humanities and information studies. This report, *Our Cultural Commonwealth* (Welshons 2006), outlines the cyberinfrastructure needs of humanities and social science scholars and makes several recommendations about how to support their research at the institutional level. The second chapter of the report, "Challenges," begins, significantly, with data. And yet, many of the issues outlined in this chapter of the report have less to do with data management or curation than they do with digitization and preservation of the cultural record writ large.

While it comes as little surprise that large-scale digitization is a pressing need in digital humanities research, there is actually an interesting, if implicit, message here about the kinds of data that humanists value—and the point in the research life cycle when data curation might need to take place. The challenges highlighted in *Our Cultural Commonwealth* reveal that humanities data are distinct from other disciplinary outputs in their reliance on previously recorded documents (whether textual, visual, or aural). Raw humanities data tend to emphasize archives and collections of material rather than, say, measurements based on a series of specific lab-generated tests.[3] Letters to and from a particular author, court records, an artist's design drafts—humanities data are "big data" because they rely on "a critical mass of information" in order to understand "both the context and the specifics of an artifact or event" (Welshons 2006, 18–19). But more than simply big, humanities data are diverse data. And this is becoming even more the case as disciplinary boundaries blur and "scholars who in the past might have worked only with texts now turn to architecture and urban planning, art, music, video games, film and television, fashion illustrations, billboards, dance videos, graffiti, and blogs" (Welshons 2006, 19).

So what does this content expansion and disciplinary diffusion mean for humanities data publishing? For one, it means that the library will continue to be the center for humanities research data, and for humanities data services. Unlike observational or computational data typical of the sciences and social sciences, humanistic data rely heavily on their originating archive. This places the onus of curating data more squarely on the shoulders of special collections and archives, as well as researchers themselves. What we might call "camera-ready" archives—material collections that contain sufficient metadata and necessary markup for easy adaptation by digital scholars—are becoming increasingly central to digital humanities research methods. In other words, it's not enough to digitize; digital archives also need to be made ready for contemporary use as well.

Of course, it's unfair to say that libraries and librarians need to prepare their collections for new digital research methods without actually talking about what these methods are or about how specific projects might help (and are helping) spur wider construction of data publishing services for

---

3. The National Science Foundation's *Long-Lived Digital Data Collections: Enabling Research and Education in the 21st Century* (NSB 2005) identifies four separate categories of data for the purposes of institutional cyberinfrastructure: observational (measurements, surveys, etc.), computational (data based on simulation models); experimental (output from specific lab-generated experiments), and records (personal and public letters, court documents, etc.).

humanities scholarship. In the following sections, we explore varieties of digital research methods practiced by humanist scholars, then move on to a discussion of how archives can begin expanding data curation services to meet new methodological needs. In the end, we urge an approach to data publishing in the humanities that sets its sights on the archive itself, framing data publishing as generative rather than preservative, tool building rather than static warehousing of content.

Data and Humanities Research Methods

Data themselves are only part of the curation and publishing story. As Julia Flanders and Trevor Muñoz point out, "The unique features of curating digital humanities data encompass not only the data themselves but also the research methods and practices" (Flanders and Muñoz 2012, paragraph 19). Data in the digital humanities cannot be separated from the new generation of methods and research practices that create, curate, and process those data. As the objects and phenomena of humanistic inquiry are digitized—or increasingly born digital—digital humanities scholars turn to computational methods for manipulation and analysis (Wilkens 2012). With an ever-increasing abundance of digitized objects, techniques from computer science can find innovative application in the digital humanities (Jockers 2013). In the past decade, the disciplines of data mining, machine learning, and social network analysis have developed powerful and robust techniques for finding patterns within large volumes of data. Text mining and natural language processing can answer corpus-level research questions previously impossible due to challenges of access and time. Digitized text, image, and sound not only *afford* computational analysis; as their quantity increases, they'll *require* computational analysis.

The Unreasonable Effectiveness of Word Counts

While an extensive discussion of the computational methods being adopted in the digital humanities is beyond the scope of this chapter, we would like to introduce two, topic modeling and entity extraction, as concrete examples of the kinds of data-centric research practices that require data publishing and curation.[4]

Topic modeling is a catchall term for a group of computational techniques that, at a very high level, find patterns of co-occurring words in large collections of text. The word *topic* in this context can be somewhat misleading, as these topics are actually probabilistic distributions of words identified via a complex statistical model, that is, something that can be precisely specified mathematically—not the more humane "a matter dealt with in text; a subject." (New Oxford American Dictionary) Topic modeling transforms words and documents into numbers and finds patterns in those numbers, producing word lists—"topics"—and their proportion in each document. For the scholar, the output is an interesting (and sometimes surprising) new "reading" of texts. What makes topic modeling a powerful technique is its ability to find meaningfully coherent patterns without human assistance. This *unsupervised* approach to text mining gives scholars a means to explore and navigate a corpus far too large to read and without a substantial effort.

We see such an approach in Robert Nelson's (2011b) project "Mining the *Dispatch*." Nelson used topic modeling to "distantly read" one hundred thousand documents from the Richmond *Daily Dispatch*, a daily newspaper that ran from 1860 through 1865. From the model, Nelson was able to

---

4. It should be noted that we present these specific methods, and the broader application of computation to the analysis of humanist data, without critique. This is not to say digital humanities scholars, librarians, archivists, and administrators should take the claims of computation at face value; they should not. There are innumerable complexities in the cross-disciplinary application of computational methods, especially between the computational sciences and the humanities. Instead, we defer those discussions to the work of scholars like Stephen Ramsay (2011), whose book *Reading Machines* urges scholars to consider forms of "algorithmic criticism" or a critical, interpretive, and humanist understanding of algorithms, their subjective contexts, and their broader impact. Additionally, we recommend Katherine Hayles's (2012) book, *How We Think: Digital Media and Contemporary Technogenesis*, and the collection of talks and provocations from the Governing Algorithms conference held at NYU in the spring of 2013 (Governing Algorithms 2013).

trace the rise and fall of particular topics, like "anti-northern diatribes" or "fugitive slave ads," by their temporal distribution in the corpus.[5] Equipped with this high-level perspective on the *Dispatch*, Nelson could contextualize the identified patterns with historical understandings of Richmond during the Civil War.[6]

Topic-modeling algorithms typically process text in the form of document-level word counts.[7] As far as data needs are concerned, scholars do not necessarily need access to the raw sequences of text. Text analysis via word counts can produce significant insights. Ted Underwood (2013), a literary historian who uses topic modeling to study eighteenth- and nineteenth-century British literature, reminds us of their value in a blog post aptly titled "Wordcounts Are Amazing":

> We need to remember that words are actually features of a very, very high-level kind.... Working with text is like working with a video where every element of every frame has already been tagged, not only with nouns but with attributes and actions. If we actually had those tags on an actual video collection, I think we'd recognize it as an enormously valuable archive. The opportunities for statistical analysis are obvious! We have trouble recognizing the same opportunities when they present themselves in text, because we take the strengths of text for granted and only notice what gets lost in the analysis.

Techniques like topic modeling can, from mere word frequencies, construct surprising and delightful algorithmic "readings" of digital corpora.

Beyond the statistical manipulation of word counts, researchers in information retrieval and natural language processing (NLP) have developed robust techniques for a technique they call named-entity recognition (NER), which finds words (or word sequences) identifying

---

5. To see Nelson's data on this topic, see Nelson 2011a.
6. For example, the rise and fall of fugitive slave ads correlates with the campaigns that brought the Union army close to the city of Richmond.
7. The exact input format depends upon implementation; some require text sequences, others require a corpus-level word dictionary and document-level word counts.

people, places, or organizations within unstructured text. Literary scholar Matthew Wilkens (2011a) has used these techniques to find place names mentioned in novels from the Wright American Fiction collection.[8] Using geocoding and mapping software Wilkens was able to quickly extract and visualize the locations on a world map.[9]

What Wilkens found in the computationally generated map revealed more international locations and distinct clusters of locations, particularly in the American south, than he expected from a collection of distinctly American literature. What is particularly interesting is not the size of the corpus, but the speed by which Wilkens was able to process the text. While mapping the locations of thirty-seven books is entirely possible without computation, it wouldn't be achievable in a matter of hours (as was Wilkens's [2011a] case).

Computational techniques like topic modeling and named-entity recognition analyze digitized cultural materials at scale with unprecedented speed. However, such analysis requires preparation: texts must be digitized, tools must be configured, and infrastructure must be developed to enable this kind of research. As digital humanities scholars explore the methodological frontier, how can libraries support them?

If You Really Want It, Put an API on It! (Archival APIs)

The computational methods described above depend upon access to data in different forms. Humanities scholars can be quickly swamped in the data management challenges of arcane file formats or the computing needs for medium- to large-scale analysis. Libraries are well positioned to be the builders and maintainers of infrastructure to support data management, access, and curation. We argue application programming interfaces (APIs) are a vital gateway for supporting digital humanities methods and digital humanities data. Through APIs, libraries can support researchers in the digital humanities by making data repositories *usable* and *accessible*.

---

8. Only a third of which had been digitized at the time (IU 2013).
9. For more information, see Wilkens 2011b.

The API is a technical gateway enabling the automated exchange of information between software systems. APIs provide standard interfaces for computers to "talk" to one another without human intervention. API specifications—the design and documentation of APIs—enable remote software to automatically interact with an information system through requests for resources on a host system. APIs, in a perfect world, reduce human overhead when exchanging information across a network. Therefore, APIs could allow "self-service" data publishing of digital libraries, archives, or repositories, reducing the administrative costs or bottlenecks of sharing data with researchers. For example, New York Public Library has collected restaurant menus since 1900. Today they have an archive of over 45,000 menus dating back to the 1840s (NYPL 2013a). Digitized and formatted menus are available as structured data via a public API (NYPL 2013b). Programmers at NYPL used the API to build an application for browsing and searching the digital menu collection (NYPL 2013c). Because the API is public, other individuals or organizations can rapidly build their own applications for interacting with the digital collection.

The NYPL menu collection demonstrates how a library can be a data publisher. Data publishing through APIs directly supports digital humanities research, aligns with the service-centric mission of the library, and enables self-service access to digital collections and materials. Self-service reduces the procedural and structural overhead of access, a reduction that is necessary to support the rapid speed and scale of computational analysis. In a blog post provocatively titled "A Publisher's Job Is to Provide a Good API for Books" on technology publisher O'Reilly's *Tools of Change for Publishing* blog, Hugh McGuire (2013) argues that digital books are simply data and the publisher's job is to make those data accessible. What is valuable to "distant readers" are the indexes, metadata, and derived data—like word counts—of books in a publisher's catalog. McGuire argues publishers should sell access to these indices in the form of machine-readable APIs.

For the purposes of this chapter, we introduce the concept of *archival APIs* as a form of data publishing for the digital humanities. Archival APIs make the objects contained within digital collections open and accessible through programmatic interfaces. We see archival APIs as a crucial form of data publishing for supporting digital humanities scholarship by providing access to digital collections in ways that support computational analysis.

Types of Archival APIs

To help understand the ways in which digital humanities research may want to access digital collections, we divide archival APIs into three conceptual categories:
- data APIs
- metadata APIs
- derived data APIs

Data APIs are programmatic interfaces that make digital objects and collections available, in whole or in part, via standard interfaces. A data API allows users to search a digital repository and retrieve individual records or collections of records and would return the record in a standardized format, like TEI for encoded text. The data API makes available the raw state of objects and collections for researchers interested in managing and manipulating the data themselves. This form of data publishing allows the generative use of materials because raw data do not prescribe a specific kind of use. The corollary, however, is that data published in this form can be the most difficult to process and manage for individual researchers.

Metadata APIs primarily serve to publish data *about* data, about the digital objects, through searchable and retrievable interfaces and message formats. A metadata API would allow researchers to search for specific titles, authors, or types of records within a collection and return records in one or more metadata standards like METS, MARC or encoded in parsable formats like JSON or XML. The advantage of a metadata API is to find digital objects in ways that do not depend upon interacting with the digital objects themselves.

Derived data APIs, unlike metadata APIs, transform the content of digital objects for the purposes of generating a new derived data object from a single object or collection of objects. This type of API is a blend of data and metadata APIs. Derived data from digital objects are data generated through algorithmic means from the original raw data, such as in the word count example discussed above. Derived data are representations of data extracted from original digital objects. Other examples of derived data might include extraction of named entities (persons, places, or organizations) or geolocations from text. Derived data APIs are potentially the most interesting and useful because they support the non-consumptive use of copyrighted works, which may not be available via a data API for legal reasons.

We present these three types of APIs, not as fixed definitions, but as a conceptual scaffold to promote conversations around the design and implementation of infrastructure to support data curation and publishing for digital humanities research. In practice, the boundaries between these types of APIs may blur. Data APIs use metadata APIs to facilitate search and retrieval, derived data can be pre-computed and added to metadata records. In such cases, the design and implementation of such data infrastructure must pay attention to what kinds of derived data will align with scholars' research practice.

To help make these ideas more concrete, the next sections walk through two examples of archival APIs, JSTOR's Data for Research, and the HathiTrust Research Center.

JSTOR Data for Research

JSTOR, the nonprofit academic journals database, launched its service JSTOR Data for Research in 2008.[10] Data for Research exposes the JSTOR database of journal articles for researchers interested in data mining and large-scale text analysis. In API terms, Data for Research provides a faceted search interface for specifying data sets (what we might call a metadata API) and a semi-automated system for requesting data about the contents of the documents previously specified (a derived data API). While Data for Research is not fully automated, it embodies the forms of data curation and enables the kinds of data workflow we argue is necessary to support digital humanities research.

Data for Research divides data curation and publishing workflows into two practical units, *document set specification* and *derived data downloading*. In the document set specification phase, scholars search the JSTOR database to identify a set of articles of interest. The Web-based interface provides full-text and faceted search across a range of categories (year, subject, discipline, publisher, author, etc.), allowing scholars to precisely specify a set of documents through the iterative accumulation of search criteria. Once a set of documents has been selected from the eight million articles in JSTOR's database, a scholar can request data derived

---

10. For more information, see JSTOR 2014.

from the selected documents. Instead of providing human-readable PDFs, the typical JSTOR workflow, Data for Research provides machine-readable CSV or XML files representing documents as data instead of prose. The *derived data download* phase of the workflow provides a list of citations, word counts, n-grams (word phrases), and key terms for each document in the search results. The data set request gives scholars access to derived data about the documents in question, but not their full text—an important feature when dealing with issues of access and copyright.

This dual transformation—of journal articles into data and "publication" of those data via a self-service API—facilitates a completely new kind of inquiry into JSTOR's collection. Parsed citations enable bibliometric analysis, word counts and n-grams enable text mining, and named entity extraction and keywords allow researchers to follow trends in the literature. For scholars interested in meta-level questions about scholarly communication, JSTOR's Data for Research has done much of the hard work, OCR-ing documents, parsing, formatting, and transforming diversely formatted text into data suitable for computational analysis. This work is invaluable because it offloads some of the complex work of data management and enables scholars to focus on research questions without getting bogged down in the onerous tasks of digitization, parsing, and data cleaning.

JSTOR's Data for Research is an interesting illustrative example, but its derived data are valuable mainly to scholars interested in metadisciplinary questions or those studying scholarly communication; journal articles are not necessarily interesting to literary scholars or other digital humanists. In the humanities, the book is the coin of the realm.

HathiTrust Research Center

HathiTrust is a digital library dedicated to preserving and making accessible the largest collection of digitized books in the world (eleven million at the time of this writing). Beyond maintaining the repository for preservation purposes, HathiTrust makes the collection available to scholars for research, especially digital humanities research.[11] To enable computational analysis, it provides two modes of access: a bibliographic API and a data

---

11. For more information, see HathiTrust Digital Library 2014a.

API. The bibliographic API is a metadata API allowing anyone to search and retrieve metadata about books in the digital library. When you access this API, you can get information like ISBN numbers, MARC records, copyright status, and the library of origin. The data API, synonymous with our conceptual data API, give access to digitized books at the page level. Through this API, scholars can access the scanned images of pages or the OCR text from that page. Where the bibliographic API is free for anyone to use, the data API, because of copyright and contractual reasons, is available only to partner institutions.

The HathiTrust Research Center (HTRC), a partner organization dedicated to building research infrastructure for HathiTrust, is developing another set of APIs for extracting useful information from specific subcollections of the public domain HathiTrust collection. Because of the sheer volume of the HathiTrust collection (as well as copyright issues), the HTRC APIs provide self-service utilities for data curation. They give researchers an interface for building custom collections of books, called *worksets*, and a mechanism for submitting algorithms to run over those worksets. The HTRC is, in effect, building a *user-extensible* derived data API for HathiTrust's collection that will grow as new techniques for text mining are added to the platform.[12]

Rather than publishing books, the HTRC publishes an API allowing scholars to submit computation jobs to be executed on the HTRC infrastructure. This idea of "bringing computation to the data" may be new to the humanities, but it is a well-established paradigm in high-performance computing (see chapter 11 by Patricia Hswe) in data-intensive sciences. As the infrastructural needs and requirements of digital humanities increases, libraries, museums, and archives can find apt models in the sciences for the design and architecture of data support systems.

What Is Possible When You Put an API on It?

In December 2012, John Resig, creator of the well-known JQuery JavaScript library and lover of Japanese woodblock prints, launched Ukiyo-e Search

---

12. See the HTRC Portal (HathiTrust Digital Library 2014b) for more information.

(http://ukiyo-e.org), a database for browsing Japanese woodblock prints. Resig describes the purpose of the site this way: "In [my] personal research [I] saw a need for a tool that did not exist: some way of easily finding similar prints across multiple collections simultaneously. Additionally, some way of finding prints simply by uploading a picture of a print seemed like an especially critical tool for researchers and collectors alike" (Ukiyo-e.org 2013).

Ukiyo-e Search allows researchers to quickly browse the database by artist, by time period, or by metadata associated with the images. The interface is fast and uses a well-designed, modern Web-based interface. More powerfully, the site allows users to search the database by image content: a user can upload an image, and the site will return similar images. In his talk at the annual conference of the Japanese Association for Digital Humanities, Resig (2013) demonstrated how a researcher could take a picture of a print using a smartphone camera and search the database "from the field," for example, from a museum or archive. The image search functionality is possible through the use of the image analysis search engine TinEye and its public MatchEngine API (TinEye 2013). Increasingly, comprehensive techniques from data mining and machine learning are being packaged into easy-to-use, third-party APIs making advanced features like image similarity search easy to implement.

Ukiyo-e Search transforms research practice in art history by bringing together disparate library, museum, and archival collections under a single interface with advanced browsing and search capabilities. The site exists because of the heroic effort on the part of one passionate programmer who has spent considerable time scraping and parsing museum, library, and archive websites to extract images and metadata. Had more of these institutions provided APIs and semantically rich metadata to their digital collections, sites like Ukiyo-e Search would be much easier to build.

The reason we highlight Ukiyo-e is to foreground the *generative* properties of APIs. Roy T. Fielding, one of the authors of the HTTP specification, is responsible for the directive to "engineer for serendipity" (Fielding 2007), and this captures the essence of what we mean by generative. Don't make assumptions about how users will use a digital collection. And, more important, don't design exclusively for those assumptions. Libraries, museums, and archives as publishers cannot, and should not, attempt to specify a priori how scholars and passionate members of the public might want to use humanities data. Publishing via programmatic means requires relinquishing control, which may be risky, but the benefits could potentially transform research practices. The humanities are currently undergoing a period of transformation and innovation. Computational methodologies such as topic modeling and entity extraction require data to be *machine readable,* in addition to *human readable.* As the digital humanities draw on techniques from computer science—techniques like machine learning and natural language processing—they will require that digital collections be published as data for consumption by algorithms, not simply human readers.

How to Respond?

Considering the need for new data curation practices, especially within the space of the digital archive, it's worth looking at how libraries might respond. This final section explores how those working in and across various library divisions might approach API building and offers recommendations for further upskilling.

A recent University of Illinois study conducted by the Data Curation Education Program for the Humanities (DCEP-H) explores the data curation needs of humanist scholars working in both digital humanities centers and the academic library. While offering no conclusive checklist, the study findings suggest several preferred skills, including: "knowledge of interoperability and standards, metadata, markup, database design, and project management" (Muñoz and Renear 2011, 3). These are obviously broad categories of work, but they do provide a thumbnail sketch of the skills needed to properly curate data for the kinds of publication we've been addressing. Of course, with the added layer of API development, further skills might include familiarity with database conversion, application programming, and web design and development.

But preparing for a data landscape in which scholars will be looking for both human- and machine-ready access is not simply about skilling up or adding personnel. It's also about equitable divisions (or, more to the point, equitable collaborations) of labor. To avoid replicating the sorts of form/content, technology/research, service/knowledge divisions that can crop up when librarians and humanities faculty work together, we recommend an approach to projects—and to the APIs that make those projects possible—that embraces hybridity and intellectual "cross-pollination." In other words, data curators should participate in shaping research questions and, potentially, research answers. And scholars should likewise participate in the pragmatic work of markup, database creation and conversion, and, where possible, learning about application development for machine readability. This kind of collaborative approach ensures at least three things: (1) that scholars' projects are possible within the context of a particular archive; (2) that library and departmental faculty are equally invested in both the aims *and* the means of a project's development and outcomes; and (3) that each participant comes away from a project having learned a scalable skillset.

By focusing on project-level work, we don't mean to suggest that data publishing is only, or should be only, a matter of individual research endeavors. If anything, the further upstream we go (where the "stream" in this case proceeds from large-scale collections to individual archives to single projects based on those archives) the better. Meaning: fully machine-accessible and readable collections will be vastly more useful than a single archive with an API applied to its database, which, in turn, will be more widely usable than an API applied to a particular researcher's subset of that database. At the same time, the creation of published data in the form of data and metadata APIs needs to be motivated by committed research aims. "Build it and they will come" is, as has been proven time and again, a recipe for underutilization at best and wasted effort at worst. In the end, we recommend a "both and" approach to humanities data publication wherever possible. This allows research projects to signal spaces within an archive or collection where wider application interaction might be warranted. Meanwhile, such "project-outward" work continues the important individualized attention libraries justifiably pride themselves on.

With all of that in mind, there are some additional skills—and associated roles—that need to be included in the above-mentioned list: project management and general administration. Discussing the training of data curation specialists, Muñoz and Renear (2011, 6) offer this insight: "A focus on training new graduates and lower-level staff may not yield the most effective curation programs if education and training is not also directed toward creating a group of higher-level managers and advocates conversant with data curation issues." Dedicated management and the institutional memory possible with higher-level administrative roles are essential to the success of humanities data publishing. A designated project manager (and in our experience, researchers themselves seldom want—or have the capacity—to take on this role) ensures that project deadlines are planned for and met and generally keeps all participants up-to-date on needed tasks and work progress. In addition, broadcasting data publishing endeavors to top-level administrators can be a crucial step in seeking further support for these endeavors. But, just as important, administrative confirmation that humanities data publishing (and API building specifically) meets the library's mission and strategic goals will help pave the way for the wider application and scalability of such projects.

Works Cited

Choudhury, Sayeed, Mike Furlough, and Joyce Ray. 2009. "Digital Curation and E-Publishing: Libraries Make the Connection." Paper presented at the annual Charleston Conference, Charleston, SC, November 4–7. doi:10.5703/1288284314782.

Cragin, Melissa H., P. Bryan Heidorn, Carole L. Palmer, and Linda C. Smith. 2007. "An Educational Program on Data Curation." Poster presented at the American Library Association annual conference, Science and Technology Section, Washington, DC, June 25. http://hdl.handle.net/2142/3493.

Fielding, Roy T. 2007. "Re: [rest-discuss] Tim Ewald: 'I finally get REST. Wow.'" Message to REST Architectural Style List, May 7. Archived at https://groups.yahoo.com/neo/groups/rest-discuss/conversations/topics/8343.

Flanders, Julia, and Trevor Muñoz. 2012. "An Introduction to Humanities Data Curation." *DH Curation Guide: A Community Resource Guide to Data Curation in the Digital Humanities*. Last modified March 15. http://guide.dhcuration.org/intro.

Governing Algorithms. 2013. "Watch All the Talks from Governing Algorithms." July 16, http://governingalgorithms.org/2013/07/watch-all-the-talks-from-governing-algorithms.

HathiTrust Digital Library. 2014a. "Data Availability and APIs." Accessed December 8. www.hathitrust.org/data.

———. 2014b. HTRC Portal. Accessed December 8. https://htrc2.pti.indiana.edu/HTRC-UI-Portal2.

Hayles, N. Katherine. 2012. *How We Think: Digital Media and Contemporary Technogenesis*. Chicago: University of Chicago Press.

IU (Indiana University). 2013. "Wright American Fiction." Accessed September 20th. http://webapp1.dlib.indiana.edu/TEIgeneral/welcome.do?brand=wright.

Jockers, Matthew L. 2013. *Macroanalysis: Digital Methods and Literary History*. Urbana-Champaign: University of Illinois Press.

JSTOR. 2014. Data for Research (beta test website). Accessed December 8. http://dfr.jstor.org.

McGuire, Hugh. 2013. "A Publisher's Job Is to Provide a Good API for Books." O'Reilly Tools of Change for Publishing (blog), February 1. http://toc.oreilly.com/2013/02/a-publishers-job-is-to-provide-a-good-api-for-books.html.

Muñoz, Trevor. 2013. "Data Curation as Publishing for Digital Humanists." *Trevor Muñoz* (blog), May 30. http://trevormunoz.com/notebook/2013/05/30/data-curation-as-publishing-for-dh.html.

Muñoz, Trevor, and Allen Renear. 2011. "Issues in Humanities Data Curation." Working paper. http://hdl.handle.net/2142/30852.

Nelson, Robert K. 2011a. "Fugitive Slave Ads." Mining the Dispatch website. http://dsl.richmond.edu/dispatch/Topics/view/15.

———. 2011b. "Introduction." Mining the *Dispatch* website. http://dsl.richmond.edu/dispatch/pages/intro.

NSB (National Science Board). 2005. *Long-Lived Digital Data Collections: Enabling Research and Education in the 21st Century*, NSB-05-40. Washington, DC: National Science Foundation.

NYPL (New York Public Library). 2013a. About page, "What's on the Menu?" Accessed September 20. http://menus.nypl.org/about.

———. 2013b. Data, "What's on the Menu?" Accessed September 20. http://menus.nypl.org/data.

———. 2013c. "What's on the Menu?" home page. Accessed September 20. http://menus.nypl.org.

Palmer, Carol L., Nicholas M. Weber, Trevor Muñoz, and Allen H. Renear. 2013. "Foundations of Data Curation: The Pedagogy and Practice of 'Purposeful Work' with Research Data." *Archive Journal*, issue 3 (Summer). www.archivejournal.net/issue/3/archives-remixed/foundations-of-data-curation-the-pedagogy-and-practice-of-purposeful-work-with-research-data.

Parsons, M. A., and P. A. Fox. 2013. "Is Data Publication the Right Metaphor?" *Data Science Journal* 12: 32–46. doi:10.2481/dsj.WDS-042.

Ramsay, Stephen. 2011. *Reading Machines: Toward an Algorithmic Criticism*. Topics in the Digital Humanities. Urbana: University of Illinois Press.

Resig, John. 2013. "Ukiyo-e.org: Aggregating and Analyzing Digitized Japanese Woodblock Prints." Recorded September 19. Vimeo video, 20:25. http://vimeo.com/74691102.

TinEye. 2013. "MatchEngine." Accessed September 20. https://services.tineye.com/MatchEngine.

Ukiyo-e.org. 2013. "About the Site." Ukiyo-e Search. Accessed September 20. http://ukiyo-e.org/about.

Underwood, Ted. 2013. "Wordcounts Are Amazing." *The Stone and the Shell* (blog), February 20. http://tedunderwood.com/2013/02/20/wordcounts-are-amazing.

Welshons, Marlo. ed. 2006. *Our Cultural Commonwealth*: Report of the American Council of Learned Societies Commission on Cyberinfrastructure for the Humanities and Social Sciences. New York: American Council of Learned Societies. www.acls.org/cyberinfrastructure/ourculturalcommonwealth.pdf.

Wilkens, Matthew. 2011a. "Contemporary Fiction by the Numbers." *Post45*. March 11. http://post45.research.yale.edu/2011/03/contemporary-fiction-by-the-numbers.

———. 2011b. "Maps of American Fiction." MattWilkens.com (blog), March 28. http://mattwilkens.com/2011/03/28/maps-of-american-fiction.

———. 2012. "Canons, Close Reading, and the Evolution of Method." In *Debates in the Digital Humanities*, edited by Matthew K. Gold, 249–58. Minneapolis: University of Minnesota Press.

CHAPTER 11

Peering Outward
Data Curation Services in Academic Libraries and Scientific Data Publishing

Patricia Hswe

Introduction

In the sciences, data are so pivotal they can be considered a chief currency the domain deals in—in more than one sense. First, data are central to the reproducibility of research results, which aid in verifying science. As such, they signify an asset, and dissemination of them enhances their value. Second, data enable existing research to be expanded upon and transformed. The recycling and reuse of data can lead to new types of experimentation, adding, as well, to the value of data. Third, data help keep science itself current, making the timely sharing of them all the more essential. It is little wonder that, embodying the dependency for the way science is done, data are viewed—in

This work is licensed under the Creative Commons Attribution License 4.0 (CC-BY 4.0).

particular, of late, by federal grant-funding agencies and the US Office of Science and Technology Policy (OSTP)—as worth sharing and thus worth making broadly discoverable and accessible. Freely available data are public goods.

As this "democratization of data" continues apace, spurred by federal mandates, data publishing offers a new frontier for various entities having a vested interest in their currency and in their longevity. Besides governments and grant agencies, these stakeholders include—but are not limited to—researchers, scholarly publishers, archives, data repositories, and academic libraries. For many of them, the publication of data offers both challenges and opportunities, though for a range of different reasons (Kratz and Strasser 2014). For example, while a majority of researchers may support broader dissemination of quality data that publishing standards would likely foster, the reward structure for most promotion and tenure cycles in the humanities, social sciences, and sciences continues to favor the publication of articles and monographs over that of data sets (Griffiths 2009). For many science journal publishers, how to publish data remains a puzzle to be solved, although there are communities of interest, such as in biodiversity research, making sizable strides toward the creation of frameworks for data publishing (Chavan and Ingwersen 2009) and advocating for journal-based data publishing policies (De Wever et al. 2012). There is also debate about the use of the term *publication* in this arena and how it functions as a metaphor, though not necessarily the most felicitous one. Because scientific data are a special case, consisting of many variables in the sense of formats, types, metadata, versions, and standards, and because *publication* is innately connected, in the production of research literature, with articles and monographs, it may not be appropriate to apply *publication* to describe the wide dissemination of data (Parsons and Fox 2013).

For academic libraries, traditionally viewed as keepers of data and content, the concept of data publishing—while still a new frontier—is less strange than it may initially appear, largely because important groundwork has already been laid. First, efforts to develop and promote standards for data citation, which is closely tied to data publication, have long involved libraries, as reflected in the library membership of DataCite, the organization that has led work in this area;[1] libraries are in the business of facilitating discovery and access—it makes sense that data about data, such as citations, matter to them. Second, many academic libraries, whether on their own or in collaboration with a university press, run scholarly publishing operations and are familiar with the processes thereof, including the implementation and customization of software applications for publishing, the establishment of criteria for publishing, and the design and development of production workflows. Third, a great number of libraries also manage institutional repositories (IRs), a primary purpose of which is to preserve and ensure persistent access to the scholarly record; as part of this mission, some libraries are sharing data sets via their IRs.[2] Finally, even before the data management plan (DMP) requirement from the National Science Foundation (NSF) came into effect, libraries had started building out services for e-science data support and anticipating needs for data publishing (Soehner, Steeves, and Ward 2010). The NSF DMP mandate mobilized many libraries to respond with new services and tools, such as the DMPTool (https://dmptool.org), and to revamp existing services for enhanced relevance to faculty and students in light of the requirement. Because it is early days yet for library-based data curation services, professional development opportunities for librarians to become more informed about data curation infrastructure, practices, and services have also been on the rise. Examples are the E-Science Institute (offered by DuraSpace and the Digital Library Federation), the Data Scientist Training for Librarians course at the Harvard-Smithsonian Center for Astrophysics, and the New England Science Boot Camp for Librarians, which has an e-science focus. Academic libraries are also creating new roles, such as data management services librarian positions, to concentrate on this area more

---

1. DataCite members consist of data services and centers, information science and technology institutes and councils, research institutes, and libraries. Library members include the British Library, California Digital Library, the German National Library of Medicine, Purdue University Libraries, and Harvard Library.
2. Examples of IRs that accept and preserve data sets are Penn State's ScholarSphere (https://scholarsphere.psu.edu), Purdue University Research Repository (PURR, https://purr.purdue.edu), University of Minnesota's Digital Conservancy (http://conservancy.umn.edu), and University of California at San Diego's Digital Collections (http://library.ucsd.edu/dc).

strategically. The Council on Library and Information Resources (CLIR), which has sponsored a library-based postdoctoral fellowship program for the humanities since 2004, received funding in 2013 from the Alfred P. Sloan Foundation to make possible new postdoctoral opportunities, also centered in academic libraries, for data curation in the sciences and social sciences (CLIR 2013). All of these related activities and tactics are preparing academic libraries well for collaboration with other stakeholders, such as researchers and publishers, in advancing data publishing for the sciences.

Data curation services in libraries are poised to help make strides in science data publishing. A chief objective in data curation is ensuring that data are shareable. To provide curation services for research data is, in part, to foster channels of access to those data, such as through citation and publication. This chapter teases out the synergy between publishing services and data curation services in libraries. It reports on the current status of each type of service, providing context and drawing out comparisons between library publishing and data publishing. The complications surrounding peer review of data sets are also examined. Such background sets the stage for assessing the state of data publishing in the sciences by looking in brief at data policies currently enacted by journal publishers for associating articles with data sets, data repositories that publishers and researchers use for linking data with publications, and the genres of the data journal and the data paper. It also captures briefly what some programs and services in publishing and data curation at academic libraries are currently accomplishing in data publishing. As the chapter suggests, the paradigm for publication of data in the sciences seems always to be shifting. The goal of the chapter, however, is to lay a foundation for understanding scientific data publishing, as well as the role that data curation services in libraries can play in it.

But First, the Basics: Data Curation and Sharing versus Publication

In concept, data curation is the "active and ongoing management of data through its lifecycle of interest and usefulness" to the scholarly and scientific research enterprise (Cragin et al. 2007). In practice, it encompasses a range of activities: collection of data sets, often including a selection and appraisal process; documentation and description of them in accordance with a community's best practices and standards to optimize for sharing, discovery, and retrieval; assurances for dissemination, access, use, and reuse so that analysis, integration, and visualization of data may take place; and storage, preservation, and migration for persistent access. (Higgins 2008; Michener et al. 2012) Important to mention, as well is that curation tracks usage not only for repurposing possibilities but also to inform future deaccessioning measures and decisions. Library services for data curation can address both external needs, such as those of researchers, and internal needs, such as those of library professionals who work with researchers. They also address the needs of library collections, such as digital collections, including those that are IR-based. As a conduit for access and sharing, the publication of data may be considered an integral activity in the curation of data.

To afford an appreciation of the data publishing landscape, it helps to know what is generally meant by *data publication*. Read (2013) offers a well-conceived definition:

> A data publication takes data that has been used for research and expands on the "why, when and how" of its collection and processing, leaving an account of the analysis and conclusions to a conventional article. A data publication should include metadata describing the data in detail such as who created the data, the description of the type of data, the versioning of the data, and most importantly where the data can be accessed (if it can be accessed at all). The main purpose of a data publication is to provide adequate information about the data so that it can be reused by another researcher in the future, as well as provide a way to attribute data to its respective creator. Knowing who creates data provides an added layer of transparency, as researchers will have to be held accountable for how they collect and present their data. Ideally, a data publication would be linked with its associated journal article to provide more information about the research.

Read's précis covers chief attributes of published data, including information about data generation and processing and detailed metadata that captures versioning and leads to access. Publication of data enables adequate context for encouraging reuse and crediting the producer of the data. A tacit yet critical requirement for ongoing access to data is the preservation of them. In effect, much of this definition embodies the central activities of data curation in practice. As proposed by Read and the leaders in the field from whom he derived the above synthesis, the publication of research data hinges largely on the curation of them.

It is also worthwhile distinguishing between data sharing and data publishing. Sharing data could mean making data sets available at the website for one's research laboratory, e-mailing data at a colleague's request, depositing them into a repository, or, as Read observes in his definition, linking data to an article publication. The DMP mandates issued by the NSF and the National Endowment for the Humanities (NEH), as well as a similar policy long in effect at the National Institutes of Health (NIH), stress the sharing and availability of data, rather than the publishing of them (Costello et al. 2013)—although the publication of research results is strongly encouraged, if not required. No doubt, the emphasis on sharing is owed to a combination of at least the following factors: (1) the word *sharing* bespeaks the broadest possible sense of distributing or circulating content; (2) a progressively accepted practice, among communities of interest with stakes in NSF or NIH funding, is the sharing of data via disciplinary or data-specific repositories, such as GenBank (https://www.ncbi.nlm.nih.gov/genbank), Ocean Biogeographic Information System (www.iobis.org), and the Predicted Crystallography Open Database (www.crystallography.net/pcod); and (3) without a clear understanding of what the publishing of data means across these communities of interest, funding agencies can hardly require that data resulting from a supported project be *published* rather than simply made publicly available for sharing.

A related nuance to consider is that, just as the deposit of a research paper into an IR is often held up as an example of open-access *publishing*, albeit with a "lowercase p," so may data sets that are deposited into a disciplinary repository, or even an IR, be understood to be similarly published. Cornell University's Research Data Management Service Group (RDMSG) codifies data publishing in a comparable manner. It takes *data publication* to mean "all strategies by which an investigator might make their [sic] data available to a broader audience" (Cornell University 2014, under "Data Publication"). The RDMSG categorizes or classes these strategies accordingly: (1) deposit to a discipline-specific data repository; (2) submission to a journal publisher in conjunction with a related publication; (3) deposit to an IR; and (4) publication via an independently developed infrastructure for data distribution. Whereas the first three strategies are straightforward, the last one is less clear. The RDMSG does not elaborate on the final strategy listed, but it could be taken to mean publishing frameworks tailored for distinct types of data, such as marine science data (Brauer and Hasselbring 2013), polar scientific data (Wenfang et al. 2013), and biodiversity data (Chavan and Ingwersen 2009), or to mean the infrastructure that publishers of data journals have created—again based on the needs and expectations of distinct research communities or subfields.

Publication is a mode of sharing, nonetheless, but not vice versa. More and more, scientists and data curation experts are pushing for a formalized notion of data publishing. Callaghan et al. (2013, 194) view formal data publication as "a service over and above the simple act of posting a dataset on a website, in that it includes a series of checks on the dataset of either a technical (format, metadata) or a more scientific (is the data scientifically meaningful?) nature." Furthermore, in formal publication of data, the persistence of the data is assured, and discovery and open evaluation of the data are facilitated. Lawrence et al. (2011, 7) promote a similar definition: "In this paper we define to Publish (with a capital P) data, as: 'To make data as permanently available as possible on the Internet.' This Published data has been through a process which means it can appear along with easily digestible information as to its trustworthiness, reliability, format and content." These interpretations go several specific steps beyond the definitions from Read and from Cornell's RDMSG, particularly in terms of reviewing data for quality assurance purposes (e.g., "checks," "evaluation," "trustworthiness," "reliability") and in terms of prioritizing enduring access ("persistence of the data," "make data as permanently available as possible"). It is interesting that neither definition integrates the notion of discovery, although Lawrence et al. (2011, 10) consider "discovery metadata" essential to include in a taxonomy of metadata for "the Publication process."

Key to the notion of data persistence is the mechanism of the digital object identifier (DOI) and data citation standards in general. Per Lawrence et al. (2011), persistence also relates to repeated findability of data—that is, whether one is able to find the data set again, which constitutes an identifier issue. Data citation renders many of the benefits that scientific publication brings about: attribution and credit; data reuse and a means to verify the data; evidentiary information; and, as already mentioned, access and persistence. A critical feature for data citation is unique identification, or the DOI, which allows for machine readability of digital data. Repository services that accept and curate data are adopting data citation standards increasingly, assigning DOIs to their data sets. In February 2014, Force 11, an organization that advocates for improvement of research communication and frameworks for e-scholarship, issued a "Joint Declaration of Data Citation Principles," in which additional fundamentals of data citation are expressed: citation of data should be considered as important as citations of publications; they should lead to the data being cited as well as to any related metadata, code, and other documentation; and approaches to data citation should be responsive to diverse community needs and practices but not at the risk of jeopardizing interoperability. While data citation is not equivalent to data publication, there is evidence of concern that data published with a DOI may be considered a previous publication—as if assignment of a DOI, which enacts persistence, is akin to publication. For example, the data policies for *F1000Research*, an open science journal that relies on a post-publication, open peer-review process, list journals that "have confirmed that they would not view publication of datasets with a DOI and associated protocol information as prior publication, if a more standard (analysis/conclusions) article based on the data was subsequently submitted to them" (*F1000Research* 2014).

The foregoing assertions about data publishing capture key tenets of data curation. Data that are curated should be persistently accessible, too, and give credit and attribution. If curated data are quality data, and curation adds value to data, then are these data not equivalent to published data? With respect to repository services and the question of whether they qualify as publishers of data or not, the name changes of the data repository Pangaea tell a revealing story. From 1996, when it was launched, until 2003, the repository service was called Pangaea: Network for Geological and Environmental Data. In 2004, it became known as Publishing Network for Geoscientific and Environmental Data. Since 2011, Pangaea has billed itself as Data Publisher for Earth and Environmental Science, explicitly signaling its key purpose for data. Pangaea offers rich metadata for its data sets, which themselves are rigorously reviewed by an editorial board of earth and environmental scientists for "completeness and consistency" (Pangaea 2014). It also assigns each data set a DOI for persistence (particularly in terms of the ability to be located and accessed) and to render the data citable and discoverable. In addition, the journal *Earth System Science Data* includes Pangaea among its recommended repositories (Pangaea 2014; ESSD 2014). Few may dispute data sets in Pangaea as being of published quality. It is not clear, however, how Pangaea is facilitating discovery and interoperability, which—as Muñoz (2013, citing Parsons and Fox 2013) rightly points out—should be prominent concerns in data publishing, as should exposing the issues of big data through "latency, rapid versioning, reprocessing, and computational demands" (Muñoz 2013, citing Parsons and Fox 2013, WDS37). Indeed, how to publish "big data" currently stands as an intractable issue. For this reason, and for other reasons mentioned later in this chapter, the terminology of *publishing* and *publication* may not be appropriate for data. Yet, *publishing* and *publication* have such cultural weight in academia that not to try to accord data sets the legitimacy and resources they deserve as tenure-worthy products through some form of publication may be ill-advised, both for data and for scientists.

If data curation in practice is intended to ensure quality data, as well as access to and use of that data, then as library-based services in data curation evolve, they present an immense opportunity for shaping how data publication may be done. Services in data curation may also be ripe for collaboration with publishing services within academic libraries and beyond.

Data Curation Services and Library Publishing Services: Context and Comparison

Data curation services in US academic libraries are still in their infancy; likewise with library-based data publishing. *Academic Libraries and Research Data Services,* an ACRL white paper, notes that only a very few libraries have such services, which it defines as focusing on the demands of the complete data lifecycle (Tenopir, Birch, and Allard 2012). Based on survey responses from libraries at associate's colleges, baccalaureate colleges, and research/doctoral universities, Tenopir, Birch, and Allard report that approximately 25 percent to 30 percent of respondents intend to begin services in this area in the next couple of years. Similarly, in *Research Data Management Services: SPEC Kit 334*, issued a year after the ACRL white paper, Fearon et al. (2013, 11) refer to the "'growing pains'" and "early stages" of developing these services in libraries. They differentiate between services for broad data support and services for research data management (RDM). A key finding is that for most libraries (93 percent of respondents, or sixty-eight libraries out of a total of seventy-three that responded), broad data support services primarily constitute assistance to faculty and students in search of data sets for their own use. Tenopir, Birch, and Allard (2012) also present a comparable takeaway in their white paper. Fearon et al. (2013, 12) describe RDM services as "providing information, consulting, training or active involvement" for areas such as data management planning and guidance, metadata, and sharing and curation of research data. In this sense, however, fewer libraries—though still almost three-quarters of respondents (or fifty-four libraries)—can claim active participation. The SPEC Kit authors encouraged respondents to document that they were providing RDM services, even if the services amounted to only Web-based resources for data management planning guidance and reference. Another significant survey response, because of its implications for infrastructure and data sharing, is the number of libraries running IRs—sixty-four, or 88 percent of respondents. Neither the ACRL white paper nor the ARL SPEC Kit mentions data publishing per se, although the latter delves into data archiving as a mechanism for data sharing.

By contrast, library publishing services seem relatively mature. Far more established operations exist for this area than for data curation. Data curation services are probably at the stage where library publishing services stood in 2007, when ARL surveyed its member libraries about publishing services. The survey found that 44 percent of the responding libraries (which numbered eighty in total) already had some form of such services, and 21 percent disclosed plans to develop them (Hahn 2008). If the current edition of the *Library Publishing Directory* (Lippincott 2013) gives any indication, libraries have gained further traction in scholarly publishing since then. According to the directory, there are ninety-eight academic libraries in North America engaged in publishing services. (The directory includes listings for seven additional libraries outside the United States and Canada.) Most of these libraries publish faculty-led, peer-reviewed journals, and more than half support the publication of journals started by students; many also publish electronic theses and dissertations (ETDs). Monographs, conference proceedings, and technical/research reports make up most of the remaining types of publications covered by these services. Publications that are open-access are the norm for most services.

The directory also hints at a kind of "data publishing readiness" among library-based publishers. Many of the libraries—more than half—note in the Formats field of the directory that they publish data (albeit in what sense is not clear). Also relevant to data publishing are some of the additional services the directory highlights in its introduction: metadata, analytics, outreach, and DOI assignment/allocation of identifiers. Another worthwhile statistic, which the directory does not surface explicitly, is the number of libraries specifying "dataset management" among their additional services—just under one-third, or roughly 27 percent. In addition, most library publishing services are at institutions with IRs; they acknowledge a digital preservation strategy; and roughly one-third are considering the integration of digital preservation services. As digital preservation and data reflect burgeoning concerns, these statistics imply that library-based publishing, though long operational at many institutions, is still evolving and may have more in common with data curation services as these services, too, mature.

These statistics convey that building capacity to support researchers in data publishing is not an unreasonable ambition. Hahn (2008, 10) veritably indicated such in her summary of the 2007 ARL survey, with particular reference to the repository service component of library publishing: "Evolving repository services, which house and disseminate institutional records, theses and dissertations, pre-prints, post-prints, learning objects, and research data, can inspire a range of inquiries about potential publishing services." As further evidence, Mullins et al. (2012), in their report on a series of library publishing workshops held in spring 2011, note the attendees' openness to developing such services to address research life cycle issues, including data management, and to test out different modes of disseminating scholarly content. Indeed, the publication of science data qualifies as an example of both: a research life cycle endeavor—one consonant with data curation concerns—as well as an experimental service. In addition, library publishing and data publishing have comparable missions. For library publishing, the overarching mission is to provide unfettered access to peer-reviewed scholarship and allow authors to retain their copyright. Data publishing, as a formalized mode of data sharing, echoes such an aim, especially in terms of availability, discovery, quality, standards, and attribution. Like the publishing done by libraries, data publishing contributes to a public good. There is more to the ethos of scientific data publishing in comparison with typical library publishing, however, which tends to favor humanities content (although social sciences are also represented): the sciences depend on access to reliable data and other research results for purposes of verifiability and accountability (Borgman 2008). Moreover, applying data curation practices to scientific research aids in ensuring overall reproducibility. In this sense, the publication of data may be viewed as a curation tactic and thus about more than access.

Conceptually and operationally, scholarly publishing that is library-based is better defined than data publishing vis-à-vis data curation services in libraries—and not only because library publishing has been around longer. Another pivotal reason is the homogeneity of the content and the format that academic libraries commonly publish: the subject matter stems mainly from the humanities and social sciences, and the publication format is overwhelmingly text, though in a variety of genres. Furthermore, as the *Library Publishing Directory* (Lippincott 2013) implicitly confirms, with few exceptions libraries are publishing what they have always *collected*. The containers—for example, the monograph and the journal—have also not changed for most library-based publishers, even in online environments. It is true that experimentation in this area, such as CommentPress, a MediaCommons Press product (http://futureofthebook.org/commentpress), for example, has enabled innovative leaps in recent years, particularly in the practice of open peer review. Data publishing may be more likely to occur in an academic library if its collection policies and mission statements were formally articulated to include, and thus promote, data set collection, particularly as produced by the researchers of the library's institution. If publishing services and data curation services in libraries had adequate infrastructure and other support for experimental, even risk-taking ventures, then perhaps collaborative pilot projects for data publication would be the norm rather than the exception.

Data Publishing and Peer Review: Peas in a Pod, or Strange Bedfellows?

Speculation about what is possible for data publishing as part of a suite of data curation services in a library ultimately raises questions about peer review and quality assurance standards for data. Namely, what determines these standards for data? In the text-based scholarly publishing performed by library publishing services, the standards for quality work are well understood. Library publishing typically observes peer review and other quality assurance processes through practices long in place in academic communities. Scholars who review article manuscripts for journal publications know whereof they evaluate; they write, as well as review, in genres familiar to them—genres that also count toward tenure. Criteria for peer evaluation of data for publication are currently less concrete (Parsons and Fox 2013; Parsons, Duerr, and Minster 2010; Griffiths 2009). Scientists frequently advocate for progress toward such criteria and argue that data sets, like journal articles, should be treated as first-rate research products and thus inform promotion and tenure decision making (Gorgolewski, Margulies, and Milhan 2013; Reilly et al. 2011; Callaghan et al. 2013; Lawrence et al. 2011; Parsons, Duerr, and Minster 2010). In the case of articles linked to data files, the assignment to peer review a data set, in addition to the published article, can also prove burdensome, as the experience of reviewers for the *Journal of Neuroscience* ultimately conveyed (Socha 2013, citing Maunsell 2010). Reviewers found the task of refereeing article manuscripts along with supplemental materials, which could include data sets, increasingly insurmountable. The extent of the additional files (which in time were equaling the length of the articles), the growing tendency of them to reflect content that actually belonged in the main article, and, thus, the challenge that referees faced in assessing supplemental materials with any depth, drove editors of the journal to cease their acceptance (Maunsell 2010). Parsons and Fox (2013, WDS39) have noted how slow the review process can be for substantial sets of data; current approaches for refereeing "will not scale to handle the growing deluge of data." The lack of scalability affects time to publication, a serious impediment in the peer-review process (Bornmann 2011), and was arguably a factor for the *Journal of Neuroscience* in its management of review practices for supplemental materials.

Deciding upon principles of review of scientific data for publication is a daunting endeavor. Data are heterogeneous and dynamic in nature. Data formats and types vary considerably across science disciplines, making "standardization" a slippery, if not also hollow, concept. As Tenenbaum, Sansone, and Haendel (2014, 2) caution, "even data standards experts do not agree on what constitutes a data standard." Such disparity makes metadata for data sets an especially intractable problem. Communities of interest have their own data models and metadata schemas, eroding the likelihood of interoperability and data that are shareable and reusable (Willis, Greenberg, and White 2012). Or scientists may understand the value that metadata brings to their data but are not well informed about standards for it (Cragin et al. 2010). Even when metadata standards are established, they are infrequently used or incorrectly implemented, making them "almost standards" (Edwards et al. 2011, 683). Unsurprisingly, the lack of metadata use is also a persistent issue. A DataONE survey conducted by Tenopir et al. (2011) found that of the 1,329 scientists who responded, almost 60 percent disclosed that they do not apply any metadata standards; another roughly 20 percent said they "use their own lab metadata standard" (9). In addition to these metadata hurdles is the complication of data versioning, a significant aspect of managing data. Data versions must be tracked, thereby raising the question of which version of a data set to subject to review for publication or how to capture for publication a changing data set, especially given the general understanding of publication as an act that finalizes and fixes for perpetuity a research investigation and its findings. Because data sets can evolve over time, their use and value may not be fully realized until well into the future, which renders current practices for peer review inadequate for them (Parsons and Fox 2013). The validity of a data set also is neither uniformly nor easily determined within science disciplines, let alone across subsets of them (Parsons, Duerr, and Minster 2010). An ever-moving target, data—and thus their publication—resist a "one size fits all" solution. And, as Parsons and Fox (2013, citing de Waard et al. 2006, de Waard and Kircz 2008, Kuhn 1996, and Latour 1987) also caution, the tendency to model the peer-review publishing of data on that of scientific articles is itself problematic. The substance and intent of each differ radically: based on investigative findings, articles are "designed to persuade" (Parsons and Fox 2013, WDS38), while data constitute fact.

Although it may seem that data publishing and peer review make strange bedfellows, there are signs hinting at an enhanced perception and treatment of data as meriting peer review and thus being tenure-worthy. One sign is the Peer Review for Publication and Accreditation of Research Data in the Earth Sciences (PREPARDE) project (PREPARDE 2014). Based in the United Kingdom, PREPARDE has been working on deliverables for five aspects of data publishing: journal and data repository workflows, scientific review of data sets, cross-linking between repositories and data publishers, data repository accreditation, and stakeholder engagement and dissemination. The project has partnered with Wiley-Blackwell and its new *Geosciences Data Journal,* an open-access, online-only, peer-reviewed publication, on the workflows piece and on the creation of procedures and policies for scientific review of data sets to guide scientists refereeing for the data journal. Formal publication of just the data—that is, minus the preparation of an article manuscript—also holds the promise of swifter dissemination and thus access. Some in the sciences and the social sciences, as well as in academic libraries, have argued for publication outputs that are solely devoted to accounts of research data, such as data articles, or data papers, and data journals (Callaghan et al. 2013; Guy and Duke 2013; Kansa and Kansa 2013; Chavan and Penev 2011; Kunze et al. 2011). The rise in prominence of these types of data publication may, in time, lend them the cachet they need to be considered as scholarship that counts toward promotion and tenure. Other encouraging signs come from the NSF. Since 2012 it has permitted researchers applying for grant funding to cite data sets and software code in their biosketches; for this purpose, the agency changed the heading for Publications to Products in its biosketch format. In early 2014 it issued a "Dear Colleague" letter to solicit collaborative workshops and exploratory research proposals in the areas of data citation and attribution and of metrics reflecting the impact of these practices: "Unlike generally accepted citation-based metrics for papers, software and data citations are not systematically collected or reported. NSF seeks to explore new norms and practices in the research community for software and data citation and attribution, so that data producers, software and tool developers, and data curators are credited for their contributions" (Tornow and Farnam 2014). If the NSF is going to require DMPs and thus expect scientists to care for their data more systematically, then shifting policy and supporting research efforts to prioritize citation, attribution, and metrics for data mark logical developments. Yet, just as proper attribution via use of data citation standards can serve as an impetus for sharing data (McCallum et al. 2013; Socha 2013), more incentives for researchers to publish data must also be created if researcher culture, attitudes, and behaviors are to change—an awareness that cuts across the sciences and social sciences (Costello et al. 2013; Gorgolewski, Margulies, and Milhan 2013; AGU 2012; Lawrence et al. 2011; Barton, Smith, and Weaver 2010; Griffiths 2009; Swan and Brown 2008).

Toward Publication: Data Policies, Data Repositories, Data Journals

The paradigm for scientific data publishing is in flux, but there are policies, systems, standards, and publication genres being engaged and interconnected for dissemination of data that are germane to this paradigm. These include publishers' data policies, data repositories, and data journals and data papers, as well as new genres for data publishing, such as the Data Descriptor, formulated by the journal *Scientific Data* and intended to present a detailed, peer-reviewed data set, complete with the methods and analyses associated with producing it and understanding it. The examples of these genres discussed below arise mainly from nonlibrary publishing enterprises. The act of peering outward at these models for data publishing not only reveals possibilities for similar or complementary operations in academic libraries, especially in the context of data curation services, but is also aspirational. Libraries should strive to be peers with those outside that are meeting and anticipating the needs of researchers effectively. In this sense, too, libraries should be "peering outward."

With the growing expectation for science journals to link published articles to the relevant data sets, publishers' data policies have also risen in importance. The trend toward open data has impelled many publishers to require researchers to ensure that data from their articles are available for others to access on publication. The Public Library of Science (PLOS) is one of the latest publishers to revise their data policies: as of March 2014 it requires researchers to make their data sets for articles completely available upon submission, thus before publication, and to include a "Data Availability Statement" asserting PLOS policy compliance (Bloom 2013). The practice of associating published articles to data sets also works well for scientists who would rather not share data until their research has been published (Tenopir et al. 2011). Some journals host the data themselves, like *CODATA Data Science Journal* and the journals published by the Ecological Society of America (ESA), which also maintains a data registry. The *CODATA Data Science Journal* accepts data in any format, including proprietary ones, while ESA journals take in data only for data papers that are in open formats. The ESA also demands fairly detailed metadata for the data sets, and it charges a one-time fee for publishing data papers.

Rather than hosting data sets themselves, many journals offer recommendations for repositories where researchers may deposit their data. In its list of data-sharing options (Bloom 2013), PLOS recommends deposit of data to public repositories, preferably ones that are certified as trusted and with open licensing policies, such as Creative Commons Attribution (CC BY). There are also data repositories that were created expressly for deposit of data sets associated with scientific article publications, such as Pangaea and Dryad (datadryad.org). An advantage for authors submitting to journals collaborating with Dryad is the repository's Submission Integration service, detailed on the Dryad website, which is essentially a workflow that couples processes for article submission with those for data deposit. Through automated notice, journals let Dryad know when a manuscript is about to be processed; Dryad establishes a placeholder for the data set record; journals encourage authors to archive their data in Dryad when they submit, giving them access to the link for the placeholder record, where they may upload the files for their data; the author deposits data files into Dryad, which approves the data set and generates a DOI for it; and the DOI is then passed onto the relevant journal and applied to the article so the data set can be accessed, tracked, and cited. The goal of Dryad's Submission Integration service is to make deposit of data into the repository as seamless an experience as possible for researchers. It also activates two-way access, or linking, between the journal article and the data set, which allows each to gain more visibility. Dryad is able to furnish such a service largely because of its membership-based business model, a development that occurred after its NSF funding ended in 2012. Each journal that integrates with Dryad does so for a fee, or the integration occurs as a benefit of organizational membership in Dryad.

Close partnerships between data repositories and publishers, such as that which Dryad enjoys and from which it is able to create a valuable service, are not as common as they should be, however. For the most part, publishers provide authors with a list of recommended repositories but little more. The onus is still on the researcher, who must figure out which repository is best for the data (or what to do in the event that no suggested repository appears suitable), learn the guidelines of that repository, and prepare the data for submission—in addition to the other work that is required to finalize an article manuscript for publication. Resources have surfaced in the last few years that offer some guidance on data repositories. One of these is DataBib (http://databib.org), a well-curated registry of information about data repositories that researchers can use to locate repository services relevant for their data types. Data journal publishers in particular, such as Ubiquity Press, are selective in the repositories they advise authors to use; the ones they list adhere to the publisher's standards for peer review of data. (Although data journals are devoted to publishing data sets, they also must advise their authors on where to deposit the data being featured and discussed in the data paper or data article to allow other researchers to access and use the data sets.) The website for the *Earth System Science Data (ESSD) Journal* (www.earth-system-science-data.net) explicitly displays the requirements that repositories accepting authors' data sets must fulfill: the repository has to mint a DOI for the data set; it must make the data set freely available (i.e., charge no fees for access); it accords the data set the equivalence of a Creative Commons Attribution license; and the repository satisfies the topmost criteria for ensuring ongoing access. While *ESSD* displays a short list of repositories at its site, cautioning that the list is not exhaustive, it also urges authors to see whether data repositories they are familiar with meet the journal's criteria.

In 2014 a new online, open-access data publication, *Scientific Data*, emerged that introduced an inventive genre for data publishing—the peer-reviewed Data Descriptor: "a combination of traditional scientific publication content and structured information curated in-house… designed to maximize reuse and enable searching, linking and data mining" (NPG 2013). A main motivation for creating *Scientific Data* is to assist researchers in complying with data management requirements. Six principles lie at the core of what *Scientific Data* is trying to achieve: credit, reuse, quality, discovery, openness, and service. As part of its focus on service, *Scientific Data* strives to lower barriers for researchers submitting their data sets, such as automating deposit of them into Dryad, or the figshare repository service (in the event that there is not a community-driven repository available for the data); provide professional services in data curation to make certain standards are observed so that content is discoverable; facilitate visual interpretations of the content, as well as pathways *to* the content via robust linking and searching; and rapid evaluation and decision processes, resulting in prompt publication of the data. *Scientific Data* recommends as part of its data policies that data be submitted in the "rawest" form that will benefit the scientific community and bring out the broadest possible repurposing of the data. It urges authors to use data repositories that are discipline-specific for their data and community-driven. Its data policies include criteria for trusted data repositories that scientists are expected to consult when deciding which one to use. The criteria call for expertise in curation; implementation of "relevant, community-endorsed reporting requirements"; provision "for confidential review" of the data; application of "stable identifiers" for the data; and "public access to data without unnecessary restrictions" (NPG 2014). *Scientific Data* provides a template for the Data Descriptor manuscript, which incorporates sections for, among other things, background and summary of the data, methods, data records, technical validation, and usage notes (which are optional).

With multiple senses of "data publishing" at play—is it sharing, dissemination, or publication?—and without conducting a formal environmental scan via a survey, it is difficult to know who is doing what in data publishing and at which US academic libraries. A few examples do come to the fore, though, that, because of the high level of curation involved, could be called data publishing. Cornell has repurposed its Datastar repository, originally for staging data, as a metadata-rich data registry, taking advantage of Semantic Web technologies such linked open data and VIVO, a networking tool (Wright et al. 2013). Another is the data publishing investigation on which the California Digital Library (CDL) has partnered with the PREPARDE project. CDL has been a leader in the

United States promoting data citation through its EZID identifier service, as well as data preservation and access via Merritt, its repository service. CDL hired a CLIR postdoctoral fellow to take the lead in exploring data publishing possibilities. It is creating specifications, toward implementation, for a data paper, at minimal cost and minimal effort for the researcher, that would be formed from a record for an EZID citation; it would "identify a publishable dataset, complete with author, title, date, abstract, and links to stored data" (PREPARDE 2014). Also within the PREPARDE project, CDL is partnering with UC Berkeley in curation of medium-to-large data sets. As part of developing a service model for data publishing, CDL issued a survey to determine how researchers think about, and engage in, data publication. Another academic library that is testing the waters with data publishing is Purdue. By coordinating workflows among its data repository, IR, and university press, Purdue has been able to automate linking of technical and project reports shared through its IR with their related data sets, which are deposited separately (Scherer, Zilinski, and Matthews 2013). Finally, as active collaborators with faculty in research activities, librarians at Johns Hopkins are paving new paths for how data, as a result of these partnerships, can be accessed—such as through interactive visualizations of data, projected on a wall, that are transformed via hand and body motions, making the wall "a new form of publishing" (Monastersky 2013). Johns Hopkins has also developed a program in which it will contract, for a fee, with researchers who have been awarded project funding: the libraries will commit to curation and storage of the research data produced by projects for a period of five years, renewable thereafter (Monastersky 2013). A key benefit of such a commitment is the rich, contextual information that curation will engender for the data sets, making the sharing, if not also the publication, of data uncomplicated.

Conclusion

Data curation services, especially those that leverage expertise across departments and subject libraries, have many roles to play in this area in support of researchers managing, and perhaps publishing, their data. Topics for instruction in academic libraries tend to focus on vended database resources and tools for management of citations, generally helping researchers look for and find materials in support of their research and organize those materials. However, there could be regular instruction offerings that complement creation and collection of data sets, such as sessions on data repositories, data publishing and citation principles, data publication genres, tools like the Open Data Commons toolkit for providing and using open data, and what scientific publishing entails overall, as well as on the best practices for maintaining data files locally. This instruction could be geared toward postdocs, beginning graduate students, and advanced undergraduates, as well as early-career faculty—particularly those who play the role of "data keeper" in their research labs. It could also complement instruction already being done on data management planning. Since the Data Descriptor template for *Scientific Data* effectively helps researchers tell the story of a data set, the template could serve as an "inreach" tool for librarians wishing to learn more about what data sharing and publishing are about. Another resource, the Data Curation Profiles Toolkit (http://datacurationprofiles.org), developed by Purdue and the University of Illinois at Urbana-Champaign, could be applied for similar purposes.

In a slight reversal of collection development responsibilities, librarians could familiarize themselves with the types of data that faculty and students are collecting and consider approaches for strategically developing collections of their institution's data sets—to assist in curating them with an eye toward their dissemination and reuse. Based on overall knowledge about their constituents' data, and with the assistance of a resource like DataBib, librarians could also become familiar with the repository services that are applicable to the data being generated by their researchers. In the event that an IR is not appropriate, then familiarity with DataBib would help them have suggestions at the ready when meeting with faculty and students about data management planning. Metadata librarians, working with their libraries' IR managers and liaison librarians, could engage with researchers on various outreach efforts, such as metadata education and training that would include best practices for file naming and management, data normalization and cleanup, information on data standards for specific disciplines, and approaches to making researchers' data discoverable and accessible.

Since many library publishing services are well versed in copyright and fair use, they could collaborate with data curation services to establish guidance on intellectual property rights and data. A hopeful trend is that of open data, particularly given the data-sharing policy put into effect by PLOS. Along this line, libraries could repurpose position responsibilities of appropriate staff to include monitoring of external developments regarding policies for data sharing, at the national level as well as at the publisher level. Such monitoring, itself an example of peering outward, is useful not only for reasons of internal apprising. It can also inform possible discussion in the context of university governance—for example, how an institution needs to respond to decisions made by the OSTP so that it acts as a whole in compliance. Keeping track of the pulse of initiatives at funding agencies, such as the NSF, opens up possibilities for direct participation from academic libraries, particularly when the initiative addresses areas in which many libraries already have strengths, such as in citation standards and bibliometrics. The best practices for data citation, attribution, and metrics tracking, supported by the NSF's "Dear Colleague" letter mentioned earlier, constitute an area in which library-based services in data curation and in publishing could partner with information schools and with relevant departments in the sciences and social sciences on workshops and research proposals appropriate for this call.

Libraries should also partner formally with the research institutes on their campuses, as well as with the Office of the Vice President for Research (OVPR), in developing more centralized, scalable, and programmatic efforts and services toward improved data management practices for faculty, students, and staff. An institution's OVPR is often the campus entity that provides guidelines for the responsible conduct of research, under which best practices for data management would fall. There are opportunity costs too dear for libraries, information technology services, and the OVPR to afford if an institutional approach to data curation programs is not realized. Perhaps the steepest costs are data loss and lack of access to data, which are ultimately tied to an institution's ability to foster and gain more research funding and more research partnerships. Vines et al. (2014) note the adverse effects of "article age" on availability of data sets. In summary, the older the publication, the harder it was for Vines et al. to contact researchers for access to the relevant data sets, primarily because of obsolete e-mail information, loss of data, and barriers to data due to "inaccessible storage media" (95). As Vines et al. suggest, support on an institutional scale for author identity services, such as the Open Researcher and Contributor ID (ORCID), as well as guidance on ORCID and on researcher networking opportunities evident in Google Scholar and ResearchGate, could ultimately help increase researcher access and data set availability, regardless of the age of the article. Libraries could expand their instruction offerings to include such guidance, advising researchers on identity and research reputation management tools, which offer additional channels for discovery of data set citation and attribution. Programs in the responsible conduct of research should encompass an understanding of these and other issues related to proper management of data sets produced by an institution's researchers.

As early as 2002, Gray et al. connected curation of scientific data with publication and archiving, stating, "Librarians would describe documenting the metadata as *curating* the data. They have thought deeply about these issues, and we would do well to learn from their experiences." (104, emphasis in the original). In the same article, summarizing, they say, "Data publication is really data curation," thus binding together the library's central role in publishing and curation of data, if not as data publisher. Others have made similar parallels between publishing and curation (Muñoz 2013; Ray, Choudhury, and Furlough 2009), suggesting new models for library organizational structures and collection development and management practices. As data policies, particularly at the level of publishers, funding agencies, and the federal government, move toward more openness and transparency, opportunities are opening up in tandem for libraries to participate and partner in data sharing and publishing efforts. There is also much that services in data curation and in library publishing can learn from each other, perhaps to the extent that peer review and data sets might make sense instead of seeming at odds—as long as libraries keep peering outward.

Works Cited

AGU (American Geophysical Union). 2012. "Earth and Space Science Data Should Be Widely Accessible in Multiple Formats and Long-Term Preservation of Data Is an Integral Responsibility of Scientists and Sponsoring Institutions." Adopted May 29, 1997; revised May 2009, February 2012. http://sciencepolicy.agu.org/files/2013/07/AGU-Data-Position-Statement_March-2012.pdf.

Barton, C., R. Smith, and R. Weaver. 2010. "Data Policies, Practices, and Rewards in the Information Era Demand a New Paradigm." *Data Science Journal* 9: IGY95-IFY99. doi:10.2481/dsj.SS_IGY-003.

Bloom, Theo. 2013. "Data Access for the Open Access Literature: PLOS's Data Policy." Public Library of Science (PLOS) website, December 12. www.plos.org/data-access-for-the-open-access-literature-ploss-data-policy.

Borgman, Christine L. 2008. "Data, Disciplines, and Scholarly Publishing." *Learned Publishing* 21, no. 1 (January): 29–38. doi:10.1087/095315108X254476.

Bornmann, Lutz. 2011. "Scientific Peer Review." *Annual Review of Information Science and Technology* 45, no. 1: 197–245. doi:10.1002/aris.2011.1440450112.

Brauer, Peter, and Wilhelm Hasselbring. 2013. "PubFlow: A Scientific Data Publication Framework for Marine Science." Paper presented at PubMan Days conference, Munich, Germany, October 23–24, 2013. Accessed January 24. http://eprints.uni-kiel.de/22400/1/vortrag_pubmanDays.pdf.

Callaghan, Sarah, Fiona Murphy, Jonathan Tedds, Rob Allan, John Kunze, Rebecca Lawrence, Matthew S. Mayernik, and Angus Whyte. 2013. "Processes and Procedures for Data Publication: A Case Study in the Geosciences." *International Journal of Digital Curation* 8, no. 1: 193–203. doi:10.2218/ijdc.v8i1.253.

Chavan, Vishwas S., and Peter Ingwersen. 2009. "Towards a Data Publishing Framework for Primary Biodiversity Data: Challenges and Potentials for the Biodiversity Informatics Community." *BMC Bioinformatics* 10, Supp. 14: S2. doi:10.1186/1471-2105-10-S14-S2.

Chavan, Vishwas, and Lyubomir Penev. 2011. "The Data Paper: A Mechanism to Incentivize Data Publishing in Biodiversity Science." *BMC Bioinformatics* 12, Supp. 15: S2. doi:10.1186/1471-2105-12-S15-S2.

CLIR (Council on Library and Information Resources). 2013. "CLIR Receives Sloan Foundation Grant for Data Curation Fellows." News release, April 1. www.clir.org/about/news/pressrelease/sloan-data-curation-award.

Cornell University. 2014. "Sharing Data." Research Data Management Service Group website, accessed February 24. http://data.research.cornell.edu/content/sharing-data.

Costello, Mark J., William K. Michener, Mark Gahegan, Zhi-Qiang Zhang, and Philip E. Bourne. 2013. "Biodiversity Data Should Be Published, Cited, and Peer Reviewed." *Trends in Ecology and Evolution* 28, no. 8 (August): 454–61. doi:10.1016/j.tree.2013.05.002.

Cragin, Melissa H., P. Bryan Heidorn, Carole L. Palmer, and Linda C. Smith. 2007. "An Educational Program in Data Curation." Poster presented at the American Library Association Science and Technology Section Conference, Washington, DC, June. https://www.ideals.illinois.edu/bitstream/handle/2142/3493/ALA_STS_poster_2007.pdf?sequence=2.

Cragin, Melissa H., Carole L. Palmer, Jacob R. Carlson, and Michael Witt. 2010. "Data Sharing, Small Science and Institutional Repositories." *Philosophical Transactions of the Royal Society A: Mathematical, Physical and Engineering Sciences* 368, no. 1926 (September): 4023–38. doi:10.1098/rsta.2010.0165.

de Waard, Anita, Leen Breure, Joost G Kircz, and Herre Van Oostendorp. 2006. "Modeling Rhetoric in Scientific Publications." Paper presented at the International Conference on Multidisciplinary Information Sciences and Technologies, Mérida, Spain, October 25–28.

de Waard, Anita, and Joost Kircz. 2008. "Modeling Scientific Research Articles: Shifting Perspectives and Persistent Issues." In *Open Scholarship: Authority, Community, and Sustainability in the Age of Web 2.0: Proceedings of the 12th International Conference on Electronic Publishing*, edited by Leslie Chan and Susanna Mornatti. Toronto:

ELPUB, 21: 234–45.
De Wever, Aaike, Astrid Schmidt-Kloiber, Mark O. Gessner, and Klement Tockner. 2012. "Freshwater Journals Unite to Boost Primary Biodiversity Data Publication." *BioScience* 62, no. 6: 529–30. doi:10.1525/bio.2012.62.6.2.
Edwards, Paul N., Matthew S. Mayernik, Archer L. Batcheller, Geoffrey C. Bowker, and Christine L. Borgman. 2011. "Science Friction: Data, Metadata, and Collaboration." *Social Studies of Science* 41, no. 5 (October): 667–90. doi:10.1177/0306312711413314.
ESSD (Earth System Science Data). 2014. Website. Accessed January 6. www.earth-system-science-data.net.
Fearon, David, Jr., Betsy Gunia, Barbara E. Pralle, Sherry Lake, and Andrew L. Sallans. 2013. *Research Data Management Services: SPEC Kit 334*. Washington, DC: Association of Research Libraries, July.
F1000Research. 2014. "Can I Publish an Analysis of My Published Dataset in Other Journals?" Accessed February 26. http://f1000research.com/data-policies.
Force 11. 2014. "Joint Declaration of Data Citation Principles: Final." February. www.force11.org/datacitation.
Gorgolewski, Krzysztof J., Daniel S. Margulies, and Michael P. Milham. 2013. "Making Data Sharing Count: A Publication-Based Solution." *Frontiers in Neuroscience* 7, no. 9. doi:10.3389/fnins.2013.00009.
Gray, Jim, Alexander S. Szalay, Ani R. Thakar, Christopher Stoughton, and Jan vandenBerg. 2002. "Online Scientific Data Curation, Publication, and Archiving." In *Proceedings of SPIE* 4846, "Virtual Observatories," edited by Alexander S. Szalay, 103–7. Bellingham, WA: SPIE. doi:10.1117/12.461524.
Griffiths, Aaron. 2009. "The Publication of Research Data: Researcher Attitudes and Behaviour." *International Journal of Digital Curation* 4, no. 1: 46–56. doi:10.2218/ijdc.v4i1.77.
Guy, Marieke, and Monica Duke. 2013. "The Rise of the Data Journal." Presentation at IASSIST, Cologne, Germany, May 31. www.slideshare.net/MariekeGuy/the-rise-of-the-data-journal .
Haendel, Melissa A., Nicole A. Vasilevsky, and Jacqueline A. Wirz. 2012. "Dealing with Data: A Case Study on Information and Data Management Literacy." *PLOS Biology* 10, no. 5 (May 29): e1001339. doi:10.1371/journal.pbio.1001339.
Hahn, Karla L. 2008. *Research Library Publishing Services: New Options for University Publishing*. Washington, DC: Association of Research Libraries.
Higgins, Sarah. 2008. "The DCC Curation Lifecycle Model." *International Journal of Digital Curation* 3, no. 1: 134–40. doi:10.2218/ijdc.v3i1.48.
Kansa, Eric C., and Sarah Whitcher Kansa. 2013. "We All Know That a 14 Is a Sheep: Data Publication and Professionalism in Archaeological Communication." *Journal of Eastern Mediterranean Archaeology and Heritage Studies* 1, no. 1: 88–97. http://muse.jhu.edu/journals/journal_of_eastern_mediterranean_archaeology_and_heritage_studies/v001/1.1.kansa01.html.
Kratz, John, and Carly Strasser. 2014. "Data Publication: Consensus and Controversies" [v2; ref status: indexed, http://f1000r.es/3hi]. *F1000Research* 3, no. 94 (May 16). doi:10.12688/f1000research.3979.2.
Kuhn, Thomas S. 1996. *The Structure of Scientific Revolutions*. 3rd ed. Chicago: University of Chicago Press.
Kunze, John, Trisha Cruse, Rachael Hu, Stephen Abrams, Kirk Hastings, Catherine Mitch-

ell, and Lisa Schiff. 2011. *Practices, Trends, and Recommendations in Technical Appendix Usage for Selected Data-Intensive Disciplines*, version 2011.01.18. Oakland: California Digital Library. www.cdlib.org/services/uc3/docs/dax.pdf.

Latour, Bruno. 1987. *Science in Action: How to Follow Scientists and Engineers through Society*. Cambridge, MA: Harvard University Press.

Lawrence, Bryan, Catherine Jones, Brian Matthews, Sam Pepler, and Sarah Callaghan. 2011. "Citation and Peer Review of Data: Moving towards Formal Data Publication." *International Journal of Digital Curation* 6, no. 2: 4–37. doi:10.2218/ijdc.v6i2.205.

Lippincott, Sarah K., ed. 2013. *Library Publishing Directory*. Atlanta: Library Publishing Coalition. www.librarypublishing.org/sites/librarypublishing.org/files/documents/LPC_LPDirectory2014.pdf.

Maunsell, John. 2010. "Announcement Regarding Supplemental Material." *Journal of Neuroscience* 30, no. 32: 10599–600. www.jneurosci.org/content/30/32/10599.

McCallum, I., H.-P. Plag, S. Fritz, and S. Nativi. 2013. "Data Citation Standard: A Means to Support Data Sharing, Attribution, and Traceability." In *Proceedings of the 16th International Conference on Heavy Metals in the Environment*, edited by Nicola Pirrone. *E3S Web of Conferences* 1: 28002. doi:10.1051/e3sconf/20130128002.

Michener, William K., Suzie Allard, Amber Budden, Robert B. Cook, Kimberly Douglass, Mike Frame, Steve Kelling, Rebecca Koskela, Carol Tenopir, and David A. Vieglais. 2012. "Participatory Design of DataONE—Enabling Cyberinfrastructure for the Biological and Environmental Sciences." *Ecological Informatics* 11 (September): 5–15. doi:10.1016/j.ecoinf.2011.08.007.

Monastersky, Richard. 2013. "Publishing Frontiers: The Library Reboot." *Nature* 495, no. 7442 (March 27): 430–32. doi:10.1038/495430a.

Mullins, James L., Catherine Murray Rust, Joyce L. Ogburn, Raym Crow, October Ivins, Allyson Mower, Daureen Nesdill, Mark P. Newton, Julie Speer, and Charles Watkinson. 2012. *Library Publishing Services: Strategies for Success*. Final Research Report. Washington, DC: SPARC, March. http://docs.lib.purdue.edu/cgi/viewcontent.cgi?article=1023&context=purduepress_ebooks.

Muñoz, Trevor. 2013. "Data Curation as Publishing for Digital Humanists." Paper presented at the CIC Library Initiatives Conference, Columbus, OH, May 22–23.

NPG (Nature Publishing Group). 2013. "NPG to Launch *Scientific Data* to Help Scientists Publish and Reuse Research Data." News release, April 4. www.nature.com/press_releases/scientificdata.html.

———. 2014. "Scientific Data: Data Policies," under "Data Deposition Policy." Accessed February 24. www.nature.com/scientificdata/for-authors/data-deposition-policies.

Pangaea. 2014. Website. Accessed January 6. http://pangaea.de.

Parsons, Mark A., Ruth Duerr, and Jean-Bernard Minster. 2010. "Data Citation and Peer Review." *Eos, Transactions American Geophysical Union* 91, no. 34 (August): 297–98. doi:10.1029/2010EO340001.

Parsons, Mark A., and Peter A. Fox. 2013. "Is Data Publication the Right Metaphor?" In "Proceedings of the 1st WDS Conference in Kyoto 2011," special issue, *Data Science Journal* 12 (February 10): WDS32–WDS46. doi:10.2481/dsj.WDS-042.

PREPARDE (Peer Review for Publication and Accreditation of Research Data in the Earth Sciences). 2014. Project website, accessed October 13. http://proj.badc.rl.ac.uk/preparde.

Ray, Joyce, Sayeed Choudhury, and Michael J. Furlough. 2009. "Digital Curation and

E-Publishing: Libraries Make the Connection." Presentation, 29th Annual Charleston Library Conference, Charleston, SC, November 6. http://docs.lib.purdue.edu/cgi/viewcontent.cgi?article=1065&context=charleston.

Read, Kevin. 2013. "Data Publishing: Who Is Meeting This Need?" *Kevin the Librarian* (blog), June 11. http://kevinthelibrarian.wordpress.com/2013/06/11/data-publishing-who-is-meeting-this-need.

Reilly, Susan, Wouter Schallier, Sabine Schrimpf, Eefke Smit, and Max Wilkinson. 2011. *Report on Integration of Data and Publications, Opportunities for Data Exchange report.* Yetminster, UK: Alliance for Permanent Access, October 17. www.alliancepermanentaccess.org/wp-content/uploads/downloads/2011/11/ODE-ReportOnIntegrationOfDataAndPublications-1_1.pdf.

Scherer, David, Lisa Zilinski, and Courtney Matthews. 2013. "Opportunities and Challenges of Data Publication: A Case Study from Purdue." Presentation, 33rd Annual Charleston Library Conference, Charleston, SC, November 8. http://docs.lib.purdue.edu/lib_fspres/38.

Socha, Yvonne, ed. 2013. "Out of Cite, Out of Mind: The Current State of Practice, Policy, and Technology for the Citation of Data." *Data Science Journal* 12 (September): CIDCR1–CIDCR75. doi:10.2481/dsj.OSOM13-043.

Soehner, Catherine, Catherine Steeves, and Jennifer Ward. 2010. *E-Science and Data Support Services: A Study of ARL Member Institutions.* Washington, DC: Association of Research Libraries. www.arl.org/storage/documents/publications/escience-report-2010.pdf.

Swan, Alma, and Sheridan Brown. 2008. *To Share or Not to Share: Publication and Quality Assurance of Research Data Outputs.* London: Research Information Network, June. www.rin.ac.uk/our-work/data-management-and-curation/share-or-not-share-research-data-outputs.

Tenenbaum, Jessica D., Susanna-Assunta Sansone, and Melissa Haendel. 2014. "A Sea of Standards for Omics Data: Sink or Swim?" *Journal of the American Medical Informatics Association* 21, no. 2: 200–3. doi:10.1136/amiajnl-2013-002066.

Tenopir, Carol, Suzie Allard, Kimberly Douglass, Arsev Umur Aydinoglu, Lei Wu, Eleanor Read, Maribeth Manoff, and Mike Frame. 2011. "Data Sharing by Scientists: Practices and Perceptions." *PLOS ONE* 6, no. 6 (June 29): e21101. doi:10.1371/journal.pone.0021101.

Tenopir, Carol, Ben Birch, and Suzie Allard. 2012. *Academic Libraries and Research Data Services: Current Practices and Plans for the Future.* An ACRL white paper. Chicago: Association of College and Research Libraries, June.

Tornow, Joanne, and Farnam Jahanian. 2014. "Dear Colleague Letter: Supporting Scientific Discovery through Norms and Practices for Software and Data Citation and Attribution." NSF 14-059. Washington, DC: National Science Foundation, April 11. www.nsf.gov/pubs/2014/nsf14059/nsf14059.jsp.

Vines, Timothy H., Arianne Y. K. Albert, Rose L. Andrew, Florence Débarre, Dan G. Bock, Michelle T. Franklin, Kimberly J. Gilbert, Jean-Sébastien Moore, Sébastien Renaut, and Diana J. Rennison. 2014. "The Availability of Research Data Declines Rapidly with Article Age." *Current Biology* 24, no. 1 (94–97). doi:10.1016/j.cub.2013.11.014.

Wenfang, Cheng, Zhang Jie, Zhang Beichen, and Yang Rui. 2013. "A Multidisciplinary Scientific Data Sharing System for the Polar Region." In Proceedings: *12th International Symposium on Distributed Computing and Applications to Business, Engineering and Science: DCABES 2013,* edited by Souheil Khaddaj, 167–70. doi:10.1109/

DCABES.2013.54.

Willis, Craig, Jane Greenberg, and Hollie White. 2012. "Analysis and Synthesis of Metadata Goals for Scientific Data." *Journal of the American Society for Information Science and Technology* 63, no. 8 (August): 1505–20. doi:10.1002/asi.22683.

Wright, Sarah J., Wendy A. Kozlowski, Dianne Dietrich, Huda J. Khan, Gail S. Steinhart, and Leslie McIntosh. 2013. "Using Data Curation Profiles to Design the Datastar Dataset Registry." *D-Lib Magazine* 19, no. 7/8 (July). doi:10.1045/july2013-wright.

About the Authors

Maria Bonn is a Senior Lecturer at the Graduate School of Library and Information Science at the University of Illinois at Urbana-Champaign where she teaches courses on the role of libraries in scholarly communication and publishing. Prior to her teaching appointment, she served as the associate university librarian for publishing at the University of Michigan Library, with responsibility for publishing and scholarly communications initiatives, including the University of Michigan Press, the Scholarly Publishing Office, the institutional repository (Deep Blue), the Copyright Office, and the Text Creation Partnership. She has also been an assistant professor of English at Albion College and taught at Sichuan International Studies University (Chongqing, China) and Bilkent University (Ankara, Turkey). She received a bachelor's degree from the University of Rochester, master's and doctoral degrees in English Literature from SUNY Buffalo, and a master's in information and library science from the University of Michigan.

Amy Buckland recently moved to the University of Chicago where she is the Institutional Repository Manager. Previously she was Coordinator of Scholarly Communications at McGill University Library, where she was responsible for open access initiatives, publishing support, copyright, digital humanities, and research data services. She has a Bachelor of Arts degree from Concordia University (Montreal) where she studied political science and women's studies, and an MLIS from McGill

University. Prior to joining the library world, she worked in publishing for 14 years, and thinks academic libraryland is ripe for a revolution.

Matt Burton is Visiting Assistant Professor at the University of Pittsburgh. His research explores digital scholarship in the social sciences and humanities. He has a PhD from the University of Michigan School of Information where his dissertation study was on the use of blogs as a mode of scholarly communication in the Digital Humanities.

Dan Cohen is the Founding Executive Director of the DPLA, where he works to further the DPLA's mission to make the cultural and scientific heritage of humanity available, free of charge, to all. Prior to his tenure, Cohen was a Professor of History and the Director of the Roy Rosenzweig Center for History and New Media at George Mason University. At the Center, he oversaw projects ranging from new publishing ventures (PressForward) to online collections (September 11 Digital Archive) to software for scholarship (the popular Zotero research tool). His books include *Digital History: A Guide to Gathering, Preserving, and Presenting the Past on the Web* (with Roy Rosenzweig) and *Equations from God: Pure Mathematics and Victorian Faith*. Dan was an inaugural recipient of the American Council of Learned Societies' Digital Innovation Fellowship. In 2011 he received the Frederick G. Kilgour Award from the American Library Association for his work in digital humanities, and in 2012 he was named one of the top "tech innovators" in academia by the *Chronicle of Higher Education*. Cohen received his bachelor's degree from Princeton, his master's degree from Harvard, and his PhD from Yale.

Paul Courant is the Harold T. Shapiro Collegiate Professor of Public Policy, Arthur F. Thurnau Professor, professor of economics, and professor of information at the University of Michigan. Courant has served as provost and executive vice president for academic affairs, as university librarian and dean of libraries, as associate provost for academic and budgetary affairs, as chair of the Department of Economics, and as director of the Institute of Public Policy Studies (predecessor of the Gerald R. Ford School of Public Policy). Courant has authored half a dozen books, and over seventy papers covering a broad range of topics in economics and public policy. More recently, his academic work has considered the economics of universities, the economics of libraries and archives, and the effects of new information technologies and other disruptions on scholarship, scholarly publication, and academic libraries, with an eye to developing intellectual property policies that will work well in the digital age. He was a founding board member of both the HathiTrust Digital Library and the Digital Public Library of America, and serves on several other nonprofit boards, including the Council for Library and Information Resources and the DuraSpace Foundation. He is also a member of the Advisory Board of the Authors Alliance. Courant holds a BA in history from Swarthmore College, an MA in economics from Princeton University, and a PhD in economics from Princeton University.

Kathleen Fitzpatrick is Director of Scholarly Communication of the Modern Language Association and Visiting Research Professor of English at NYU. She is author of *Planned Obsolescence: Publishing, Technology, and the Future of the Academy* (NYU Press, 2011) and of *The Anxiety of Obsolescence: The American Novel in the Age of Television* (Vanderbilt University Press, 2006). She is co-founder of the digital scholarly network MediaCommons, where she has led a number of experiments in open peer review and other innovations in scholarly publishing.

Mike Furlough is Executive Director of HathiTrust Digital Library. Furlough leads an organization that includes over 90 academic and research institutions working to transform scholarship and research in the 21st century. Furlough's research has focused on how libraries and universities develop organizational support for emerging scholarly communication practices. He has presented work at the Digital Library Federation Forum, the American Association of University Presses, the Charleston Conference, the Bloomsbury Conference, and Educause, among others. From 2011-2013 he served as faculty for the ARL/DLF/Duraspace E-Science Institute. Furlough studied English and American Literature at the University of Virginia. After joining the University of Virginia Library in 1997 he led the GeoStat lab, initiating support for GIS in digital humanities research, and later led planning for and development of the Scholar's Lab. From 2006-2014 served as Assistant and later Associate Dean for Research and Scholarly Communications at Penn State University Libraries, where he led content stewardship services that support the life cycle of scholarly production.

Kevin S. Hawkins was appointed director of library publishing for the University of North Texas Libraries in May 2014 and since October 2014 has served as the first president of the board of directors of the Library Publishing Coalition. Previously he was director of publishing operations for Michigan Publishing, the hub of scholarly publishing at the University of Michigan Library which includes the University of Michigan Press and other brands and services. Hawkins has also worked as visiting metadata manager for the Digital Humanities Observatory, a project of the Royal Irish Academy. He has contributed to major standards for digital publishing—most notably, the Journal Article Tag Suite (ANSI/NISO Z39.96-2012), EPUB 3.0, and the Text Encoding Initiative (TEI) Guidelines. His involvement with the TEI includes co-editing the 2011 revision to the Best Practices for TEI in Libraries and serving as the first managing editor of the Journal of the Text Encoding Initiative. He has BAs in Russian and linguistics from the University of Maryland and an MS in library and information science from the University of Illinois. For more information, see http://www.ultraslavonic.info/.

J. Britt Holbrook is Visiting Assistant Professor in the School of Public Policy at the Georgia Institute of Technology and a member of the Committee on Scientific Freedom and Responsibility of the American Association for the Advancement of Science (AAAS). Holbrook published the first scholarly article on the US National Science Foundation's Broader Impacts Merit Review Criterion in 2005, and has published widely on peer review and related topics since then. Recent publications include: "What is interdisciplinary communication? Reflections on the very idea of disciplinary integration." *Synthese*, 190 (11): 1865-1879, DOI: 10.1007/s11229-012-0179-7; J. Britt Holbrook and Adam Briggle (2014), "Knowledge kills action—why principles should play a limited role in policy-making," *Journal of Responsible Innovation* 1 (1): 51–66, DOI: 10.1080/23299460.2014.882554; and Holbrook, J. Britt, and Carl Mitcham, eds. *Ethics, Science, Technology, and Engineering: A Global Resource*, 2nd edition. 4 vols. Farmington Hills, MI: Macmillan Reference USA, 2015. You can also find him on Twitter: @jbrittholbrook or on his blog: jbrittholbrook.com.

Patricia Hswe is Digital Content Strategist at the Pennsylvania State University Libraries and heads user services for Penn State's repository service, ScholarSphere. She also co-leads the Libraries' department of Publishing and Curation Services (PCS). PCS is establishing a framework of programs, services, and support to help researchers put into practice a lifecycle management approach to the enterprise of scholarly inquiry. It offers training and consultation in data management planning; advises on scholarly publishing activities, including starting open access journals and conference proceedings; and plans, develops, and carries out digital projects in collaboration with faculty, students, and staff. Hswe holds an M.S. in Library and Information Science and a Ph.D. in Slavic Languages and Literatures. In her free time, when she doesn't have PCS on the brain, she tries to indulge in her love of cooking, knitting, photography, hiking, board games, and reading novels for fun—though not all at once.

Korey Jackson is the Gray Family Chair for Innovative Library Services at Oregon State University. Before coming to OSU, Jackson was an American Council of Learned Societies (ACLS) Public Fellow at Anvil Academic, a digital humanities publisher sponsored by the Council on Library and Information Resources (CLIR) and the National Institute for Technology in Liberal Education (NITLE). While at Anvil he served as Program Coordinator, helping to create editorial partnerships, engage in social media relations, and implement digital publishing strategies for a number of humanities projects. Prior to Anvil he held a CLIR Postdoctoral Fellowship at the University of Michigan's Michigan Publishing, where he developed campus-wide outreach efforts around open access publishing and digital humanities training and discussion. Jackson earned PhD in English Language and Literature from the University of Michigan.

Elisabeth A. Jones is a Postdoc/Lecturer at the University of Washington Information School and a Research Associate at the University of Michigan Libraries. Her current research explores the social, political, and institutional issues that arise alongside changing modes of information access in the digital world, especially in the context of large-scale digitization initiatives like the Google Books Library Project and the now-defunct Open Content Alliance. She is particularly interested in what these types of initiatives mean for the future of libraries and for the policy dynamics that surround them. Jones holds a PhD in Information Science from the University of Washington and an MSI in Information Economics, Management, and Policy from the University of Michigan. Before entering academia, she worked in several capacities within various academic libraries, including cataloging maps at the University of Chicago, providing reference assistance at the University of Michigan, and conducting research on libraries' role in cyberinfrastructure initiatives at the University of Washington.

Sarah Lippincott is Program Manager for the Library Publishing Coalition and bears primary responsibility for all LPC development duties, including attracting and retaining member institutions, developing and maintaining relationships with relevant service organizations, research/market analysis, event hosting/organization, and creation/dissemination of outreach activities. Lippincott received her MSLS from The University of North Carolina at Chapel Hill and her BA in the College of Letters and French Studies from Wesleyan University. Before joining Educopia, she worked as a communications consultant for ARL, SPARC, and the open access journal *eLife*.

Monica McCormick is Program Officer for Digital Scholarly Publishing at New York University, reporting jointly to the Division of Libraries and NYU Press. She develops strategies and supports services for digital publishing at both organizations, and manages collaborations between them. She received her MSLS from the University of North Carolina, Chapel Hill. Before moving in to her hybrid publisher/librarian role, she served as a sponsoring editor for history and ethnic studies at the University of California Press for fifteen years.

Cyril Oberlander is the Library Dean at Humboldt State University since July 2014. Previously, he served as the Director of Milne Library at the State University of New York at Geneseo since 2011, and as the Principal Investigator of the Open SUNY Textbook Project, a multi-institutional, $120,000 grant and library funded open textbook publishing initiative. Prior, he served as the Associate Director of Milne Library at SUNY Geneseo and as an internal consultant to the IDS Project, a 75 library cooperative in New York, since 2008. Prior experience includes: Director of Interlibrary Services at the University of Virginia Library from 2005-2008; the Head of Interlibrary Loan at Portland State University from 1996-2005, as well as various roles in Access Services at Portland State University since

1987. Oberlander has more than 25 years of academic library experience and over 10 years of experience as an independent library consultant. As a consultant he has worked with a variety of public, academic, and special libraries, providing workflow and space use analysis, as well as effective technology and innovation integration. His extensive scholarly record includes more than 26 published articles and over 100 presentations at the state, national, and international level. Oberlander is an experienced and innovative leader in libraries, committed to and passionate about creating a vibrant and positive role for libraries and higher education in the 21st century.

Dr. Katherine Skinner is the Executive Director of the Educopia Institute (http://www.educopia.org), a not-for-profit educational organization that advances cultural, scientific, and scholarly institutions by catalyzing networks and collaborative communities to support the publishing, dissemination, and preservation of knowledge. She is the founding program director for the MetaArchive Cooperative, a community-owned and community-governed digital preservation network founded in 2004 that now has more than 50 member institutions in four countries. She also directs the Library Publishing Coalition project, a two-year initiative to create a new organization to support library publishing and scholarly communications activities in conjunction with more than 50 academic libraries. Skinner received her Ph.D. from Emory University. She has co-edited three books and has authored and co-authored numerous reports and articles. She regularly teaches graduate courses and workshops and provides consultation services to groups that are planning or implementing collaborative networks.

Julie Speer is Associate Dean for Research and Informatics at Virginia Tech Libraries and Director of Virginia Tech's Center for Digital Research and Scholarship. Prior to her time at Virginia Tech, Speer served as Head of the Scholarly Communication and Digital Services department at Georgia Tech Library overseeing repository, publishing, and digital media production services.

Lisa Spiro serves as the Executive Director of Digital Scholarship Services at Rice University's Fondren Library. She has published on topics such as collaboration in the digital humanities, digital humanities values, alternative academic careers, the prospect for an all-digital academic library, and the impact of digital resources on research into American literature and culture. Prior to her current position at Rice, she served as the Director of NITLE Labs and Program Manager of Anvil Academic press.

Tyler Walters is Dean, University Libraries and Professor, Virginia Tech. He is a Research Libraries Leadership Fellow of the Association of Research Libraries. Walters serves on many boards such as the steering committee, Coalition of Networked Information (CNI); Board of Directors, DuraSpace; Board of Directors, National Information Standards Organization (NISO); and editorial board, *International Journal of Digital Curation*. Walters is a founding member of the MetaArchive Cooperative, a digital preservation federation and serves on the board of its management organization, the Educopia Institute. Walters recently completed a Ph.D. from Simmons College Graduate School of Library and Information Science. His research focuses on changes in knowledge creation and production in research universities, organizational change, and authentic and transformational leadership. Currently Walters is also serving as founding director of SHARE, which is networking digital repositories across the US to provide public access to federally funded research.

Charles Watkinson is Associate University Librarian for Publishing at the University of Michigan Library and Director of University of Michigan Press. Previously he was Head of Scholarly Publishing Services at Purdue University Libraries and Director of Purdue University Press from 2009 to mid-2014, when his contribution to this book was written. From 2004 to 2009 he was Director of Publications at the American School of Classical Studies, and prior to this worked for Oxbow Books in various capacities in both the US and UK. He has been on the boards of directors of the Association of American University Presses and Society for Scholarly Publishing and played an initiating role in the creation of the Library Publishing Coalition.

Index

A

Academic context, 131–132
Academic degree programs, 125
Academic disciplines, library support, 20
Academic freedom
    contextual variation, 45–46
    disciplinary terms, 50–51
    negative notion, 52
    positive liberty, relationship, 51
    risk/reputation/revaluation, 52–54
Academic liberty, 45–46
Academic librarians, faculty (interaction), 178–179
Academic librarianship, humanities data publishing (relationship), 203
Academic libraries. *See* Small academic libraries
    data curation services, 221
    examination, 49–50
    publishing services, 141
        defining, 144–147
        method, 142–143
    publishing support services, 10
    works, non-rivalrous characteristic, 31–32
Academic Libraries and Research Data Services (ACRL), 229–230
Academic presses, initiation, 17–18
Academic publishers, project search, 38–39
Academic units, alliances, 165
Acquisitions, function, 134–135
Against the Grain (Furlough/Alexander), 87
Alexander, Patrick, 87

All-digital publishing, assumptions, 63
Alliance networks, absence, 109
Alliance of Digital Humanities Organizations, 71–72
ALPSP. *See* Association of Learned and Professional Society Publishers
Alt-metrics, 72
Amazon
    attention, 77
    negotiator aggressiveness, 63
American Association of University Professors (AAUP), *1940 Statement of Principles on Academic Freedom and Tenure*, 46
American Communal Societies Quarterly (publication), 154
American Council of Learned Societies, report, 205
American Historical Association (AHA), dissertation embargo, 195–196
American Library Association Midwinter Conference, 178
Ames Library (Illinois Wesleyan University), 150
Amherst College
    initiatives, 142
    library publishing, case studies, 155–157
Amherst College Press, 155–156
    initiation, challenges, 156–157
    launching, 6–7, 168–169
    monographs, publication, 108
Amherst Library (press), 156

Andrew W. Mellon Foundation, grants, 161
Application programming interfaces
  (APIs), 210-211. *See also* Archival APIs
    generative properties, 216-217
    machine-readable APIs, 211
    metadata, 215
    usage, possibilities, 215-217
Applications developer, 124
Archival APIs
  types, 212-213
  usage, 210-211
Aristotle, 44
ARL SPEC Kit, data publishing, 230
Armato, Douglas, 74
Article age, effects, 242-243
Article submission, processes, 237-238
Arts Undergraduate Research Fair (McGill
  University), 200
arXiv.org
  endorsements, 70
  preprint acceptance, 68
  work, sharing, 72
Association for Nepal and Himalayan
  Studies (ANHS), 148
Association of American Publishers
  (AAP), 122-123, 126
Association of American University Presses
  (AAUP), 126
    Reporting Structure Survey, 85-86
Association of College and Research
  Libraries (ACRL), 178
Association of Learned and Professional
  Society Publishers (ALPSP) webinar
  series, 126
Association of Research Libraries (ARL)
  membership, survey, 5
  "Strategic Thinking and Design," 2
Attribution-NonCommercial-NoDerivs
  license, 116
Atypon, 63, 77
Audiences, identification, 127-128
Australian National University Press, 78
Australian Universities Publishers Group,
  86
Authors
  agreements, 117-118
  calls, 185
  rights, importance, 194
  strategies, 183
Autonomy, 51, 52. *See also* Disciplinary
  autonomy
Auxiliary unit, classification, 98-99

B

Baseline digital edition, 38
Bell, Steven J., 179
Berkeley Electronic Press, 5
Berline, Isaiah, 46
Bibliography of Asian Studies, 3
Bibliometric analysis (enabling), parsed
  citations (usage), 214
Big data, publishing process, 229
BioOne, partnership, 7
Bonn, Maria, 1, 118, 133, 135
Book Publishers Bureau, 122-123
Books
  distinction/usefulness, 37
  fields, 41
  marketing, difficulty, 166
  publication, review, 69
Bowker, 77
Bryn Mawr Classical, 3
Buckland, Amy, 8, 193
Budapest Open Access Initiative, 116
Burke Library (Hamilton College), 154
Burton, Matt, 9, 203
Business models, 49, 53-54
  future, 123-124
Business planning/management, 132-133

C

California Digital Library (CDL)
  CLIR postdoctoral fellow, hiring, 240
  PREPARDE, partnership, 239-240
California State Auditor, faculty interview,
  180-181
Camera-ready archives, 206
Campus-based partnerships, 8
Campus-Based Publishing Partnerships
  (Crow), 141
Campus publishing, support
  (development), 153-154
Capstone projects, 195
Captive Audiences/Captive Performers
  (DeWitt Wallace Library), 147

Index 259

Center for Digital Research and Scholarship (CDRS) (Columbia University Library), 68
Choudhury, Sayeed, 205
Citation-based metrics, 235–236
Claremont Colleges, 142
 Consortium, 144
 digital scholarship, expansion, 146–147
 repository, 200
Claremont Colleges Library (CCL), 149
 journals, proposals, 165
 provisions, 161
 publishing, case studies, 149–150
CLCWeb: Comparative Literature and Culture, 103
Clement, Rick, 99
CLIR. *See* Council on Library and Information Resources
Club goods, 31
Coble, Zach, 145, 153, 164
Co-curricular activities, impact, 162–163
CODATA Data Science Journal, 237
Colby College, 142
 copy editor contract, 168
 Libraries, LPC membership, 144–145
 library publishing, case studies, 148–149
Colby Environmental Assessment Team, 149
Colby Libraries, 149
Colby Quarterly back issues, Digital Commons digitization, 149
Collaboration, 83, 86–92
 challenges, 79–80
 conversion, challenges, 95–99
 cross-institutional collaboration, rarity, 98
 economic/operational convenience, 102
 opportunities, 99–103
 synergies, 99
 type 1 relationships, 87–88
 type 2 collaboration, 88–89
 type 3 projects, 89–90
 type 4 collaboration, 90
 type 5 collaborations, characterization, 90–91
Collaboration opportunities, 75–79

Collaborative arrangements, 35–36
Collection development responsibilities, reversal, 241
College Open Textbooks Collaborative, 182
Columbia International Affairs Online (CIAO), 4, 88
Columbia Publishing Course, 125
Columbia University Library, Center for Digital Research and Scholarship, 68
Columbia University, University of California (relationship), 87–88
CommentPress, usage, 69, 76
Commercial publishing houses, submissions, 26
"Committee on Professional Education for Publishing" (AAP), 123
Communication, improvement, 79
Constraints, freedom, 50
CONTENTdm, 146
 CLIC access, 167
Content expansion, impact, 206
Content management
 skills/practices, 123–124
 systems, 75–76
Content selection, support, 71–72
Contractual arrangements, 34
Co-occurring words, patterns (discovery), 208
Cooperating Libraries in Consortium (CLIC), CONTENTdm access, 167–168
Copyrighted works, non-consumptive use (support), 212
Core knowledge/skills, identification, 130–135
Cornell Libraries, joint project, 89
Cornell University Library, 68
 arXiv.org site, hosting/maintenance, 72
 Duke University Press, collaboration, 88, 89
Cornell University, Research Data Management Service Group (RDMSG), 226–227
Council on Library and Information Resources (CLIR)
 library-based postdoctoral fellowship program sponsorship, 224
 postdoctoral fellow, hiring, 240
Couper Press (Hamilton College), 154

book marketing difficulty, 166
publication charges, 161
targeting, 155
Courant, Paul N., 17, 1334
CreateSpace, 6
Creative Common (CC)
  Attribution, 237
    license, 238
  licenses, 59, 117–118, 185
    adoption, 158
  open-access content, sharing, 116
Cross-fertilization, opportunities, 136
Cross-institutional collaboration, rarity, 98
Crow, Raym, 95, 109, 129, 141
  emphasis, 132–133
Cultural challenges, 96–97
Cultural differences, 96
CUNY Grad Center, 69
Cupola, The: Scholarship at Gettysburg College, 153
Curation. *See* Data curation
  usage, 225
Curatorial services, impact, 204–205

D

Dangerous Citizens (Fordham University Press), 88
Dartmouth, partnership, 7
Data access process, 240
Data APIs, 212
DataBib, 238
Data citation, 235–236
  standards, 227–228
    promotion, 222–223
DataCite, library membership, 222–223
Data curation, 204–207, 243
  basics, 224–229
  library services, 225
  occurrence, 205–206
  responses, 217–219
  services, 221, 224
    context/comparison, 229–233
  sharing/publication, contrast, 224–229
"Data Curation as Publishing for Digital Humanists" (Muñoz), 205
Data Curation Education Program for the Humanities (DCEP-H), 217

Data Curation Profiles Toolkit, 241
Data democratization, 222
Data Descriptor, 236, 238–239
  template, 241
Data dissemination, 222
Data for Research. *See* Journal Storage
Data journals, 236–240
  genres, 224
Data management plan (DMP), 223
  NEH/NSF mandates, issuance, 226
  NSF requirement, 236
Data management services librarian
  positions, creation, 223
Data paper genres, 224
Data persistence, 227–228
Data policies, 236–240
  revision, 237
Data publication, 225, 243
  classification, 227
  meaning, 226–227
Data Publisher for Earth and Environmental Science, 228–229
Data publishing, 204–207
  assertions, 228–229
  frameworks, creation, 222
  peer review, relationship, 233–236
  RDMSG codification, 226–227
  readiness, 231
Data, reading, 217
Data repositories, 236–240
  name changes, 228
  publishers, partnerships, 238
  workflows, 235
Data research methods, 207
Data scientist, 124
Data Scientist Training for Librarians, 223
Data set
  assignation, 229
  change, 234–235
  hosting, 237–238
  peer review, assignment, 233
Dataset management, specification, 231
Data standards, 234
Davis-Kahl, Stephanie, 145, 150–151, 160–162
Debates in the Digital Humanities, 69
Denver Publishing Institute (DPI), 125, 127
Derived data APIs, 212

Derived data download, 214
Derived data downloading, 213
DeWitt Wallace Library
 publishing program, 147–148
 scholarly journal publication, 148
dh+lib journal, sponsorship, 71
Dickens, Charles, 74
Digital age, scholarly production
 (optimization), 36
Digital asset management, 123–124
Digital business models, purpose
 (convergence), 33–36
Digital Commons, 160
 Colby Quarterly back issues,
 digitization, 149
 repository platform, 88
 subscription, 151
Digital Culture Books (Michigan
 Publishing), 78
"Digital Curation and E-Publishing:
 Libraries Make the Connection"
 (Choudhury, et al.), 205
Digital data, machine readability, 228
Digital formats, library publisher
 production, 65
Digital humanities, computational
 methods (usage), 207
Digital Humanities Now blog, 71–72
Digital Humanities Quarterly, 71
Digital humanities scholarship, profile
 (growth), 205
Digital Library Federation, 223
Digital media, education coverage, 126
Digital object identifiers (DOIs), 152
 assignment/allocation, 231
 mechanism, 227–228
 minting, 238
Digital publications, careers, 158–159
Digital research methods, preparation,
 206–207
Digital scholarly publishing, vision, 58–60
Digital Scholarship Council (DSC), 93
Digital scholarship, expansion, 146–147
Digital sustainability, NSF Blue Ribbon
 Task Force report, 23
Digital technologies, usage, 35–36
 consequences, 20
Digital tools, usage, 133–134

Digital work, server presence, 33
Digress.it, usage, 69
Directory of Open Access Journals
 (DOAJ), 198
Disciplinary autonomy, 51
Disciplinary diffusion, impact, 206
Disciplinary practices, scholarly publisher
 knowledge, 131–132
Disruptive models, 133
Dissertations, 195
 AHA embargo, 195–196
 distributions, 74
Distance education programs, 126
Distant readers, value, 211
Distribution
 sales, relationship, 77–78
 technology/workflows, 133–134
Dixon, Donna, 184
DMP. *See* Data management plan
DMPTool, usage, 223
DocSouth Books (UNC Press), 73
Documenting the American South
 (University of North Carolina), 73
Document set specification, 213
DPubS, creation, 5
Dr. Jekyll and Dr. Hyde problem, 96
Drupal, content management systems, 75
Dryad (repository), 237–239
DSpace, 4–5
Duke University Press, Cornell University
 Libraries (collaboration), 88, 89

E

Earth System Science Data (ESSD) Journal,
 229, 238
E-books, distribution, 77
EBSCO, 78, 156, 198
Ecological Society of America (ESA), 237
EdiKit, usage, 153, 160
Edington, Mark D.W., 156
Editorial functions, 134–135
Editorial process, overseeing, 143
Editorial workflow/design (Open SUNY
 Textbooks), 185–188
Editors
 agreements, 117–118
 libraries, agreements, 115–116

non-exclusive agreement, 115
presses, competition, 134
warranty, 116
Education. *See* Publishing education
Educational resources (library-based publishing), 177
"Education for Publishing Program" (AAP), 123
Edward S. Curtis Photo Gravure collection, 146–147
Electronic Publishing Initiative at Columbia (EPIC), closure, 88
Electronic Resources Committee, 101–102
Electronic Theses and Dissertations (ETDs), 120, 143
publishing, 231
Elementa, 116
Elementa: Science of the Anthropocene, 7–8
Embedded librarians, 96
Endowed Digital Scholarship Services Student Assistant, hiring, 201
EPUB editions, 185–186
E-reading technologies, improvement, 39
Ericson, Randall, 154
E-Science Institute, 223
Espresso Book Machine, 78
services, 39
Essays in Philosophy (journal), transfer, 152
ETDs. *See* Electronic Theses and Dissertations
Ethnography of the University Initiative (EUI) (University of Illinois), 197
Experimentation, usage, 164
Expertise, deferral, 48
EZID identifier service, 240

F

F1000Research data policies, 228
Faculty
academic librarians, interaction, 178–179
alliances, 165
California State Auditor interview, 180–181
options, 183
Fathom, closure, 88
Fielding, Roy T., 216–217

Filtering
social practice, description, 68–69
usage, 67–68
Financial support, sources (discovery), 100
First copy, distribution, 40
Fishel, Terri, 148, 161, 164
Fister, Barbara, 168–169
Fitzpatrick, Kathleen, 70
Flanders, Julia, 207
Florida Student Textbook Survey, 178
Force 11, 228
Forerunners: Ideas First (series), 74–75
Freedom
contextual variation. *See* Academic freedom.
meaning, 47
Freelance editors/designers, impact, 59
Free riders
example, 32
problems, 32–33
solutions, absence, 33
Free space, 100–101
Frugé, August, 37, 38
Full publishing, 37
Functions
alignment, 18–22
missions, relationship, 19–20
Furlough, Michael, 1, 87, 100, 118, 205

G

Geffert, Bryn, 155–156
GenBank, 226
Geneseo Libraries (SUNY), 87
George State University, lawsuit, 97
Georgia Institute of Technology, 11
partnership, 7
Geosciences Data Journal, 235
Gettysburg College
library publishing, case studies, 153–154
Musselman Library, 153
Gettysburg College Journal of the Civil War Era, 153–154
Gettysburg Historical Journal, 153
Gilman, Daniel Coit, 43, 143, 163, 166, 201
Gilman, Isaac, 152
Gold, Matt, 69

Index   263

Google Scholar, usage, 20
Graduate student publications, library publishing support, 199
Graves, Diane, 144
Greenstein, Daniel, 102–103
Griffin, Stephen, 129
Guthrie, Kevin, 109
Guthro, Clem, 144–145

H

Hahn, Karla, 5, 121, 141
Hamilton College
    Burke Library, 154
    Couper Press, 154
        publication charges, 161
    library publishing, case studies, 154–155
Harvard-Smithsonian Center for Astrophysics, 223
Harvard University Press, 22
HathiTrust, 38
HathiTrust Research Center (HTRC), 214–215
Hawkins, Kevin S., 113
Hayles, Katherine, 208
Higher Education Opportunity Act (HEOA), 179
Higher education, transformation, 181
"High-Impact Educational Practices" (AAC&U), 163
HighWire Press, 3, 63, 77
History E Book Project, 7–8
Holbrook, J. Britt, 11, 43
How We Think (Hayles), 208
Hswe, Patricia, 9, 221
HTRC. *See* HathiTrust Research Center
HUBZero platform, 106
Human-Animal Bond Research Initiative (HABRI), 106
    HABRI Central, 106
Humanities
    computational methods, usage. *See* Digital humanities.
    curatorial services, benefits, 204–205
    data publishing
        academic librarianship, relationship, 203

content expansion/disciplinary diffusion, impact, 206
        research methods, 207
Humanities Commons Open Repository Exchange (Humanities CORE), 68
Human readable data, 217
Hybridity, 218

I

IDEALS. *See* Illinois Digital Environment for Access to Learning and Scholarship
Ideas (movement), ecological metaphor (proposal), 74
IITG. *See* Innovative Instruction Technology Grant
Illinois Digital Environment for Access to Learning and Scholarship (IDEALS), 197
Illinois Wesleyan University, 142, 144
    Ames Library, 150
    library publishing, case studies, 150–151
Images, metadata (association), 216
Information
    literacy instruction, 162
    non-rivalry, 33
    science, training, 49
Information Resources Council (IRC), 93
    membership, 101–102
Information technology (IT)
    infrastructure, 65
Infrastructure professionals, JTRP technical report, 105
In-house training programs, 127
Innovative Instruction Technology Grant (IITG) (SUNY), 183–185
    grant funding renewal, 186–187
Institute for the Study of the Ancient World (ISAW), 78–79
    digital publications, XHTML production/conversion, 79
Institute of Museum and Library Services (IMLS), 2
Institutional departments, arm's-length relationship, 99
Institutional library, funding sources, 95
Institutional repositories (IRs)
    running, 230

Institutional repositories (IRs), management, 223
Integration, 83, 86–92
    conversion, challenges, 95–99
    opportunities, 99–103
    synergies, 99
Intellectual cross-pollination, 218
Interdisciplinary Journal of Problem-Based Learning, 103
International Association of Scientific, Technical and Medical Publishers, 126
International Group of Publishing Libraries, 45
International Standard Serial Numbers (ISSNs), registration, 152
    library assistance, 198
Internship programs, 127
Interoperability/standards, knowledge, 217
IRs. *See* Institutional repositories
ISAW. *See* Institute for the Study of the Ancient World
Ivins, October, 121, 131

J

Jackson, Korey, 9, 203
Japanese Association for Digital Humanities, 216
JavaScript Object Notation (JSON), 212
Jefferson, Thomas, 28
Johns Hopkins University Press
    creation, 27
    Project MUSE, creation, 109
"Joint Declaration of Data Citation Principles," Force 11 issuance, 228
Joint Transportation Research Program (JTRP) (Purdue University), technical report, 105, 107
Jones, Elisabeth A., 17
Journal Editing and Publishing (undergraduate course), 163
Journal-hosting services, library offering, 198
Journal Incubator (University of Lethbridge), 199–200
Journal of Aviation Technology and Engineering, 103
Journal of Humanistic Mathematics, 150
Journal of Neuroscience reviewers, 233–234
Journal of Pre-College Engineering Education Research, 103
Journal of Purdue Undergraduate Research (JPUR), 104, 199
    white labeling, 104–105
Journals
    articles, transformation, 214
    availability, 32
    production workflow, 114–115
    publication. *See* Scholarly journals.
Journal Storage (JSTOR), 3, 64, 78, 213
    Data for Research, 213–214
    Data for Research, automation (absence), 213
JQuery JavaScript library, 215–216
JSON. *See* JavaScript Object Notation
JSTOR. *See* Journal Storage

K

Karaali, Gizem, 150

L

Large-scale digitization, 205–206
LaTeX, 184
LCPS. *See* Local Collections and Publication Services
Learning
    holistic approach, 135
    orientation, 141
    publishing/scholarly communications, integration, 162–164
Legal arrangements, 34
Lever Initiative (Oberlin Group), 168–169
    initial research phase, 169
Liberty. *See* Academic liberty
    negative liberty, 46, 50
    positive liberty, 46
Librarians
    cultural differences, 96
    digital research method preparation, 206–207
    embedded librarians, 96
Libraries. *See* Academic libraries
    agreements, entry, 115–116
    collaboration, 83, 166–167
    collections

digital research method preparation, 206–207
purpose, 24
data curation services, 224
de-accession, 100
dissemination model, 35
economic opportunity, 101
editors, agreements, 115–116
expense, 31
faculty, interaction (Pacific University), 200–201
holdings, digitization, 5–6
hosting platforms, 73
integration, 83
IT specialists, impact, 101
long-term usability, 36
OA policy promotion, 50
processes, 61–67
production activities, 121–122
services, 200–201
success, 10–11
skills, 64
university presses
collaboration, 86, 102, 107–109
report, 85t
vacated space, occupation, 100
works, publication ability, 41
Libraries-as-publishers
disciplines, impact, 53–54
legitimation, crisis, 53
Library-as-publisher, 119
Library-based publishing, 1–2
credibility, 158–159
educational resources, 177
growth, 98
increase, 107
LPC definition, 143
operations, formation, 113–114
textbooks, usage, 177
Library-based scholarly publishing, 232–233
Library presses, 35
expectation, 38–39
Library publishers
audiences, identification, 127–128
impact, 127–128
selection, 66
skills, 64

uniting, 57
university presses, relationship, 107–108
Library publishing
activity, 7
case studies, 147–157
definition, 120–122
differentiation, 120–121
efforts, increase, 2–3
focus, 3
initiatives, 141–142
IT infrastructure, 65
practices
application, 72
range, 65–66
programs
focus, 9
funding models, 160–161
roots/branches, 1
services, maturation, 119–120
skills, 60–61
subfield, capacity building, 119
Library Publishing Coalition (LPC), 1, 142
directory, library list, 5
library-based publishing definition, 143
participants, 120
praise, 167
Library Publishing Directory, 201, 232–233
indication, 230–231
Library Publishing Forum, 2
Library Publishing Services, 167
Library publishing services
context/comparison, 229–233
copyright/fair use, 241–242
students, impact, 194
support, increase, 183
Library Publishing Toolkit, 87
Lightning Source, 6
Limited Liability Corporation (LLC), 116
Linked Data, 79
Lippincott, Sarah, 119
Literature, the Humanities, and Humanity (Steinberg), 185
Local Collections and Publication Services (LCPS) (Pacific University), 152–153
Local environment, understanding, 164
Local university community interests,

harm, 35–36
Long Civil Rights Movement, 88
Long-Lived Digital Data Collections (NSF), 206
Luther, Judy, 130
Lynch, Clifford, 108
Lyotard, Jean-François, 44

M

Macalester College, 144
    DeWitt Wallace Library, *Captive Audiences/Captive Performers*, 147
    library publishing, case studies, 147–148
    open access (OA) commitment, 161
    policies, development, 165–166
Machine-readable APIs, 211
Machine readable data, 217
Machine-ready access, 217–218
Making of America (digitization projects), 6
MARC, reliance, 76–77, 212
Marginal cost, zero level, 32
Marginson, Simon, 43
Marketing, discovery, 76–77
MatchEngine API, 216
McCollough, Aaron, 118
McCormick, Monica, 7, 57, 89–90
McGill University, Arts Undergraduate Research Fair, 200
McGuire, Hugh, 211
MediaCommons Press, 69
    open review, 70
    scholar network, 72
Medieval Reviews, 3
Mellon Foundation, 89
Memoranda of understanding (MOU), 114–115
MERLOT. *See* Multimedia Educational Resource for Learning and Online Teaching
Metadata
    absence, 234–235
    APIs, 212
    inclusion, 225
    metadata-rich data registry, 239
    offering, 77
    standards, IT specialist understanding, 101
Metalmark Books, creation, 6
Metrics, usage, 72–73
METS, 212
Michigan Publishing (M Publishing), 90–91, 114
    contracts, evolution, 118
    Digital Culture Books, 78
    rebranding, 115
Middlebury College
    initiatives, 142
    skunkworks, development, 146
Milton S. Eisenhower Library, 109
"Mining the *Dispatch*" (Nelson), 208–209
Mission-driven business models, 23–36
Mission-enhancing revenues, 35
Missions, 157–158
    alignment, 18–22
    functions, relationship, 19–20
    mission-driven orientation, 22
MLA International Bibliography, 156
MLS/MLIS certification, 97
Modern Language Association, 68
Monographs
    Library of Congress deposit, 143
    production, timeframe, 40
    publication, 107–109
    series, 37–38
Motivation, 157–158
Mullins, James L., 92
Multimedia Educational Resource for Learning and Online Teaching (MERLOT), 181, 182
Multimedia publications, 75–76
Multimodal publishing (support), Scalar (usage), 75
Muñoz, Trevor, 205, 207, 229
Musselman Library (Gettysburg College), 153

N

Named-entity recognition (NER), 209–210
National Academies Press (NAP)
    books, OA versions (availability), 38
    models, 34
    open-access policy, 39

National Endowment for the Humanities (NEH), 226
National environment, understanding, 164
National Science Foundation (NSF), 226
    Blue Ribbon Task Force, digital sustainability report, 23
Native Peoples of North America (Stebbins), 185
Natural language processing (NLP), 209–210
Negative liberty, 46, 50
Nelson, Robert, 208–209
NER. *See* Named-entity recognition
Network, publishing, 78–79
New England Science Boot Camp for Librarians, 223
Newfound Press, open-access book publishing, 89
New-model publishing
    practices, 67–80
    skills, contribution, 61–62
New-model scholarship
    communication, definition, 59
    discovery, 59–60
    publishing, processes, 60–61
New York Public Library (NYPL), menu collections, 211
New York University (NYU), 124
    initiatives, 84
    M.S. in Publishing: Digital and Print Media, 125
    NYU Press, 78–79
    type 3 projects, 89–90
Nicomachean Ethics (Aristotle), 44
Nietzsche, Friedrich, 44
1940 Statement of Principles on Academic Freedom and Tenure (AAUP), 46
NLP. *See* Natural language processing
Non-rivalrous goods
    existence, 30–31
    pricing, 30
    usage, restriction, 31
Non-rivalrous information, 32
Non-rivalrousness, 29
Non-rivalry
    implication, 29
    information, 33
NSF. *See* National Science Foundation
NYU Press, 78–79

O

OASPA, 116
Oberlander, Cyril, 9, 177
Oberlin Group
    FTE allocation, 159
    Lever Initiative, 168–169
        initial research phase, 169
    publishing services, 144
    virtual workshops, 169
Ocean Biogeographic Information System, 226
OCLC, 77
OER. *See* Open Educational Resources
Office of Digital Scholarly Publishing, existence, 90
Office of the Vice President for Research (OVPR), 242
OMP. *See* Open Monograph Press
ONIX metadata, usage, 76–77
Online distributions/booksellers, negotiator aggressiveness, 63
Online education programs, 126
Online privacy, discussions (enhancement), 194
Online publishing, possibilities, 150
Online works, discoverability, 59–60
Open Access (OA), 196
    advocacy, 96–97
    books
        Newfound Press publication, 89
        series, 106
    commitment, 161
    content, sharing, 116
    digital edition, library-based publication, 41
    format, 94
    journal articles/monographs, impact, 39
    mandates, lessons, 50–51
    movement, 49
    options, possibilities, 150
    policies, library promotion, 50
    publishing, scholarly communication, 101
    Week, impact, 196–197

Open annotation data model, proposal, 70–71
Open Book Publishers, 78
Open Educational Resources (OER), 178
  authoring, increase, 183
  Commons, 182
Open educational resources, awareness/adoption (increase), 182–183
Open Humanities Press, models, 34
Open Journal Systems (OJS), 8, 65, 77
  track, impact, 126
Open Monograph Press (OMP), 8
  PDF, usage, 185
  usage, 185–186
Open peer review, 68–71
Open Researcher and Contributor ID (ORCID), 242–243
Open review, white paper, 70
Open-source software, hosting platform reliance, 65–66
Open-source WordPress platform, usage, 69
OpenStax, 182
Open SUNY Textbooks
  authors/selection, calls, 185
  cooperative pilot, 183–188
  editorial workflow/design, 185–188
  pilot
    benefits, 184
    editorial workflow, 186
Open Textbook Library (University of Minnesota), 182
  launching, 181
Orange Grove, 182
ORCID. *See* Open Researcher and Contributor ID
Oregon State University textbooks, 103
OSTP. *See* U.S. Office of Science and Technology Policy
Our Cultural Commonwealth (Welshons), 205–206
Oxford (University Press Scholarship Online), 64
Oxford English Dictionary, 3

P

Pacific University, 142, 144
Digital Commons platform, 152
Editing and Publishing Center, 200–201
education/research services, 166
library, faculty interaction, 200–201
library publishing, case studies, 152–153
Local Collections and Publication Services (LCPS), 152–153
Pangaea: Network for Geological and Environmental Data, 228–229, 237–238
Paper books, storage/moving (process), 25
Parsed citations, usage, 214
PEAK, 3
PeerJ, 116
PeerJ (open-access journal), 72–73
Peer review, 67–68
  concept, understanding, 194
  data publishing, relationship, 233–236
  formalized peer review, impact, 197–198
  methods, implementation, 69–70
  observation, 233
  perspective, problems, 47–49
Peer-review area, identification, 130
Peer-reviewed Data Descriptor, 238–239
Peer-reviewed journals, editorial board, 165–166
Peer-reviewed publications, candidate record, 48
Peer-reviewed publishers, stereotyping, 109
Peer-reviewed scholarship
  access, 232
  connection, 102–103
Peer Review for Publication and Accreditation of Research Data in the Earth Sciences (PREPARDE) project, 235
  CDL, partnership, 239–240
Peers (defining), disciplines (impact), 48
Penn State University Press
  collaboration, organization, 90
  initiatives, 84
  type 3 projects, 89–90
Perseus, 3
Persistence, DOI assignment, 229
Personal communication practices, 68
Pets and People, open-access book series, 106

Planning and Operations Council (POC), 93
PLOS. *See* Public Library of Science
PLOS ONE, 38
  works, publication, 70
Pomona College, senior thesis seminar, 200
Positive liberty, 46
  academic freedom, relationship, 51
Predicted Crystallography Open Database, 226
PREPARDE. *See* Peer Review for Publication and Accreditation of Research Data in the Earth Sciences
Preprints
  arXiv acceptance, 68
  distribution, 74
Preservation
  costs, 33
  impact, 64
  technology/workflow, 133–134
PressBooks (platform), 75, 76
Presses. *See* University presses
PressForward, 71, 76
Printing, outsourcing, 26
Print-on-demand vendors, impact, 59
Print-on-demand volume, assembly, 78
Print world
  university library business models, 23–25
  university press business models, 26–27
Production, technology/workflows, 133–134
Professional development workshops, 126
Project Euclid, 4
  usage, 88
Project management, 218–219
Project MUSE, 3, 78
  founding, 109
  University Press Content Consortium, 64
Project-outward work, continuation, 218
ProQuest, 3, 78
ProQuest Dissertations and Theses Database (PQDT), 195
Publication
  data policies/repositories/journals, 236–240

  fees, 59
  sharing mode, 227
Public goods
  non-rivalrous characteristics, 31–32
  optimal price, implication, 29–30
  provision, 32
  term, codification, 28–29
Public Knowledge Project (PKP) (Simon Fraser University), 5
  School, courses (impact), 126
Public Library of Science (PLOS), 237, 242
Public Philosophy Journal (PPJ),
  PressForward usage, 71
Publishers
  acquisitions, functions, 134–135
  core functions, 129–130
  core knowledge/skills, identification, 130–135
  cultural differences, 96
  data repositories, partnership, 238
  editorial functions, 134–135
  education, categories, 125–127
  libraries, skills (uniting), 57
  pathways, productivity, 135–136
  processes, 61–67
  soft skills, 132
  software development skills, usage/necessity, 134
  traditional value, 129
  training, history, 122–124
  value, delivery, 133
Publishing
  academic degree programs, 125
  agreements, evolution, 113
  alternative venues, 52
  approaches, 143
  certification, absence, 97
  collaborations, opportunities, 84
  cross-fertilization, opportunities, 136
  curriculum, library involvement, 163–164
  environments, exploration, 194
  fields, 97
  freedom, 52–54
  hands-on experiences, 136
  in-house training programs, 127
  internship programs, 127
  methodologies, freedom, 121

models, focus, 128–129
monolithic operation, contrast, 203–204
online/distance programs, 126
operations, integration, 117–118
professional development workshops, 126
programs, innovation, 144–145
services
    FTE, Oberlin Group libraries allocation, 159
    librarian connections, 187–188
services, defining, 144–147
summer institutes, 125–126
term, usage, 60
timeliness/modularity, 136
transformation, 123
vanity publishing, 99
vision. *See* Digital scholarly publishing.
Publishing education
    needs, 124–127
    programs, scalability/sustainability, 124–125
    roles, evolution, 128–130
    skills, adaptation, 128–130
Publish, OED definition, 36
Publish or perish system, 24
Publish-then-filter
    model, implementation, 71
    sequence, 67–68
Purdue University, 240
    Libraries, collaboration, 94
    Marketing and Media, 199
    Online Writing Lab, 199
    Studies, establishment, 92
Purdue University Press
    collaboration end products, 103–107
    collaboration/integration conversion, 91–92
    case study, 94–95
    Director, title, 94
    e-Pubs repository, 104
    experimental projects, 104
    human/animal interaction studies series, 105–106
    inventory, movement, 93
    responsibility, transfer, 92–93
    white labeling, 104–105

Pure public good, 28

R

Radcliffe College
    immersion model, implementation, 125–126
    "Summer Publishing Procedures Course," 122
Ramsay, Stephen, 208
Raschke, Greg, 182
Ray, Joyce, 205
Reading Machines (Ramsay), 208
Recording series, 38
Relationship-building skills, 132
Relationship types, taxonomy, 86–87
Reporting Structure Survey (AAUP), 85–86
Repositories
    inclusion, 196
    pedagogical tool, 196
    student work, 195–197
Res Cogitans (conference), 152
Research data management (RDM), data support/services, 230
Research Data Management Service Group (RDMSG) (Cornell University), data publishing codification, 226–227
Research Data Management Services: SPEC Kit334 issuance, 2230
Research library
    impact, 20–21
    scholarly works, populating mechanism, 21–22
Research Library Publishing Services (Hahn), 141
Research orientation, 23–24
Research paper, production, 163
Resig, John, 215–216
Resource Description Framework (RDF), 76–77
Rhodes, Jane, 164
Rice University Press, 156
Rights management, 123–124
Risk/reputation/revaluation, 52–54
Ross, Jerry L., 103
Royalty revenue, loss (risk), 117–118
Roy Rosenzweig Center for History and

New Media, 71
RSS feeds, capture, 71

S

Samuelson, Paul, 29
Santo, Avi, 70
Scalar, usage, 75
Schema. org (HTML standard), 77
Schlosser, Melanie, 118
Scholarly blogs, usage, 69
Scholarly communication
    crises, 131
    disruptive models, 133
    economic challenges, 101
    economics, 28–33
    landscape, change, 128–129
    libraries, focus, 178
    support, 129
Scholarly communications specialist librarian, responsibility, 10
Scholarly journals, DeWitt Wallace Library publication, 148
Scholarly monograph
    expenditures, 155
    publication, 143
Scholarly production, optimization, 36
Scholarly publication, 34
    business models, 53–54
    commercial system, 21–22
    economic perspective, 37
Scholarly publishing
    apparatus, orientation, 18
    characterization, 60
    context, 130–131
    economic public good, 17
    issues, incorporation, 194
    libraries, assistance, 43
    library basis, 232–233
    vision. See Digital scholarly publishing.
Scholarly Publishing and Academic Resources Coalition (SPARC), 4, 87, 178
    membership, 147
"Scholarly Publishing Certification Course: A Training Program" (2013), 126
Scholarly Publishing Office (SPO), 4
    creation, 114–115
Scholarly record, permanence, 38

Scholarly resources, access, 35–36
Scholarly work
    open-access digital edition, library-based publication, 41
    usage/production, 26
Scholars, collaboration (absence), 44–45
Scholarship
    creation/discovery/preservation, 58
    purposes, 33
    service, research library (impact), 20–21
Science data publishing, 224
    example, 232
Science journals, published articles (linking), 236–237
Science, technology, engineering, arts and math (STEAM), 145, 150
Scientific data
    publishing, data curation services, 221
    review, principles, 234
Scientific Data (journal), 236
Scientific Data (open-access data publication), 238–239
    Data Descriptor template, 241
Scientific, technical, and medical (STM), 124–125, 127
Search engine optimization (SEO), usage, 156
Seeborg, Michael, 151, 162
Selection
    calls, 185
    guidance, 73–74
    peer review, impact, 67–68
    support, metrics (usage), 72–73
    technology, impact, 71–72
Semantic Web technologies, advantage, 239–240
Senior academics, work (presentation problems), 196
Serial publishing, 73–75
Shakespeare Quarterly, 69
Shanks, Shelby, 182
Sharing
    publication, relationship, 227
    term, usage, 226
Shirky, Clay, 67–68
Skinner, Katherine, 10, 119
Skunkworks, development, 146

Small academic libraries
  prestige, absence, 146
  publishing programs, innovation, 144–147
  publishing services, 141
    definition, 144–147
    method, 142–143
Small colleges, library publishing
  campus, education, 166
  case studies, 147–157
  experimentation, embracing, 165
  faculty/academic units, alliances, 165
  funding models, 160–161
  integration, 162–164
  libraries, collaboration, 166–167
  local/national environment, understanding, 164
  mission/motivation, 157–158
  organizational structure, 159
  patterns, 157–164
  policies, clarity (development), 165–166
  programs, establishment/maintenance, 158–159
  publications visibility, increase (strategies), 166
  publishing/scholarly communications, teaching/integration, 162–164
  staffing, 159
  technology infrastructure, 160
  value, demonstration, 166
Small libraries, identity problem, 168–169
Small niche markets, Couper Press targeting, 155
Small universities, library publishing (case studies), 147–157
Smith, Kevin L., 118
Social media assistant, 124
Social referrals, 72–73
Social Science Research Network (SSRN), 68
Software, norms/practices, 235–236
SPARC. *See* Scholarly Publishing and Academic Resources Coalition
Speer, Julie, 119
Speers, Julie, 10
Spiro, Lisa, 8, 141
SPO. *See* Scholarly Publishing Office

Stable identifiers, application, 239
Stakeholder, engagement/dissemination, 235
Stanford University Libraries, service, 109
State University of New York (SUNY)
  Geneseo Libraries, 87
  Milne Library, 184
  Innovative Instruction Technology Grant (IITG), 183–184
  library system, 9
  Open SUNY Textbooks, 183
    cooperative pilot, 183–188
  textbook purchase, 180
STEAM journal, 166
Stebbins, Susan, 185
Steinberg, Theodore, 185
Stephen Greene Memorial Library, 123
Strategic Plan 2011-2016, 93
"Strategic Thinking and Design" process (ARL), 2
Student Public Interest Research Groups (Student PIRGs), 180–181
Students
  ABD status, 202
  content creators, 193
  graduate student publications, library publishing support, 199
  peer review, 197–198
  repository work, 195–197
  student-run journals, 197–200
    faculty advisors, resources, 198–199
  importance, 194
  support, ease, 201–202
  tribe, discovery, 194
Submission Integration service, 237
Subsidies, system (impact), 32
Subsidized space, 100–101
Summer institutes, 125–126
"Summer Publishing Procedures Course," 122–123
Sustainable Scholarship conference, collaboration model, 84
Swift, Allegra, 149–150

T

Tapestries (Fishel), 148, 164
Teaching

orientation, 141
publishing/scholarly communications, integration, 162–164
Tebbel, John, 122
Technical gateway, API (usage), 211
Technology
    impact, 49, 71–72
    infrastructure, 160
TEI, 212
Temple University Libraries, textbook program, 182
Tenure, 46–47
    decisions, 48
    granting, 47
    requirements, barrier, 53
    scholar perspective, 47
Textbooks (library-based publishing), 177
    cost
        federal/state agencies review, 189a–191a
        problem, library staff familiarity, 179
    faculty selection, 180
    market, disruption, 181–182
    opportunity, 181–183
    problems, 179–181
    Temple University Libraries program, 182
Text Creation Partnership, 3
Text mining, usage, 208
Thatcher, Sandy, 134
Thesaurus Linguae Graecae, 3
TinEye, 216
Tools of Change for Publishing (blog), 211
Topic modeling, 208, 210
TULIP, 3
Turnkey publishing platform, provision, 8
21st century publishers, core knowledge/skills (identification), 130–135

U

Ubiquity Press, 238
Ukiyo-e Search, usage, 215–216
Ulrich's (journal listing), 198
UMI. *See* University of Microfilms International
Undergraduate Economics Review (UER), 151

submission, review, 162
Underwood, Ted, 209
Universities
    contexts, embodiment, 45
    mission, 32
        functions, alignment, 18–19
    research-oriented model, 243
    space, pressure, 100
    undergraduate curriculum, change, 124–125
University libraries
    business models, 23–25
    mission/functions, alignment, 19–21
    model, 24–25
University of California, Columbia University (relationship), 87–88
University of California, Los Angeles (UCLA), library/Graduate Students Association (partners), 199
University of California Publishing Services (UCPubS), 87–88
University of California (UC) university press, 37
    book series, 37–38
    creation, 27
    initiatives, 84
    monograph series, 37–38
University of Colorado Boulder, partnership, 7
University of Firenze Press, 86
University of Göttingen Press, 86
University of Illinois, Ethnography of the University Initiative (EUI), 197
University of Lethbridge (Journal Incubator), 199–200
University of Michigan (U-M), 19
    initiatives, 84
    partnership, 7
    reprints, sale, 39
University of Michigan (U-M) Library
    publishing agreements, evolution, 113
    rights agreements, evolution, 114
University of Michigan (U-M) Press, publishing operation integration, 117
University of Microfilms International (UMI), 195
University of Minnesota
    Open Textbook Library, launching, 181

Press, direction, 74-75
University of Nebraska-Lincoln, monograph publication, 108
University of North Carolina
    Documenting the American South, 73
    Long Civil Rights Movement publication, 88
    university press, creation, 27
University of Pittsburgh, 103
    books/journals, publication, 108-109
University of Technology (Sydney), 86
University of Tennessee Knoxville Libraries, University of Tennessee Press (collaboration), 88-89
University of Washington, partnership, 7
University Press Content Consortium (Project MUSE), 64
University presses
    anti-commercial business model, 27
    auxiliary unit, 98-99
    business models, 26-28
    collaboration/integration, 83
    diversity, underestimation, 97
    economic opportunity, 101
    editors, competition, 134
    flexibility, reduction, 66
    institutional embedding, 86
    libraries, collaboration, 102
    future, 107-109
    library publishers, relationship, 107-108
    marketplace changes, challenge, 62-63
    misalignment, 22
    mission-based institutions, 23
    missions/functions, alignment, 18, 21-22
    noncommercial nature, 26-27
    objectives, 22
    outward-facing aspect, 34-35
    practices, application, 72
    predictability, 66
    publishing skills, 60-61
    service, 98
    skills, 61-62
    structural issue, 99
    success, 98-99
University Press Scholarship Online (Oxford), 64
University publishers, efficiencies, 63-64
University Publishing in a Digital Age, 99
University-subsidized faculty work, dissemination, 27-28
University-supported digital publishing, characteristics, 58-59
User-extensible derived data API, building, 215
U.S. Government Accountability Office (GAO), 177-179
U.S. Office of Science and Technology Policy (OSTP), 222

V
Value-added services, 35
Vanity publishing, 99
VIVO, 239-240

W
Walters, Tyler, 10, 119
Watkinson, Charles, 7, 83, 131, 135, 142
Wayne Booker Professor of Information Literacy assessment, 104-105
Wayne State University Press, collaboration, 88
Welzenbach, Rebecca, 118
White labeling, 104-105
    concept, 105
Wiley Open Access, 116
Wilkens American Fiction collection, 210
Wilkens, Matthew, 210
"Wordcounts Are Amazing" (Underwood), 209
Word counts, effectiveness, 207-210
WordPress
    content management systems, 75
    dashboard, 71
    platform, usage, 69
Workflows, 133-134
    creation, 61
    usage, 77
Working papers, 195
Works, archival record, 36
Worksets, 215
WorldCat, 156
World Wide Web Consortium (W3C)
    open annotation data model, proposal,

70–71
Semantic Web standards, 79
Writings, nonpublication, 37

X

XML-first workflow, conversion, 63–64